RESONANT MIND

RESONANT MIND

Life Review in the Near-Death Experience

by

DAVID LORIMER

WHITE CROW

www.whitecrowbooks.com

ABOUT THE AUTHOR

David Lorimer, MA, PGCE, FRSA is a writer, lecturer and editor who is Programme Director of the Scientific and Medical Network. He has also been President of Wrekin Trust and of the Swedenborg Society and was founding Chief Executive of Character Education Scotland. Originally a merchant banker then a teacher of philosophy and modern languages at Winchester College, he is the author and editor of over a dozen books, most recently *The Protein Crunch* (with Jason Drew) and *A New Renaissance* (edited with Oliver Robinson) He has a long-standing interest in the perennial wisdom and has translated and edited books about the Bulgarian sage Peter Deunov. His edited book *Prophet for our Times* was republished in 2015 with a foreword by Wayne Dyer.

He is also a founding member of the International Futures Forum and was editor of its digest, *Omnipedia - Thinking for Tomorrow*. His book on the ideas and work of the Prince of Wales - *Radical Prince* - has been translated into Dutch, Spanish and French. He is the originator of the Inspiring Purpose Values Poster Programmes, which have reached over 300,000 young people. See www.inspiringpurpose.org.uk and www.character-scotland.org.uk. He lives in France with his partner Marianne van Mierlo. Personal website: www.davidlorimer.co.uk

At that day ye shall know that I am in my Father,
and ye in me, and I in you.

JOHN 14:20

He who is in the oneness of love loves me in whatever he sees.
Wherever this man may live, in truth this man lives in me.

BHAGAVAD GITA VI:30

CONTENTS

INTRODUCTION TO THE
NEW EDITION

━━━━━━━━━━━━━━━━━━━

This book was first published in 1990 under the title *Whole in One - the near-death experience and the ethic of interconnectedness*. The new title, *Resonant Mind*, with the subtitle referring to the life review, better expresses the purpose and theme of the book. About 10% of those undergoing a near-death experience also have a life review in which they re-experience events in their lives not only from their own viewpoint, but also as if they were other people involved in the same event. The very fact that this is possible indicates that our seemingly separate minds are in fact connected at a deeper level, and that in truth we are all aspects and expressions of the same One Mind. Each event has as many dimensions as there are people who experience it.

Other indications of a shared mind include psychometry, or the ability to read past events out of objects like rings, and also telepathy, which for many of us is an everyday experience. Some medical intuitives are able to sense in their own bodies what is wrong with their patients. Twins and closely bonded people can also share experiences at a distance. For example, a mother may experience contractions when her daughter is giving birth. I call this phenomenon empathetic resonance. If mind were confined to the brain, this should not be possible. And yet it happens. So mind can be shared and non-local. It follows that any theory insisting that mind and consciousness are confined to the brain and body is quite incapable of explaining these well-attested experiences. We therefore need a new field theory of mind able to accommodate these experiences.

This shared mind or capacity to experience what is happening to another means that we are effectively each other. Hence what we do to others we are in fact doing to ourselves: what goes around comes around - we reap what we sow. I suggest that this model of a shared or universal mind provides a metaphysical basis for the Golden Rule and what I call an ethic of interconnectedness. We are told by the Golden Rule that we should treat others as we would like to be treated. Now we find that we are one another, so there is no fundamental separation between us. The highest expression of this insight lies in the principles of Love and Wisdom: loving one's neighbour as oneself and realising that the cultivation and personal embodiment of Love and Wisdom is the ultimate human achievement, the one we most admire. I hope that this book will help you on your journey.

David Lorimer,
St Colombe sur l'Hers, August 2017

Editorial note: extensive footnotes from the original publication have been removed from this edition but all the references are listed in the bibliography.

FOREWORD

It has now been clearly established, by numerous independent clinical investigators working in many parts of the world, that a significant proportion of people who are revived following close calls with death describe a remarkable spiritual experience that dramatically alters the subsequent course of their lives. Furthermore, it appears that these experiences conform to a common pattern - on the whole they are quite similar from case to case, whatever the patient's age, sex, religious, cultural or educational background, or socio-economic status.

Such people frequently relate that at the point at which they undergo cardiac arrest, far from losing consciousness they experience a heightening of awareness. They float out of their bodies, they say, and watch the resuscitation procedure from above. From this vantage point they clearly see their own physical bodies lying below. Some events of a transcendental and indescribable nature appear to unfold before them and they find themselves moving through a passageway towards an incredibly loving light. Here they find themselves in the presence of departed friends and relatives, who seem to be there to meet them and help them with their transition into this new realm. They describe seeing the whole of their lives displayed around them in a panoramic vision, and they are overwhelmed by a sense of the essential importance of love for self and for others as the purpose of existence.

So fulfilling is the ecstasy they feel in this state that many of them have reported that they were disappointed on learning that they had to return to life. Some actually express anger towards the physicians who revive them.

That, simply stated, is the type of account that patients give us of their otherworldly journeys. What is of more concern to those of us who have not had such a vision, however, is what happens to them after they return. It seems clear to me, after twenty-five years of investigating near-death experiences, that on the whole these people are affected in an overwhelmingly positive way by what happens to them. They are no longer fearful of death; they focus on the importance of love and concern for others; they live in the present moment; and they become calmer, happier people.

This much modern medical science has determined with a fair degree of certitude. What medicine alone cannot establish, however, is what the ultimate meaning of such experiences may be. Here, as in perhaps no other issue faced by modern medicine, it is clear that the ancient alliance between the physician and the philosopher must be forged anew. For, embarrassing as it may be for those of us who have been educated in the postitivist tradition, near-death experiences raise the question of whether there is survival after bodily death. This problem is plainly beyond the province of medicine, but it has long been one of the most engaging puzzles of philosophy.

I am delighted to have been asked by my friend David Lorimer to write the foreword for his fine new book about the philosophical implications of the remarkable experiences related to us by people who have returned from the brink of death. I have been inspired by my friendship with David, who combines in his person an incisive intellect and erudition, genuine compassion for others and an eagerness to explore ground at the frontiers of human knowledge. He is therefore uniquely qualified to undertake this endeavour. His book is a major contribution to the study of near-death experiences (and of other spiritual experiences as well) and will be discussed and admired for a long time to come.

Raymond A. Moody Jr.
March, 1990

INTRODUCTION

Among all my patients in the second half of life – that is to say, over thirty-five – there has not been one whose problem in the last resort was not that of finding a religious outlook on life. It is safe to say that every one of them fell ill because he had lost that which the living religions of every age have given their followers, and none of them has been really healed who did not regain his religious outlook. This of course has nothing whatever to do with a particular creed or membership of a church.

C G JUNG

My conviction is that the goal of Man's existence is not happiness but spiritual growth.

ALEXANDER SOLZHENITSYN

We live in an age of moral confusion in which we disagree not just about moral choices but about the basis of our moral diagnosis and the very concepts in which we try to tackle it.

JOHN HABGOOD, ARCHBISHOP OF YORK

For many people, death is the end: modern materialistic science informs them that consciousness is a function of the brain, and that they perish as self-ware individuals at brain-death. A corollary of this world-view is that there is no ultimate basis for values or moral order. Values can only be derived from the society in which we live.

The aim of this book is to suggest a new metaphysical basis for moral order, the insights for which arise in the empirical soil of the near-death experience. Two aspects are of fundamental importance: the life-review, in which people relive events through the consciousness of the person with whom they were interacting at the time; and unitive consciousness, in which they feel themselves at one with the Divine. From these two aspects I have derived the theory of 'empathetic resonance', by which we are able to enter into the consciousness of another as if it were our own.

For the purposes of this book, I have introduced various terms to characterize the context of the moral order of a society. By moral order I understand the framework used to explain and evaluate our moral life. A Christian and an atheist will have different frameworks and terms of reference. I will use the following scheme of our 'orders' in which we live.

1. The *social order*, including the family, tribe and other groups to which individuals may belong; subsumed under the social order one can list the economic order, the political order and the ecclesiastical order of established religion. These orders exert more or less influence according to prevailing historical circumstances.

2. The *physical order*, including the natural world, 'natural laws' such as gravity and the forces of physics, and the (systemic) ecological order of the planet. The physical body clearly belongs to the physical order and is unable to transcend it unless refined to an extraordinary degree, which seems to be the case with certain spiritual masters capable of materialization and dematerialization.

3. The *meta-physical* (literally 'beyond the physical'; I have deliberately used an unconventional spelling here in order to highlight the meaning of 'meta' – beyond) order encountered in the afterlife of religious traditions and, in my view, in the

near-death experience. Its nature varies according to the overall belief system, as do its relationships to the social, physical and moral orders.

4. The *divine order*, attained in supreme mystical experience or unitive consciousness. It may manifest as love and peace in the emotional sense, as wisdom and enlightenment in the intellectual sense, as beauty and harmony in the aesthetic sense, and as power and life-force in the will.

In spiritual world-views the physical and metaphysical worlds are part of (or an emanation from) divine creation and manifestation and subject to divine laws and providential guidance. God is creator and sustainer, immanent and transcendent, ruler and ultimate judge. In materialist world-views, however, the metaphysical and divine orders are denied, so that the framework for moral order must be derived solely from the relative physical and social orders. This can be expressed diagrammatically as in Figure 1. Likewise, concepts about the nature of the self are narrowed or expanded in relation to one's acceptance of the existence of the metaphysical and divine orders (Figure 2). One's ideas about lifetimes can be similarly expressed (Figure 3).

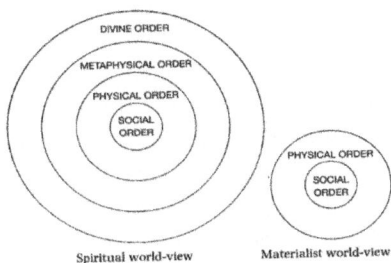

Figure 1

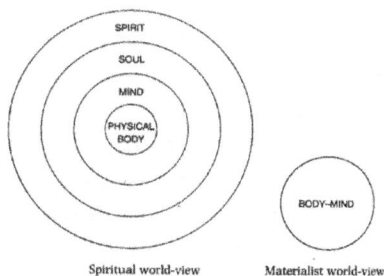

Figure 2

The book begins with a survey of memory and life-review in the near-death experience (NDE), and then moves on to compare NDE life-reviews with post mortem reports of the same experience. I then develop the idea of empathetic resonance through examples drawn from various disciplines such as medicine, psychology and parapsychology. Travelling to the East, and back to the twentieth-century West, we consider moral order in relation to the theory of karma and reincarnation. Having completed the experimentally based part of the study, I then investigate the way in which, historically, moral order was introduced into the notion of the afterlife. Turning to Christianity, we look at eschatology and the idea of post-mortem judgement as the ultimate divine and metaphysical moral sanction. With the decline of religious belief and the rise of the modern scientific spirit, however, many people have abandoned divine and metaphysical frameworks for moral order, falling back on social relativism.

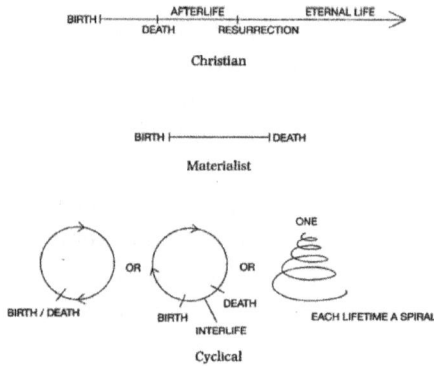

Figure 3

The concluding chapter draws together the threads to propose a new ethic of empathetic resonance, based on the essential metaphysical and divine insight that all our consciousnesses are interconnected. The ultimate moral order is the Golden Rule in action: we seek to benefit both others and ourselves, recognizing ourselves in the other. In a world moving towards a dynamic ecological and political interdependence, the study of spiritual and near-death experience shows us that we are connected on an inner level as well. Just as the planet seen from space shows us the oneness of life, so our explorations of inner space reveal the underlying oneness of consciousness.

CHAPTER ONE

MEMORY AND LIFE-REVIEW IN THE NEAR-DEATH EXPERIENCE

We live in succession, in division, in parts, in particles. Meantime within man is the soul of the whole: the wise silence; the universal beauty, to which every part and particle is equally related; the eternal ONE.

R. W. EMERSON

Rightly is the Kosmos so named; for all things in it are wrought into an ordered whole by the ... immutable necessity that rules it, and by the combining of the elements, and the fit disposal of all things that come into being.

HERMES TRISMEGISTUS

Each of us is the Universal Mind but inflicted with limitations that obscure all but a tiny fraction of its aspects and properties.

HENRY MARGENAU

Background

Although we have long since abandoned the belief that the Earth is flat and that we might fall off the edge if we sailed far enough, there is a sense in which many modern Westerners now live in Flatland. Some of the more sophisticated have denounced the spiritual world-view as an infantile superstition quite outmoded by the wizardry of modern technology and communications. It is true that we live in a larger world by being aware of events in other parts of the planet, but our overall view is for the most part confined to the 'horizontal' dimension of the physical universe. The 'vertical', metaphysical dimension has all but disappeared, so that human life is stripped of any metaphysical context and purpose: we are born, we live, we perish at death. Or do we?

Modern resuscitation techniques are capable of reviving many people who would have died twenty years ago. Up to 40 per cent of such people report that their conscious experience continued in the absence of any outward signs of life such as breathing, heartbeat and measurable electrical brain activity. Such people are clinically dead, although by definition not biologically dead since they return to physical life. These survivors have undergone what is known as a near-death experience (NDE), first publicized in 1975 with the appearance of Dr Raymond Moody's book *Life after Life*, which has sold over ten million copies worldwide. Subsequent scientific studies have broadly substantiated his findings and added detail to our knowledge of the phenomenon. The most common features are a sense of peace, freedom from pain, physical and emotional detachment from the body (extending in some instances to verifiable out-of-body perception), the passage through a tunnel, an encounter with a being of light, entry into a heavenly environment, a review of one's life, and a decision to return to the physical world, people return having lost their fear of death and with the conviction that their consciousness does indeed survive the death of the body; they have experienced themselves as separable from it.

Is all this just *hallucination* or wish-fulfilment? Such is the immediate reaction of many people who have not closely studied the NDE, and are influenced by a mental climate that hypnotizes us into supposing that only the physical world really exists. Research opinion agrees that the NDE does occur, but there is no general consensus of theoretical interpretation. Some investigators favour physical explanations such as seizure of the brain's temporal lobe or cerebral anoxia (shortage of oxygen to the brain); some put forward psychological explanations such as the psychological defence mechanism of depersonalization; a few evangelical Christians denounce the experiences as satanic deception because we are meant to sleep until the last trump, while others treat the phenomenon as a function of the religious imagination; but there are many who take it more or less at face value. These theoretical wrangles will doubtless continue; I shall have occasion to return to them later in the chapter. Meanwhile I shall focus specifically on the life-review.

Many readers will be familiar with folk tales relating how a person's life flashed in front of them as they were drowning or perhaps falling. The earliest systematic study of this phenomenon was carried out by Professor Albert Heim, a Swiss geologist, who published a monograph, *Notes on Deaths from Falls*, in 1891. He found common features in reports by people who had faced sudden accidental death: they were unafraid, quite calm in fact, and realized that their thought-processes were tremendously accelerated to hundreds of times faster than normal; they might also have retrospective views of their past lives in series of pictures. Helm's interest was stimulated by his own fall in the spring of 1871. Although the fall lasted only a few seconds, his time-sense expanded so that one second seemed like five minutes. He writes:

> I saw my whole past take place in many images, as though on a stage at some distance from me. I saw myself as the chief character in the performance. Everything was transfigured as though by a heavenly light and everything was beautiful without grief or anxiety, and without pain. The memory of very tragic experiences I had had was clear but not saddening. I felt no conflict or strife: conflict had been transmuted into love. Elevated and harmonious thoughts dominated and united the individual images, and like magnificent music a divine calm swept through my soul.

The emotional tone here combines detachment - the sense of being a spectator with an atmosphere of transforming love: a feature that will become more apparent as we consider other cases.

Two researchers who have made a special study of the life-review, or 'panoramic memory', as they call it, are psychiatrists Russell Noyes and Ray Kletti. They collected data from questionnaires filled in by 189 respondents, who *described* 215 life-threatening incidents: 57 falls, 48 drownings, 54 car accidents, 27 miscellaneous accidents and 29 serious illnesses. Two-thirds of the sample were men, and one third women, while the median age for the experience was 23. They found that the highest percentage of those reporting revival of memories was 47 per cent for drowning, while the lowest, *pace* Professor Helm, was 16 per cent of the 57 surviving falls. The percentage is 42 for those with serious illnesses or surviving miscellaneous accidents, and 34 for car accident survivors.

In Dr Kenneth Ring's *Life at Death*, 12 of 49 'core experiencers' (those whose experiences were sufficiently detailed) reported the life-review; 55 *per* cent of the accident victims reported the phenomenon, compared with only 16 per cent of the others. The small sample made him tentative about drawing any firm conclusions; rightly, as we have just seen that revival of memories is reported by Noyes and Kletti in 42 per cent of their larger sample. Ring speculates, however, that the review may be precipitated by the suddenness and unexpectedness of a life-threatening accident, an explanation consistent with Helm's case, but *which* could equally apply to a cardiac arrest. Other studies show considerable variation in incidence: Bruce Greyson found it in 22 per cent of a sample of 74, while Michael Sabom's study of 116 cases unearthed only two examples. We therefore have a minimum incidence of under 2 per cent and a maximum of 47 per cent. Similar variations can be established for other NDE variables, suggesting caution in deducing standard patterns; but experiencers' descriptions do exhibit striking enough similarities for some solid conclusions to be drawn. Before proceeding any further, however, it is helpful to gain a clearer idea of the state of consciousness in which the panoramic life-review takes place.

At this stage we shall draw a distinction between the panoramic memory and the life-review: by panoramic memory we shall understand a display of images and memories with little or no direct emotional involvement; while the life-review, although superficially similar, has the essential additional element of emotional involvement and a degree of moral assessment of the consequences of thoughts, feelings and actions. It is this depth of experience which is significant in our search for the criteria of an underlying moral order in our lives.

Studies of NDEs and out-of-the-body experiences (OBEs), especially in spontaneous and non-drug-induced instances, frequently refer to the clarity of mental processes during the experience, as well as an altered sense of perception and time. Return to the physical body is likened to re-entry into a cage or prison. In order to elaborate on these changing states of consciousness we shall look at one vivid individual account, written in 1931 by Leslie Grant Scott: 'Dying as a Liberation of Consciousness'.

Scott's experience took place in Ceylon during a protracted illness. In this case the panoramic *memory* occurred early on; she saw her life unrolling so as to reveal its purpose (this does not always seem to be the intention). She viewed it impersonally and understood everything extremely lucidly. She realized that she was dying, and yet felt comfortable and happy, with her mind 'unusually active and clear'. When the doctor arrived she was starting to become conscious of what was going on in the minds of others, perceiving hope in his mind as he gave her a hypodermic shot; this turned swiftly to disappointment as he realized that the medicine was having no effect: 'Meanwhile my consciousness was growing more and more acute. It seemed to have expanded beyond the limits of my physical brain. I was aware of things that I had never contacted. My vision also was extended so that I could see what was going on behind my back, in the next room, even distant places.' Compare the words of Sir Auckland Geddes, also apparently near death: 'Gradually I realized that I could see, not only my body and the bed in which it was, but everything in the whole house and garden ... in fact wherever my attention was directed.'

Scott then lost all physical sensation and connection with the body, and with it any control over it. She tried to close her eyes, 'but found that I could not ... I was dead. Yet I could think, hear and see more *vividly* than ever before.' With this sharp perception came an equally acute emotional sensitivity: 'From the next room came great, engulfing waves of emotion, the sadness of a childhood companion. My increased sensitiveness made me feel and understand these things with an intensity hitherto unknown to me.' This made her wish to return to her body, at which point she experienced fear and suffering: 'The effort to return to my body was accompanied by an almost unimaginable sensation of horror and terror. I had left without the slightest struggle. I returned by an almost superhuman effort of will'; she knew that she was back by a sensation in the solar plexus. There followed some days of intense fighting for life, but with a continuing expanding state of consciousness. This starkly contrasted with anger and frustration at being 'compressed, caged, in a dull stupid prison of flesh'; the body felt like the proverbial Orphic and Platonic tomb. Many experiencers, including Jung, resent the constriction and narrowness of subsequent physical perception. He speaks of returning to the 'box system', and refers to life and the whole material world as a prison.

One of the implications of the continuation of extended or expanded consciousness for Scott was an extremely vivid sense of the oneness of life. The 'skin-encapsulated ego' became porous with this heightened sensitivity. Things were no longer seen with or through the Cartesian lens which obscures the relatedness of the part to the whole: 'Immediately I saw them in their entirety and in their relation to all other things. I have never lost this sense of the underlying unity of all things but I was obliged to narrow my vision so that it might fit the brain which I had to use.' She adds that this narrowing process was an essential survival strategy which prevented mind and body from being completely shattered by the vastness and intensity of knowledge and experience. Such phrasing recalls the 'four-fold vision' of William Blake, threatened by reduction to a claustrophobic single vision; and it hints at the theories of Henri Bergson, for whom the brain was a filter and reducing valve, an instrument to keep one's focus on the present moment in the physical dimension.

The oneness and resultant connectedness of the parts and the immanence of the Whole in each part is perceived in the NDE more especially in the encounter with the being of light, which we shall look at more closely in Chapter 3. Suffice it to say that the above experience convinced Scott that there was no death, since life continues in other states of consciousness, and of the existence of one power manifesting in every created thing. Such underlying unity implies an order, a plan 'and a law that works with mathematical precision. What we sow we reap - if not now, later since we are living in infinity. I know that every cause has its effect and that perfect justice rules.' Bold and unfamiliar statements in a largely agnostic century.

Panoramic Memory

The foregoing case sets the scene for an analysis of cases of panoramic memory. It exemplifies a number of typical features in its description of the expanded state of consciousness in which the display of panoramic memory occurs, which mark it off from our normal waking reality - especially when one remembers that many near-death experiencers are in acute physical distress immediately prior to the NDE. I referred above to the sequence of experiences which may unfold at those critical moments at the threshold of death and which invariably end with an often abrupt return to physical reality on being informed that 'it is not yet your time' or as a result of a personal decision to come back.

The most prevalent features of the panoramic memory are the speed, vividness, reality and accuracy of the images which dash across the mind. The time sequence varies considerably: some go back from the present, others start in early childhood and move forwards, while still others are seen in a holographic clump. In any event the panorama seems to last only a few seconds. Many such experiences take place in the presence or atmosphere of a radiant and loving being of light; the subject feels totally accepted and understood. Before considering a few cases in more detail, we shall quote some short extracts to convey the flavour of the panoramic memory.

Rapidity, Vividness, Reality, Accuracy

> My whole life was just going in front of me like a very fast computer and I kept thinking about all the different things I had done or perhaps I hadn't done.

> I could remember everything; everything was so vivid. It was so clear in front of me ... the best thing I can think of to compare it to is a series of pictures; like slides. It was just like someone was clicking off slides in front of me, very quickly. Highlights of various very happy points in my life came up ... all fanned in front of me. Very rapidly. Just kind of went past me like a million and one thoughts ... I was a spectator, I was just watching them.

Time Sequences

It's like a picture runs in front of your eyes, like from the time you can remember, up to the present.

> The first thing I remembered was following my father as he walked along the beach; it was when I was two years old. And there were a few other things, in order, from my early years, and after that I remember breaking my new red wagon I had gotten for Christmas when I was five ... then I went to work in a grocery store, and it brought me right up to then, just before beginning my second year in college.

Unconscious as I was, I saw, as if it had been on a film, several pictures out of my earlier life, which curiously enough ran backwards from the present to the past.

It was like I was going through this memory, and ... like my whole memory was retaping. I was in reverse. And everything was just back-tracking so that I could go over it again like a tape recorder. But it wasn't in sequence.

Individual Cases

One of Raymond Moody's subjects saw his entire life flashing in front of him at the end of a tunnel: 'It was not exactly in terms of pictures, more in the form of thought, I guess.' This interesting comment suggests the limitations of the literal picture or slide analogy, especially when he goes on to say that 'it was lost all there at once, I mean, not one thing at a time, blinking off and on, but it was everything, everything at one time.' This comment corresponds to the state of relative time-lessness experienced at the out-of-body stage of the experience. The subject went on to think about the mean things he had done as a child, thus introducing an element of self-assessment, but no other presence or atmosphere was mentioned.

Janis, whose experience is reported by Ring, nearly died in a car smash in 1973. She found herself in an atmosphere of peace, and had a feeling of warmth, acceptance and home-coming. The presence in the light asked if she was ready to stay and informed her that she would have to make a decision. It seems that the panoramic memory was part of this process. She likened it to a 35-millimetre film which passed in a split second: 'It was black and white and I saw everything. I saw my whole life pass right by me ... all chronological. All precise.' She described herself as a spectator without any emotions. The unusual feature here is the black and white impression, which ostensibly turned to colour when she arrived at events which had not yet occurred - referred to by Ring as the dash-forward and very occasionally associated with the retrospective panorama, perhaps on account of the expansion of consciousness. Accurate precognition naturally raises some of the most profound philosophical questions, consideration of which I shall set aside until a later chapter.

The next case was also triggered by a car accident. The subject, Hank, found himself immersed in a total 'surrendering-type love', and was asked, telepathically, what his decision was. He then had complete recall of everything he had known from the beginning of his life, 'and what was also kind of scary was that I knew everybody else in the room knew I knew and that there was no hiding anything - the good times, the bad times, everything ... even little minute things that I had forgotten.' The lesson that he drew from the experience is that people come to Earth to learn to share more love, to be more loving towards one another: 'to discover that the most important thing is human relationships and love and not materialistic things. And to realize that every single thing you do in your life is recorded and that even though you pass it by not thinking at the time, it comes up later.' He then gives an example of a seemingly trivial event like impatience at a traffic light - you forget that you too may be in front one day. The significance of the impatience lies in its demonstration of a lack of understanding of the power of thought, and a consequent failure to realize the destructive effects of rampant negative emotions - but these observations are somewhat in advance of our case material.

The Life-Review.

The deeper the panoramic memory becomes - the more it includes an element of self-judgement and emotional reaction to it, so it more closely resembles the medieval idea of a post-mortem encounter or judgement of one's deeds. There is an externalization and hence confrontation with the memory of events as they are displayed, as it were, outside the individual. It is as if, to use David Bohm's language, what is implicate or implicit in these memories is now unfolded and made explicit in order for the person to realize the full implications of their actions, feelings and thoughts. Inward states are projected outwards: hence the impression of being both a participator and a spectator at the same time; the nearest analogy is Gurdjieff's technique of self-remembering, the attempt to be fully aware of what one is thinking, feeling and doing at a given moment, but such awareness, however perfect, is unlikely to extend to perceiving the full consequences of one's actions and thoughts.

Reviewing literally means looking again, achieving a fresh perspective, which may give rise to reflections and the reassessment of values. It is more than reminiscence, and has something in common with the process described by T. S. Eliot when he depicts the gifts reserved for old age: first comes the 'cold friction of expiring sense without enchantment'; then 'the conscious impotence of rage at human folly'; and last:

The rending pain of re-enactment
Of all that you have done, and been; the shame

9

Of motives late revealed, and the awareness
Of things ill done and done to others' harm
Which once you took for exercise of virtue.

The only relief envisaged by Eliot is restoration by the refining fire, presumably a purgatorial image rather than one of love. We shall certainly come across feelings of shame and reassessment of motives with their implication of self-judgement and remorse, but we shall also find some relief for the exasperated spirit in the balm of all-encompassing love.

Two cases cited by Margot Grey refer to the shame and embarrassment, but also make it clear that the people were learning from their mistakes. One subject found himself surrounded by a radiation of love as the memories of long-forgotten incidents surfaced: 'Things that I had completely forgotten about I was made cognisant of and these were the things that were important' - such as working on a tubercular survey of schoolchildren at the age of nineteen.

The review is often initiated by a question such as 'What do you have to show me that you have done with your life? What have you done for others? What have you done to benefit the human race? What is in your heart? - searching enquiries which go to the core of ethics and values. Dr. George Ritchie was informed that he was in the presence of the Son of God and sensed the immense love the Being has for him: 'far more even than power, what emanated from this presence was unconditional love. An astonishing love. A love beyond my wildest imagining. This love knew everything unlovable about me ... and accepted and loved me just the same.' He then relived many incidents of his childhood (the experience took place when he was a young man). With the all-inclusive view came the question, 'What did you do with your life?', an enquiry, according to Ritchie, not about facts but about values. All he saw was 'an endless, shortsighted, clamorous concern for myself', reflected in his proud choice of the achievement of becoming an eagle scout - 'That glorified you.' He then protested that he had not had time to do anything with his life, to which the gentle response - in the Tibetan tradition - 'Death can come at any age', was spoken with infinite love.

It then dawned on Ritchie that it was he, not the Presence, who was judging the events so harshly, seeing them as trivial, self-centred, unimportant. No condemnation, blame or reproach - only love - was coming from the Glory shining around him. He then realized that his frantic efforts to come up with an impressive answer to the questions were misguided, as the Presence was not so interested in accomplishments as in how Ritchie had showed love in his life. Had he loved others unconditionally, as the Presence was loving him? His immediate response was that no one had told him that this kind of love was so essential - even intrinsic - to the meaning of life. It was as if he had discovered in the exam hall that he was going to be tested on a subject which he had never studied in the standard syllabus. The centrality of unconditional love will become clearer as we analyse further cases.

J.T. was twenty-five and an agnostic at the time of her NDE, which occurred after she had spent several months in bed with an undiagnosed illness. The experience does not begin with the usual feelings of peace and release, but rather with terror accompanying an ego-death, a stripping away of the superficial self. At the same time there was an awareness of another part of herself witnessing the struggles of the personality. Surrender led to being surrounded and suffused by a loving presence, with a sense of peace and total harmony. Then came the judgement or review, with the life experience in one clump, 'its essence and totality'. The judge was more than the creator, 'it was the totality of my Self; my larger SELF, my True Self, judging my little self, the ego, the habits and patterns or tendencies of J.T. within the context of the twentieth century.' She was ashamed and dismayed, even though her life had been pretty normal, 'but I loved entirely for the gratification of the little self, the ego ... I had used all that was at my disposal for my personal small ego-self, and not for larger mankind.' It was then communicated that 'the aim in my life was to bring the Love that Jesus, Buddha, Ramana Maharshi, etc., spoke of, into actuality my life.' Ring develops the idea of self-judgement within the context of Paul Brunton's 'Overself', to which we shall return in Chapter 4. Unconditional love is once again the leitmotiv, indeed the *very* atmosphere in which the 'judgement' is played out.

Belie's NDE took place after heart failure during surgery. She found herself surrounded by an all-consuming love, and was shown her life. The fact that she had given away six dollars to someone and felt proud of it was perceived as unimportant, while the small things - Wordsworth's little, nameless, unremembered acts of kindness and of love - assumed a greater significance: 'maybe a hurt child you helped or just to stop to say hello to a shut-in'. There was a sense of having been forgiven, but the judgement was coming from herself - could she forgive herself?

Two more short extracts bring out the feature of self-judgement. The first case is that of Elizabeth Blakely: during a serious illness she found herself, as it were, awakening in the middle of the night with her consciousness 'strangely calm and clear', and without any sensation of pain. Her consciousness became condensed in the head and then projected upwards out of the body. After a timeless pause, she saw the most important events of her life flash before her inner sight: She was both actor and witness and 'became my own judge of my own actions, for good or bad, throughout my preceding life'.

The second case is that of S.V.J., victim of a car accident, whose remarkable OBE I have cited elsewhere. The pervasive feeling was of happiness, but, as in Blakely's case, there was no other presence witnessing the process, and J. described himself as 'both observer and protagonist ... my whole soul was a Sensitive instrument, my conscience immediately weighed up my actions and judged me and what I did'. He adds, though, that his evil actions were not included in the drama, but then contradicts himself later on when he asserts that there was harmony even in scenes portraying what would be called evil action. Perhaps some scenes were repressed at the time, only to come up at a later stage when J. would be more prepared.

While the foregoing cases certainly exhibit a self-judgement and reassessment of values and priorities, they do not reach the deepest stratum of the life-review in which an empathetic resonance or connection is perceived with the experiences of other people. The word sympathy is derived from the Greek and literally means to feel with, while empathy means to feel into something – thus at one level to identify oneself with it, to sense it as one's own. The word resonance is used to indicate the patterns set in motion by the thoughts, feelings and actions of an individual, a wave which travels outwards from the epicenter and affects others at a distance and unconsciously. Thus in tuning in to the memories, one is also tuning in to their radiating effects within a kind of empathetic magnetic field. The following cases will provide further insight into some possible constants and variables in the moral order revealed in the metaphysical context of the NDE.

In September 1971 Darryl was electrocuted when lightning struck his house while he was telephoning a friend. In the course of his NDE he encountered an awesome and loving being of light, who asked him if he knew where he was. Then suddenly 'my life passed before me ... what occurred was every emotion I have ever felt in my life, I felt. And my eyes were showing me the basis of how that emotion affected my life. What my life had done so far to affect other people's lives using the feeling of pure love that was surrounding me as the point of comparison.' The function of the atmosphere of love is made more explicit in this case, where the tone of the review was predominantly emotional: love actually became the criterion of assessment. It is not simply, as in previous cases, that the lesson to be learned was to love more unconditionally; rather that love is the active principle, the constant through which the variables of human experience are viewed and weighed. The insight is extended beyond Darryl's own emotional experience to its effect on other people, which he then felt.

This connectedness of empathetic resonance comes out clearly in some cases of life-review cited in Raymond Moody's 1988 study. One subject, laconically characterized as 'a con artist and outright criminal', experienced the life-review in the presence of a being of light, seeing and feeling the effects of his actions on others. The outcome was salutary in that the man realized that he would have to undergo the process again when he really died. For another of Moody's subjects, this connectedness with others led to a greatly enhanced sense of responsibility. She relived an incident from her childhood when she had yanked away her little sister's Easter basket because it contained a toy she wanted: 'I felt her feelings of disappointment and loss and rejection.' The review process made this feeling conscious and therefore enabled her to learn from her own unkindness: there could be no covering up, since 'I was the very people that I hurt, and I was the very people I helped to feel good.' The subject treated this empathetic resonance as a challenge which made her consider more carefully how she interacted with others.

In his 1977 study, Raymond Moody comments on the theme of exposure in the NDE, already referred to when considering the review as an unfolding display; but one can also add that there is a kind of spiritual nakedness as dimensions of life and truth are unfurled. Question-begging rationalization and petty excuses are swept aside in this extended picture. One of Moody's subjects described how he was surrounded by light and how everything in his life went by for review. He had a 'different knowledge', whereby the light showed him what was wrong, as if through eyes 'with omnipotent knowledge', helping him to see. In this state he saw not only what he had done, 'but even how what I had done had affected other people. And it wasn't like I was looking at a movie projector because I could feel these things; there was feeling, and particularly since I was with this knowledge ... I found out that not even your thoughts are lost ... every thought was there.' The feeling of being protagonist or actor as well as witness is here extended to include experience of the consequences of one's actions in others, an empathetic participation in other consciousnesses; this is made possible through the sharing perspective of omnipotent knowledge, itself a kind of pervasive memory which stores and links related effects in an eternal present.

The implications of Phyllis Atwater's review are even more far-reaching. She described the great bliss she had felt before the onset of what was more of a reliving than a review:

> For me it was a total reliving of every thought I had ever thought, every word I had ever spoken, and every deed I had ever done; plus the effect of each thought, word, and deed on everyone and anyone who had ever come within my environment or sphere of influence whether I knew them or not (including unknown passers-by on the street); plus the effect of each thought, word and deed on weather, plants, animals, soil, trees, water, and air.

She was astonished to discover that thoughts, words and deeds were remembered and accounted for (a feature already noted above) and even had a life of their own once released as an energy form which 'directly affected all [they] touched or came near'. She likens the process to existing in a vast 'sea or soup of each other's energy residue and thought waves', and being 'held responsible for our contributions and the quality of the "ingredients" we add'.

The only picture within which the above account makes sense is one of an interconnected web of creation, a holographic mesh in which the parts are related to the Whole and through the Whole to each other by empathetic resonance. It must be the sort of Whole in which we and the rest of creation live and move and have our being, a consciousness-field in which we are interdependent strands. It is precisely this oneness and connectedness with the rest of humanity and creation – that is the basis of our responsibility: if we were not connected, there could be no possible feedback loop of the kind described above, no tuning in to the memory and consciousness of other forms of life. These ideas will be more fully developed when we come to reflect on the overall significance of the life-review later in this chapter and in the next.

Our final case in this section is the experience of a prisoner, Starr Daily, who was suffering from an intestinal condition brought about by prolonged ingestion of soap in an attempt, eventually only too successful, to have himself transferred to the hospital wing. He was in acute pain when he found himself passing into a state of mental and emotional terror, dreaming while he seemed wide awake. A scroll or motion film began to unroll before his vision:

> And the only pictures on it were the pictures of people I had injured. It seemed there would be no end to it. A vast number of these people I knew or had seen. Then there were hundreds I had never seen. These were people who had been indirectly injured by me. The minute history of my long criminal career was thus relived by me, plus all the small injuries I had inflicted unconsciously by my thoughtless words and looks and omissions. Apparently nothing was omitted in this nightmare of injuries, but the most terrifying thing about it was that every pang of suffering I had caused others was now felt by me as the scroll unwound itself.

Although there is no mention of nature in this case, the reliving experience is strikingly similar in format, if not in content, to the previous case, in that indirect and unconscious effects are also relived. It is a good deal more drastically purgative, given the kind of life that Daily had been leading and the agonies which he was forced to experience for himself. Moreover, he had to endure an identical process about a dozen times over the subsequent weeks, until he awoke one morning free from pain and fear. His next spell was four months in isolation, during which period he discovered more of his hidden inner geography, 'little-known continents in the human mind'. Then followed an extraordinary event which completes and resolves the account related above. He went back to childhood dreams of Jesus Christ, meeting him as it were in a garden and receiving an outpouring of sublime love; this dream was replayed and Daily was submerged in love until for the first time he had a joyous sense of bestowing it: 'it poured from me in gratitude and blissful tears. I loved all men. I hated only the evil conditions they imposed on each other and upon themselves.' Once more the scroll unwound:

> There was no pain in it this time; it was all elation, ecstasy. All the people I had injured directly or indirectly came before me again and this time I gave them love, which seemed to soothe and heal their hurts. Then all the people who had injured me appeared. One by one I began to help them and love them. It was all exceedingly vivid. Out of the scroll a great auditorium took form. There was a huge audience. They were all the people I had injured or who had injured me.

This experience marked a turning-point in Daily's life. He discovered that it was possible for him to receive and transmit the love which healed both the injurer and the injured, thus reciprocally forgiving and being forgiven. Not that the people were literally present: we are dealing with the drama of only one person. But if this interconnecting web does indeed exist, such healing could be transmitted and received at least unconsciously, thus enhancing the harmony of the whole by a restoration of balance in some of the relationships between the parts.

Interpretations

Few researchers have offered specific interpretations of panoramic memory and life-review, since their primary interest has been other aspects of the NDE such as the out-of-body experience and encounter with the being of light. Noyes and Kletti, however, have advanced a two-pronged thesis in which one level of explanation is psychological - the 'depersonalization syndrome' - and the other neurological - abnormal firing patterns in the temporal lobe of the brain.

Depersonalization is defined as an adaptive defence pattern of the nervous system, a subjective response to life-threatening danger. Psychologically it defends the endangered personality against the threat of death by organizing and integrating the immediate experience. Three factors emerge from the research analysis: a mystical component that includes a sense of harmony and joy together with visions and sharp imagery, which are conjectured to underlie the panoramic memory; a depersonalization component including emotional aloofness and detachment from the body and the world; and a hyperalertness component which the researchers acknowledge may superficially conflict with the second component. Michael Sabom found significant differences between his own study and those of Noyes and Kletti, noting that Noyes himself admitted that the patterns experienced by those only psychologically near death (realizing that they were in danger of dying) differed from those of people who were both psychologically and physically near death. Noyes and Slyman report that factors in the mystical component are reported twice as frequently by those endangered in accidents as by those endangered in other ways.

The essential question is whether the panoramic memory and life-review can be explained as part of a symbolic fantasy based on denial of imminent death. One might plausibly argue that recourse to the past, especially to positive and happy memories, represents a form of escapism which diverts attention away from the dire emergency of the present moment. This line of argument seems much less convincing, however, when we reach the deeper strata of the life-review, with its calling into question of values and images cherished by the personality; and it completely collapses when we reach the emotional and empathetic life-review which starkly confronts the individual with the consequences of thoughts and actions. This stage leaves absolutely no room for escapism or wish-fulfilment.

A second approach is the neurological one, based on the standard orthodox position that memories are stored in the brain. Before examining this explanation in detail, we need to sketch out the background to this theory. Two basic processes are recognized in memory: learning or acquisition on the one hand, and recollection or retrieval on the other. This second process, as Eccles points out, consists of two stages: that of retrieval itself, followed by recognition or checking that the memory recovered is indeed the correct one. The mechanism by which memories are retained in the brain is supposed to be through traces or engrams which modify the synapses or gaps between neurones. In the words of Sir John Eccles: 'We have to suppose that long-term memories are somehow encoded in the neuronal connectivities of the brain. We are thus led to conjecture that the structural basis of memory lies in the enduring modification of the synapses.' Correspondingly, it is supposed that 'the recall of a memory involves the replay in an approximate manner of the neuronal events that were responsible for the experience that is being recalled.'

It can be readily appreciated that storage and retrieval draws heavily on the computer analogy and information theory. It is curiously circular to suppose that the organic brain must necessarily be fully understood by analogy with the inorganic computer which it invented! Research has concentrated on the processes of learning and recall, but it is surely going too far to assert, as Professor Rose does, that 'the observed biochemical, anatomical, and physiological changes which accompany learning form the necessary, sufficient and exclusive representations of that learning at the biological level, rather than merely being the correlates of other phenomena which occur at the same time as the learning.' Rose himself observes elsewhere that the engrams which link learning and recall are 'inferred rather than demonstrated.' And Professor J.Z. Young makes the point that although most neuroscientists believe in a theory of synaptic change, 'there is little direct evidence of the details of it.'

Earlier this century, Karl Lashley spent thirty years attempting to locate memories in the brains of rats and found that maze-running skills could not actually be obliterated by excising particular areas of the cortex; the result of such cuts was an *overall* decline in efficiency. This conclusion has led some theorists to postulate a holographic theory of memory, which sees memory as generalized in the brain as a whole and not in any one part; it is still, however, supposedly located in the brain. A rival theory of particular memory traces was seemingly given some backing by the experiments of Wilder Penfield, which form the basis of Noyes and Kletti's speculation that the panoramic memory and life-review have a neurological basis in a seizure of the temporal lobe, perhaps due to the blood supply being cut off.

Penfield's procedure involved the electrical stimulation of the cerebral hemispheres, notably the temporal lobes, during operations under local anaesthetic. (It is important to note that these experiments were all carried out on patients with a history of epileptic seizures and in precisely that region of the brain in which the seizures occur. Extrapolation of the findings in such cases on to discussion of normal brains, on which no such tests have been carried out, would be highly questionable.) Penfield found that his patients were recalling long-forgotten memories, apparently elicited by the electrical stimulation, while at the same time remaining aware of their stream of consciousness in the present. The most common experiences were visual or auditory, sometimes combined: 'times of watching or hearing the action and speech of others, and times of hearing music'. The striking feature of these recollections is their passive nature; they are events in which the patient had been an observer rather than a participator. In contrast to this, reports of panoramic memory and life-review speak of observing and participating at the same time. Moreover, there are no categories of experience omitted from NDE memories, such as Penfield found. He states that the following kinds of incident are absent from his patients' reports: times of decision-making, carrying out skilled acts, speaking or writing oneself, eating, sexual experience and painful suffering. In contrast, in the NDE, many subjects speak of total recall and at a speed far in excess of the actual remembered event.

Finally, Penfield's subjects speak of being in a dreamy state, whereas near-death experiencers stress the vividness and reality of the images. When we consider the deep life-review, it clearly becomes impossible to give an adequate account of empathetic resonance in terms of neurological activity, as we cannot conceivably store other people's engrams in our own brains. Were it not for empathetic resonance, it might be possible to argue that the panoramic memory represented the preliminary unwinding of memories or disconnection of synapses prior to their dissolution with brain death; but then near-death experiencers do not lose the memories reviewed - they are, if anything, heightened and enhanced. It looks as if we shall have to try another theoretical angle if we are to account for the full range of phenomena, especially when we look into instances of psychometry.

Memory and Resonance

'That reminds me' is an expression with which we are all only too familiar. Memory and memory techniques work by association, some courses even providing 'image hooks' on which to hang the items in a shopping list; and the more striking the image, the easier it is to recall. Suppose, for instance, that you have to buy toothpaste and a screwdriver in town. Try conjuring up an image of yourself brushing your teeth with a screwdriver or using a screwdriver to prise open a tube of toothpaste. The image is so absurd that it is easy to recall. It is also a common experience to attempt to remember something and find the memory inaccessible until it spontaneously re-emerges in a moment of inattention. It is as if the brain was actually preventing the memory from surfacing. Marcel Proust, in a famous passage about a piece of Madeleine cake, tastes a piece with a mouthful of tea and is initially incapable of conjuring up the association which the sensation has set in motion. 'Then suddenly the memory appeared to me.' It was a long-forgotten part of his childhood – his aunt used to give him a piece of madeleine soaked in tea on Sunday mornings. The sensation acted as a resonant key which unlocked memories of similar occasions in the past. The emphasis lies in the selection of similarity, the principle underlying all forms of resonance or affinity: that like elicits like, that tuning responds to particular frequencies.

Henri Bergson, F.C.S. Schiller and William James have advanced a theory of the relationship of brain to mind and memory which can begin to make sense of panoramic memory in particular and ESP phenomena in general. They take issue with the conventional view that consciousness of a certain kind is permitted or transmitted through the brain. As Schiller puts it: 'Matter is not what *produces* consciousness but what *limits* it and confines its intensity within certain limits: material consciousness does not construct consciousness out of arrangement of atoms, but

19

contracts its manifestations within the sphere which it permits.' Bergson defines the brain as the organ of attention to life, an organ which channels, limits and focuses our awareness on the practicalities of the present moment. Its function *vis-à-vis* memory, he argues, is to mask the past, only letting into present awareness data relevant to the situation in hand; and these data are retrieved by association, since the present is understood in terms of similar situations in past experience. He further contends that brain damage affects not storage but recall of memories; the brain provides a framework into which the memory can fit, but not the memory itself. He therefore concludes that it is a fallacy to make the automatic assumption that memories are actually stored in the brain.

Such limitation of consciousness acts as a survival mechanism in our everyday lives by excluding or screening out enormous numbers of impressions and memories which might otherwise impair our efficiency or even safety. It is well known that ESP impressions normally require a quiet and receptive state of mind, since the subtle is otherwise drowned by more gross sensations. But the fact that we have no immediate access to our memories does not mean that they have disappeared. Bergson himself cites panoramic memory as an indication that the past is indeed conserved. Extending his point of view, one might conjecture that moments of life-threatening danger focus our attention away from continuing material life as we begin to find our bearings in another dimension of consciousness, a wider and more intense state which some researchers have tried to explain by using the model of 'hyperspace'.

Gordon Greene, for example, postulates that time is spatialized into a fourth dimension which enables us to perceive the whole of our past life simultaneously. More generally, the hypothesis that the principal function of the brain is to limit conscious awareness to the three-dimensional physical world would predict that our consciousness would expand beyond the brain at death. This is precisely what the evidence suggests, contrary to the assumption that consciousness is produced by the brain and must therefore perish at physical death. NDE subjects (see for instance the case of Leslie Grant Scott described above) report a widening and intensification of consciousness when close to physical death. Sir Auckland Geddes, moreover, was quite explicit that his consciousness existing out of the body was clear and extensive, while on return to the body he experienced 'a glimmer of consciousness suffused with pain'. In other words, for consciousness to leave the body is a liberation, while return is a form of imprisonment.

The concepts of resonance and frequency have been central to two recent scientific developments. The first is the emergence of holographic theory to account for memory and brain function. As already observed, this approach assumes that memories are stored in the brain, but more widely distributed than was previously thought. It pictures our brains as 'mathematically constructing "hard" reality by interpreting frequencies from a dimension transcending time and space'. If the brain is understood as a frequency-analyser used by the conscious self to focus on the material dimension, then there is no intrinsic reason why we should not be able to tune in to different levels of consciousness and reality when the limitations of the physical brain are removed. The second development is the elaboration of the theory of formative causation and morphic resonance by Rupert Sheldrake. What is of particular interest here is Sheldrake's theory of memory as a form of morphic resonance. The term itself means the influence of like upon like through morphogenetic fields; thus past organisms influence the development of present organisms of the same kind through the morphogenetic field of that particular species of organism. With reference to memory, Sheldrake also argues that memories need not be stored in the brain, but that they may be accessed by morphic resonance through similarity to past states. In other words the act of retrieval or recall acts through resonance with the particular memory. A similar mechanism is posited by those who think that memories are stored in the brain when they speak of the searching for a replay of the original neuronal event. It may turn out to be as misleading to localize memories as to localize consciousness, without which there could be no memory anyway. Our brains are undoubtedly in space, but, as Lawrence LeShan argues, paranormal phenomena such as telepathy and clairvoyance suggest that our consciousness is not. There is thus no question of action at a distance because space-time is a category applicable to the physical universe and contravened by the data of psychical research. The effectiveness of telepathy and the vividness of crisis apparitions, for instance, are unrelated to distance. A more relevant variable seems to be the degree of love and sympathy existing between the two parties, a mental, emotional or spiritual closeness which penetrates the walls with which we normally surround and isolate ourselves.

Hidden Memory and Psychometry

The panoramic memory experience can be regarded as a particular manifestation of hidden memory, which also emerges in other circumstances when normal inhibiting mechanisms are not operating. The technical term for hidden memory is cryptomnesia, a word normally encountered in connection with other phenomena which seem to elicit hidden memories such as hypnotic regression, hauntings and psychometry (or object-reading). We shall start with some cases of cryptomnesia.

W. H. C. Tenhaeff cites an interesting case reported by Theodore Flournoy in which Hélène Smith had a vision, during a séance, of an Arab holding up a drawing in front of her. She copied out what she was 'seeing' from left to right. The letters turned out to be real Arab script and formed the *words* 'elqalil men alhabib ktsir', which mean 'A little friendship means a lot'. Flournoy discovered that her family doctor, Dr Rapin, spent his spare time on Oriental studies. The doctor was amazed when he saw the scrap of paper and exclaimed 'It is as if I see my own handwriting!' He went on to explain that he had written an account of a trip to North Africa and had it bound as a travelogue; on the binding he inscribed proverbs from his Arabic notebook. It turned out that the proverb in question was the first one featured in the notebook. Hélène Smith must have at some stage seen a copy of the travelogue, although she denied all knowledge of it. (This in itself is not, however, sufficient to rule out her having seen a copy: research in memory indicates that we take in far more than we realize consciously.)

An early case described by the Cambridge don G. Lowes Dickinson concerns the emergence of a latent memory under hypnosis. The subject was a clergyman's daughter, not a professional medium. She purportedly made contact in the spiritual world with a woman called Blanche Poynings who claimed to have known Maud, Countess of Salisbury in the reign of Richard II. She was able to volunteer a substantial amount of biographical material about the Countess's three husbands and various offspring. This information takes up two pages, and leads into a description of period costume and contemporary medical treatment. At a subsequent tea with 'Miss C.', the clergyman's daughter, Dickinson proposed the use of the planchette and 'Blanche Poynings' communicated, telling the company of the existence of a book called *Countess Maud* by Emily Holt. Miss C. said that she had indeed read such a book, but could not consciously recall anything about it. Dickinson's investigations revealed that all the facts were contained in the book; Blanche Poynings's character, however, was quite different, and Miss C.'s version seems to have been fabricated by her unconscious active imagination, based on the characteristics of an acquaintance of the same name.

Tenhaeff would call this last case one of 'hypnotic hypermnesia', that is acute memory under hypnosis, which has caused a weakening of inhibitions. The same principle is applied to repressed memories treated under psychoanalysis. The current vogue for hypnotic regression to 'past lives' provides some data supporting the cryptomnesia explanation. Ian Wilson documents an astonishingly detailed recollection by Jane Evans of a life as 'Livonia', a Roman matron living in fourth-century York. All this information was ultimately traced to a historical novel published in 1947 by Louis de Wohl. Tell-tale details included a fictionalized name used by both de Wohl and Jane Evans; correct identification of Roman towns, including an abbreviation from Verulamium to Verulam; and reference to other historically unknown characters appearing only in the novel. The episode appears to have been dramatized into a convincing narrative by the unconscious.

T. C. Lethbridge was a Cambridge archaeologist who made some remarkable discoveries in the course of his retirement in Devon. They have been described in his own books and by Colin Wilson. Lethbridge began experimenting with a novel dowsing technique using a much longer thread than normal. Having placed a silver dish on the door, he proceeded to hold the pendulum over it. It swung back and forth as he gradually lengthened the string; at 22 inches the pendulum suddenly went into a circular motion. He thus called 22 inches the 'rate' for silver, and soon found out that the same 'rate' applied to lead. If, as Lethbridge speculated, the pendulum was simply an extension of the mind of the dowser, it ought logically to react to thoughts and emotions as well. He tested the hypothesis by dowsing some sling stones, which reacted at rates of 24 and 40. On a nearby beach he then collected a bucketful of stones, using tongs to avoid direct contact; the next step was to test the stones - no reaction. He and his wife then threw some and retested. He established that the stones thrown by him reacted at 24 inches, while those of his wife did so at 29 inches, thus indicating 'rates' for male and female which were subsequently confirmed in other experiments.

But what about the rate of 40? Perhaps stones used in war would react to an imprint of anger? Lethbridge set the rates at 40 and thought of something annoying: the pendulum immediately various qualities and substances. Interestingly, 40 turned out to be the rate for black, cold, anger, deceit, sleep and death – related but not identical ideas; and 20 represented life, white, earth and electricity. A further fascinating observation was that the rates did not seem to decay with time. Thus

Lethbridge found that Elizabethan ironwork gave the male rate of 24 inches and the 'thought rate' of 27 (he found a thought rate associated with craftsmanship); while flint implements, perhaps 3,500 years old, also indicated masculine and feminine rates. The interested reader can follow up Lethbridge's countless examples.

Thinking in terms of force-fields surrounding objects, Lethbridge concluded that the rate for an object corresponded to the radius of its force-field. The next concept to introduce is the 'psyche-field', his term for the electro-magnetic field of the human being. (Other fields have also been suggested by Lethbridge - the dryad-field around trees, the naiad-field around springs and streamlets, the Ge-field for the Earth itself.) The reader will recall that Lethbridge managed to imprint the anger rate on a stone; if this can happen, then there is no reason in principle why emotions and thoughts should not be impressed on the fields of other objects or places. We now turn to this possibility.

Our next scene is Ladram Bay, where Lethbridge and his wife were collecting some seaweed for their asparagus bed. He describes his sensations on stepping on to the beach: 'I passed into a kind of blanket, or fog, of depression, and, I think fear.' His wife came to him ten minutes later, neither having yet spoken to the other, and remarked that she could not stand the place any longer with its horrible atmosphere. As it happened, his wife rang her mother that evening, and when she mentioned the bay her mother spontaneously observed that she had been struck by a depressing ambience on a visit to the beach some five years before. A further visit to the beach confirmed that the atmosphere seemed to have definite boundaries. On another occasion his wife remarked on a feeling at a certain point on a clifftop, apparently an urge to leap. She surmised that this may have been a resonance from someone who had committed suicide at the spot, or at any rate had seriously contemplated doing so.

We can now extend our analysis to certain classes of apparitions or ghosts. Lethbridge suggests that if thoughts can be transferred from human minds into the static fields of streams, trees, or even rocks, then resonant interaction with another psyche-field at some future date could produce a mental picture or emotional impression of a past event. G. N. M. Tyrrell advances the hypothesis that recurrent and apparently automaton-like ghosts exhibit a 'brooding reminiscence' and suggests that people living in haunted houses are drawn into 'the ghostly idea-pattern'. In Lethbridge's terms, the habits or traumas of previous occupants would have been transferred by them on to the fabric of the building and then displayed as mental images in the perception of some of the current inhabitants. This theory should by no means be taken as a blanket explanation for all apparitions, but it does make sense of certain types of apparition, where there seems to be no conscious agency animating it.

We are now in a better position to understand the phenomenon of psychometry, also called psychoscopy or object-reading, since it appears that the events recounted by the sensitive are mediated by the object. An anecdotal instance will serve as an introduction. A friend of mine handed her signet ring to a sensitive and asked what impressions she gained from it. The answer was in three parts: material relating to my friend's own life, to that of her mother, and to that of her grandfather. The ring had been given to her by her mother, who in turn had had it recast from the signet ring belonging to her father. Thus the ring had belonged to the three people whose lives had been illustrated. The simple theory that the images are somehow stored in the field of the ring fails to account for cases in which the events described either relate to the future or occurred after the object had left the owner's presence.

In such cases the only two theories remaining open are telepathy and clairvoyance: the telepathic explanation would suggest that the object enables the sensitive to make contact with the mind of the owner, whether deceased or not, and thus gain access to the appropriate memories; while the clairvoyant explanation would suppose that the object acts as a tuning fork for the sensitive to read out the images from a sort of cosmic memory or akashic record. Cases in which there is no obvious human intermediary mind favour the latter explanation. Consider the following two: a reading of a tie-pin produced both a description of the owner and that of the box lined with foreign newspaper in which it had lain for many years: a psychometrist given a book which had been stored in a bottom drawer was able to make forty statements about the contents of the drawer: only two were inaccurate. It could still be argued, however, that the information was actually obtained from the unconscious mind of the human subject who, while unable to recall the contents of the drawer, had nevertheless observed and absorbed them without being aware of the fact - a case of cryptomnesia.

Eugene Osty made an extensive study of what he called the metagnomic faculty in the 1920s and produced a classic book, *Supernormal Faculties in Man*, in which he set out his results. His work convinced him that a sensitive, or 'metagnomic subject' as he called them, is 'specially sensitive to the modalities of energy with which we impregnate the things that we touch [and] is able to cognize each of those who have touched the object as if that person were present'. This observation is consistent with Lethbridge's finding that stones which have been touched will register the male or female rate according to the sex of the handler. Osty furthermore remarks that one touch is sufficient to 'charge' the article with 'informative potentiality'. Nor does he find experimental results affected by the fact that the owner of the article was living or dead, present or distant. He, therefore, inches cautiously towards a theory of 'interpsychic communication at a distance'. His phrasing reveals that he does not consider the possibility of consciousness not actually being located in physical space; it does not seem to have occurred to him to consider the nature of the space in which discarnate consciousness resides, given the fact that he rejects non- telepathic theories. A similar problem applies to time. It looks as if we are talking about a realm beyond our ordinary notions of space-time, but which can nevertheless be translated into these familiar terms.

One of Osty's most intriguing and fascinating cases concerns reconstruction of the last moments of an 82-year-old man named Etienne Lerasle. The metagnomic subject, Mme Morel, was given a neckerchief belonging to M. Lerasie on 23 March 1914, three weeks after his disappearance; this item was naturally not with the man at the time of his vanishing. Mme Morel went into deep hypnosis and described the following:

> I see a man lying at full length, his eyes are closed, as if sleeping, but he does not breathe ... he is dead·... He is not in bed, but on the ground ... the ground is damp, very damp ... flat ground, uncultivated ... There is water not far off ... a large tree ... some very big thing quite near ... something very bushy - a wood.

When asked to follow the man on the day he went there, Mme Morel describes him leaving his house rather ill, with difficulty breathing and a confused brain, and then relates how he threw himself on the ground, wishing to die. It is clear that she is not only picking up physical impressions, to which she adds a description of the old man's face, but is also feeling states of mind. Cutting a long story short, the body was eventually found in surroundings as depicted; and the face and clothing corresponded to those described in Mme Morel's account.

I now quote Osty's own summary of the case:

On March 2nd 1914, a man who lived in the outbuildings of a country house in the department of Cher, left his house and was seen no more. He was sought for during twenty days. There was no slightest clue to what had become of him. No one knew anything of his life since he left his home. I did not even know that the man existed, and I used a metagnomic subject under hypnosis, to whom the man and his place of habitation were totally unknown. Under these conditions, where no influence from any living person could be alleged, the percipient reconstituted the last episodes in the life of the missing man, indicating step by step the path he had taken, the things he saw, his gestures (some of which were said to be characteristic by members of his family), his thoughts and the place where he awaited death, and his body was found; this place being accurately described in detail.

In considering how it is that this story subsisted somewhere, Osty wonders how it can be imagined to subsist unless it is a thought or memory of some kind. He asks whether there is a collective consciousness behind individual consciousness, 'a thought outside time and space, where every reality is represented', and answers elsewhere:

Beyond the human individualities that our senses detach from the continuity of Nature, we glimpse an immense mental world subjacent to appearances in which particular identities seem to be linked in an inconceivable collective psychic life. It is from this vast latent life of thoughts, of thought, that sensitives unconsciously draw the substance of their revelations, being endowed with a sense which enables them to distinguish the evolving schemes of individual lives.

It is important to draw a distinction between this collective consciousness and the idea developed by C. G. Jung in the 1930s of the collective unconscious. Jung makes it clear that the collective unconscious does not owe its existence to personal experience and acquisition, as does the personal unconscious: 'the contents of the collective unconscious have never been in consciousness, and therefore have never been individually acquired, but owe their existence exclusively to heredity.' The contents of the collective unconscious consist of archetypes rather than individual memories and events.

Tischner, at the end of his book *Telepathy and Clairvoyance*, also postulates the existence of some kind of non-individual or super-individual mind. He observes that supernormal phenomena are often produced 'in a state in which the consciousness of everyday life, the waking consciousness, has completely disappeared, and other strata of this mind, which are not accessible to us under ordinary circumstances, have taken command'. He goes on to argue that what he calls the subconscious mind is not as clearly separated from its surroundings as is waking consciousness, and that it 'represents a mental field which is connected with the "non-individual" or super-individual mind'. This subconscious mind does not belong to a single individual but is shared in such a way that it has 'knowledge of things which are quite unattainable and incomprehensible to the individual mind'.

Our investigations are bringing us closer to the idea of the participation of one mind in another, of the accessibility of our own private experience to other minds; in psychometry this operates via the intermediary of an object, and in haunting through a place. A curious case is cited by Herbert Bland of a person sleeping in a strange bed dreaming that he had been involved in a serious motorcycle accident. It turned out that his hostess's son had been involved in such an accident, but insufficient detail is given for the case to be regarded as more than suggestive of the bed as a psychometric medium.

The next case brings us back to Lethbridge, who made his own investigations into psychometry. He hypothesizes that the field of the object acts as a resonant conductor between the psyche-fields of the sensitive, the enquirer, and perhaps a third party whose experiences are being recorded. His observations persuaded him that he had to be present at the time of a reading; thus there was a minimum of three fields involved - the two psyche-fields and the field of the conducting object. In one experiment he gave E. a snuffbox made out of the timbers of the *Royal George,* sunk in 1787. Her immediate reaction was to go green and comment on the movement! This interrupted the proceedings for a moment, but when she resumed she gave a vivid description of a gun's crew grouped around a gun run up to an open port. Lethbridge doubted that she was reading his mind, as his own associations with the box did not include nausea. He comments that if she was tapping the information from memories of some long-dead soldier, then vivid emotional scenes from history might become available, even if not neat facts. On other occasions she referred to the stink of the dwellings in which some of the objects she was given might have been found. But we already know how seldom our ancestors washed ...

Lethbridge adds a reasonable caveat: that it is easy for the sensitive to pick up information from the mind of the observer. He illustrates his thesis by relating how he had left E. with a fragment of Anglo-Saxon glass while he went upstairs to tell one of his children a story. The tale finished with a scene of a duel between two men in Elizabethan times. On returning downstairs, he enquired about the glass, and E. launched into an account of two Elizabethans fighting a duel in a panelled room. This had come straight out of Lethbridge's mind and was elaborated with a few other items such as the looking-glass from the drawing-room itself. Despite this experience, Lethbridge did not automatically assume that the first case could be explained in the same way. The clairvoyance might have been brought about by the strength of the impression created by Lethbridge's story, which blocked access to other associations.

By a roundabout route, we are coming back to the life-review. We have seen how telepathy, clairvoyance and psychometry open up the life experience of other people to the mind of the sensitive, indicating that at one level our minds are not as separate as common sense would suggest. The implications of this observation will be developed in terms of feelings later in the book. At present we are concerned with mental phenomena. The Swiss politician and author Heinrich Zschokke had the remarkable ability of being able to psychometrize people, and illustrates this in his autobiography published in 1843 and quoted by Dr James R. Buchanan in his epoch-making *Manual of Psychometry* (1885). Zschokke asserts that he sometimes had a dream-like vision of earlier events in the life of new acquaintances; the scenes were quite distinct. For instance, he tells how he once told the secret history of a seamstress whom he had just met and who had just left the house. He and the company were astonished to learn afterwards that the details were all correct.

One day he and two companions arrived in Waldshut and went to have supper at the Vine Inn. The conversation turned around the eccentricities of the Swiss and, as it happened, one of Zschokke's companions was Swiss; his national pride was hurt by the mockery, and he asked Zschokke to make some reply, especially to a handsome young man 'who allowed himself extraordinary licence'. Zschokke continues:

> This man's former life was at that moment presented to my mind. I turned to him and asked whether he would answer me candidly, if I related to him some of the most secret passages of his life, I knowing as little of him personally as he did of me ... he promised, if I were correct in my information, to admit it frankly. I then related what my

vision had shown me and the whole company were made acquainted with the private history of the young merchant - his school years, his youthful errors, and lastly, with a fault committed in reference to the strong-box of his principal. I described to him the uninhabited room, with whitened walls, where, to the right of the brown door, on a table, stood a black money-box, etc. A dead silence prevailed during the whole narrative, which I alone occasionally interrupted by inquiring whether I spoke the truth? The startled young man confirmed every particular, and even what I had scarcely expected, the last mentioned.

As the ribald conversation had been ridiculing clairvoyance and the like, the young man must have been more than a little taken aback!

The Mind as a Whole

In drawing together the threads of our investigations so far, we can note that all the phenomena considered are consistent with underlying mind-connections. I began with panoramic memory, distinguishing it from the more emotionally charged experience of the life-review, and then considered the Bergson type of interpretation of brain/mind relation and sketched a resonance theory of memory. This theory was illustrated with reference to hauntings, atmospheres in particular places, and psychometry, all suggesting a kind of field associated with the object, place or person. This enables the sensitive to tune in to certain memory images by a process of empathetic resonance. In the panoramic memory the individual is tuning in to their own past experiences, while in the life-review they also attune to the resonant experiences of other people. This same tuning in to the experiences of others occurs in telepathy, clairvoyance, hauntings, 'atmospheres' and psychometry.

Two of the most powerful images recently impinging on our worldview have been the development of holographic techniques and the pictures of the blue Earth moving through the darkness of space. Holographic photography gives a three-dimensional representation of the whole unfolded in the parts; while the Earth seen from space displays the oneness and connectedness of life. Advances in theoretical physics have drawn of these images of oneness. Among the most significant thinkers along these lines is the physicist David Bohm, whose book *Wholeness and the Implicate Order* outlines a new world-view based on the fundamental insight of 'unbroken wholeness in flowing movement'. The wholeness is elaborated in terms of the implicate order in which 'everything is enfolded into everything'. In contrast we have the explicate (unfolded) order which displays everything as separate and distinct.

From this unbroken wholeness may be abstracted (literally 'withdrawn') what Bohm calls 'relatively autonomous sub-totalities', which are not independently and permanently existent but rather 'a product that has been formed in the whole flowing movement'. If we apply this analogy to consciousness and the findings of this chapter, we might say that our individual consciousness is a relatively autonomous sub-totality abstracted from cosmic consciousness or universal mind. At the explicate level of ordinary waking reality, it looks as if our individual consciousnesses are separate, a perception reinforced by centuries of analytical, fragmentary thinking which has lost sight of the whole. At the implicate level, however, there is this unbroken wholeness of consciousness in flowing movement, which gives us a theoretical basis for the kind of empathetic resonance noted in this chapter.

A helpful model of universal mind is advanced by the physicist Henry Margenau as he follows in the footsteps of Erwin Schroedinger's proposal of the unification of minds or consciousness. The quotation at the beginning of the chapter suggested that we were each the universal mind indicted with limitations that obscure all but a tiny fraction of its aspects and properties. More specifically, Margenau outlines three principal limitations: individual isolation, which he refers to as the personal wall which gives us identity as well as an ego; temporal restriction called the time slit, which narrows our time to the present; and what he calls 'probabilistic knowledge' imposed by the 'stochastic wall' - in other words we can view the future only in terms of probabilities.

He then suggests that these limitations are not absolute, but may vary in their strictness. Thus a widening of the time slit might allow precognition, while 'a lowering of the personal wall would enhance our sense of identity with others ... [and] might permit extrasensory perception in the form of a coalescence of information, perhaps in the form of mind reading'. Margenau's suggestion is perfectly consistent with the findings of this chapter; an expansion of consciousness in the life-review does indeed lead to an enhanced sense of identity with others, while psychometry represents one form of information coalescence through empathetic resonance. At one extreme we can isolate our consciousness and deny our connection to the whole, while at the opposite end of the spectrum are cases of identification with cosmic consciousness such as those we shall encounter in Chapter 3.

The same message, in somewhat different language, can be found in an address by C. D. Broad, a past President of the Society for Psychical Research. In it he elaborates on two common assumptions of normal cognition and perception: the 'principle of unique ownership of experiences', whereby the same experience cannot be owned by more than one mind; and the 'principle of the privacy of prehensible particulars', a long-winded phrase meaning that an existent or event can be directly apprehended by only one mind. In other words we do not normally assume that our experiences can be shared directly by other minds. What Broad calls 'telepathic prehension' (grasping through telepathy) contradicts the above two principles by giving one mind direct access to the experiences of another, thus indicating 'intermental confluence'. Such intermental confluence is usually inhibited by the brain's activity of 'attention to life', to use Bergson's phrase; the brain shuts out sundry impressions irrelevant to the business in hand. But in states of lowered inhibition, such as hypnotic trance or even a passive and receptive frame of mind, the barriers between one mind and another or between the present and the past are removed. Furthermore, it becomes apparent that the past is not lost, but is conserved in its entirety in a series of images or thought-forms; and if these images are emotionally charged, they can affect others years after the death of the originator or transmitter, as in the case of haunting apparitions or place atmospheres of various feeling tones. Our mental lives seem to be much less private than we are led to believe. With this in mind, we now move on to post-mortem review experiences.

CHAPTER TWO

POST-MORTEM
LIFE-REVIEW

———————

One day, when you return to the invisible world, you will be examined on how you have applied the law of Love ... you will find yourself confronted by the film of your earthly life, you will see the smallest details and notice the tiniest errors and you will have to reform yourself. You must therefore reflect and concentrate on what you are saying and how you are saying it. Here, you are an actor on stage, being photographed and recorded all the time.

PETER DEUNOV

People do not need to think so much what they should do, but rather how they should be. If we are good, then our works are radiant. If we are just, then our works are also just. We should not think to find sanctity on doing things, but rather on a way of being, for works do not sanctify us, rather we sanctify works.

MEISTER ECKHART

Death can be understood as the passage from one form to another, from a limited degree of life to another higher, freer one. It is wrong to assume that everything ends with death; what ends is only the temporary conditions in which people have lived on earth, that great school of purification and development towards perfection.

PETER DEUNOV

Beyond Human Personality

During his lifetime as one of the pioneers of psychical research, F. W. H. Myers wrote the classic *Human Personality and its Survival of Bodily Death*. After his death he was ostensibly instrumental in establishing the complex scholarly evidence for survival which came to be known as the cross-correspondences. A further work, entitled *Beyond Human Personality*, was written through the mediumship of Geraldine Cummins in 1935 and is subtitled: *Being a detailed description of the future life purporting to be communicated by the late F. W. H. Myers ... containing an account of the gradual development of human personality into cosmic personality*. This is not the place to discuss the problems and pitfalls associated with mediumistic communication; suffice it to say that the above book, and others on which I shall be drawing, is clearly and intelligently expressed. We can certainly apply the canons of the coherence theory of truth – the internal consistency of the reports – even if some readers would rather stop short of the correspondence theory of truth – that the reports accurately represent another level of reality. We shall also be bearing in mind the Bergsonian filter-theory of mind, which predicts that mind untrammelled by matter is not extinguished, but finds its capacities extended and enhanced.

'Myers' defines death as the passing from one speed to another, 'the adjusting of the soul to a more intense vibration, to a livelier, quicker state of manifestation'. Given that the phrasing is probably indicative rather than literal, the overall sense is that of a greater and more intense reality of thinking and feeling. Consistent with the filter-theory, 'Myers' comments that those whose consciousness is of a normal character will 'enter into a wider freedom and find their ideas of space altered and enlarged'.

In an appendix there is a revealing commentary on 'Prevision and Memory', which will illuminate some of the themes of the final chapter of this book and provide a prelude to some of the material to follow. 'Myers' explains that the Great Memory contains the record of every vibration of universal life: 'All experience has its duplicate in this register, this chronicle of eternity. Past, present and future may be said to be enshrined within the Imagination of the Supreme Mind.' It is this Mind in which our minds life and move and have their being. 'Myers' explains that this Memory should not be confused with the memory of the individual, which is like a river within the ocean; even individual memory, as we have seen, is only partially accessible, but 'after death, however, the mind is freed and less trammelled', and at a certain point in development it becomes possible to enter into the experiences and memories of its 'Group' – 'his wisdom and capacity for living intensely are thereby greatly increased'. This seems to be a learning experience, learning not just from one's own life but directly from those of other people. It is possible for the individual mind to enter momentarily into the Great Memory and thus perceive 'some image of a past or future event which is not contained within its individual memory'; the assumption here is that the Great Memory actually contains the matrices for future as well as for past events, and that it is possible for the future to feature in the extended present of an expanded mind.

'Myers' explains that imagination is the ruler and lawgiver of our being, that it has freedom to create and so 'because of its limited character when enshrined in man, it creates evil as well as good, and destroying the beautiful, seeks ugliness, creating misfortune and sorrow for others.' These cruelties invented by the human imagination are permitted by God, the Creative, Cosmic Power 'because only through such excesses may the soul of man evolve and grow, opening into the greater awareness through bitter experience of evil on the earthly level'. The rationale of this statement is set within the context of the post-mortem life-review where 'the soul is a spectator and perceives, at intervals, the episodes in the past existence. He dreams; sometimes the dream is a nightmare, sometimes it contains much that is beautiful and fine. The memories of evil must be considerable if these Hades-visions become acutely distressing in character'. This last phrase calls to mind the confrontation by Starr Daily of his past in the previous chapter.

The theme is illustrated in a section describing the fate of the tyrant, in true classical Greek tradition. Because the variety of the imagination is infinite, so too are the post-mortem experiences: a long gallery which contains scenes of the past. It is explained that the tyrant who gloated over the victim he cruelly tortured will experience similar pangs in his soul: 'His imagination has thrilled with, and delighted in, the ugliness of pain, so that ugliness surrounds, penetrates and overwhelms, in the dark places, of his creation.' The inner state is outwardly mirrored, the imagination mediates the empathetic resonance in this 'echoing hall'. The moral of the story is to realize the centrality of creative activity in each human being and the responsibility for one's creations, mental and emotional as well as physical.

Panoramic Memory and Life-review

Some of the most painstaking research into patterns of communications purportedly originating from the post-mortem world has been carried out by Robert Crookall. His analysis builds up a coherent theory about post-mortem processes, although he has been criticized for not being more selective in his resources. In *The Supreme Adventure* he differentiates between what he calls a review of the past life and the judgement. The first process is said to occur in the early stages of transition and is impersonal and non-emotional in nature. The language used to describe such experience is identical to that used for the similar event in the NDE: the events passing like a long procession or panorama, the life unfolding in a procession of images.

Such a stage is mentioned by Rudolf Steiner, the pioneering spiritual scientist to whom we shall return in Chapter 4. He speaks of the whole of the incarnation just finished coming before the soul of the dead as if in a great tableau of memories. He comments that the subjective experiences are omitted, the joys and sorrows connected with the pictures are absent: 'The human being confronts this memory-tableau as objectively as he confronts a painting; even if this painting depicts a man who is sorrowful and full of pain ... we do not experience it directly. So it is with these pictures immediately after death. The tableau widens out and in an astonishingly brief span of time man sees all the detailed events of his life.' Steiner's observations are certainly consistent with what we know about panoramic memory in the NDE.

Later in Crookall's analysis comes the judgement, 'an emotional and personally responsible review of the past earth life'. Typical features include:

1. The sense of a judgement of God through the higher self, similar to the experience of J. T. in the last chapter;
2. The judgement-bar being the innermost of oneself;

36

3. The reliving of past actions in every detail so that the pain and pleasure given to others is received back again;

4. The contrition felt by the soul at this self-revelation in which it is no longer possible to disguise one's motives.

We shall find that the cases described below elaborate on these features and enable us to understand the process and its implications in more depth.

Individual Cases

Maurice Barbanell

Maurice Barbanell was a leading spiritualist and medium. The book *The Barbanell Report* is supposed to be a report of his post-mortem existence and how it differed from his earthly expectations. The editor, Paul Beard, is in no doubt that he was communicating with his old friend. 'Barbanell' speaks of his life-review as a difficult time, 'my first uncomfortable period'. Asked if he saw his life forwards or backwards, he replied that it was a pattern, and compared it to complex toy railways with many intertwining tracks. Certain critical events stood out, in which hard decisions had had to be made. He refers to instances where it became apparent that he had been proud and vain, in spite of not realizing this at the time. Excuses did not seem so convincing from his new perspective, viewing the whole of his life at one point. He thinks that everyone eventually has to undergo this process which leads to some fundamental self-questioning arising from extended self-knowledge and scrupulous honesty. One particular episode concerned the mishandling of an incident with a reporter on his staff.

Humility is acquired through seeing through to one's underlying motivation by careful examination of past actions: cases of impatience and unkindness return as part of the learning process. 'Barbanell' adds another interesting remark about degrees of judgement when he observes that 'the more aware you are, the more aware your judgement of yourself. This is why some souls over here seem quite content, while others experience a certain amount of anguish.' In the light of his remark that everyone eventually faces this process, one can only surmise that the seemingly content souls are in a state of semi-sleep and inertia. He reiterates that the degree of self-judgement is proportional to one's knowledge, a reflection of those saintly people who often show an acute sense of their own unworthiness. It all depends on the criterion of comparison: Divine Love is much more demanding than popularity with one's cronies. In the end 'Barbanell' looks back on his period of self-analysis and disgust as a 'refining process' in which he became aware of characteristics of which he was previously unaware. Although he does not speak of direct experience of other people's feelings, this much is implied by his reliving past events from more than the personal and subjective perspectives. The key for him is the revelation and assessment of his motives.

Jane Sherwood

In her books *The Country Beyond* and *Post-Mortem Journal* Jane Sherwood reports communications from three individuals: her husband Andrew, 'Scott' (later supposedly identified with T. E. Lawrence) and 'E.K.' In describing his own transition 'E.K.' found his thought turning inward and moving at a surprising rate:

> It raced over the record of a long lifetime which it lit up with a searchlight that spared no blunders, sins or weaknesses, but impartially illumined it all, as one holds up an old, finished garment to the light and notes with dismay its rents and stains. This clear blaze of recollection showed me the honest shape and cut of the thing too. I reviewed it as though I no longer had any special responsibility for it but had to understand clearly in what I had failed and in what succeeded. I was saddened enough and humbled by what I saw, and then, with a sigh of acceptance I was able to turn to other thoughts.

The impression of speed is quite apparent, as is a degree of detachment, although the event in itself caused 'E.K.' to rethink his whole religious outlook. The other noteworthy feature is the sense of meaning derived from seeing the life as a whole. 'Scott' also comments on the panorama as a 'speeded-up run through of a film shown backwards, a swiftly moving vision of life from end to beginning, flickering rapidly past the mind's eye until it ends in the unconsciousness of one's beginning'. A later chapter explains the panoramic memory as part of a process whereby the etheric body (defined as the 'life' form which along gives sensation and power of growth and reproduction to what would otherwise be only an aggregate of mineral substances) is shed. The loosening of this body gives rise to the rapid survey of the lifetime: 'The etheric is a necessary vehicle for the clear-cut, detailed earth-memory and as the real being draws away from it, the record of that memory is exposed.' The next phase is a 'sleep' during which the subject allegedly loses the detailed memory of events, 'although their traces in the emotional body remain and can be recovered'. The implication here is that the feelings associated with events remain, even without the detailed recall of the events themselves. This is certainly consistent with the account of purgation that follows.

'E.K.' gives an extensive description of the process. He begins by describing how the astral body (feeling-body, as it were) is gradually strengthened, and concern turns to the past life; scenes and events are re-experienced in terms of their feeling content and in a much more comprehensive fashion, since the reactions of other people form part of the picture: 'Everything that happens to you affects others as well as yourself, and every event has therefore as many aspects in reality as there are consciousnesses affected by it.' Thus events are multi-faceted, and understood differently by the various parties in question; the event in one's own consciousness is only one facet. Therefore 'as an incident comes back to one's mind it brings with it the actual feelings, not of yourself alone but of the others who were affected by the event. All their feelings have now to be experienced in oneself as though they were one's own. This means that the effects of deeds on the lives of others must be experienced as intimately as though to do and suffer the deed were one.' Sorrow inflicted is sorrow actually felt rather than just known about; and it does not matter whether you were conscious of inflicting anything at the time; the process occurs regardless.

It follows that most of our deeds are performed in ignorance of their real bearing on the lives of others. Our normal perspective is to see and feel only our own side of the events, and to regard ourselves as fundamentally separate from other people. Such separation can be overcome by empathetic imagination or imaginative empathy, which enable us to put ourselves in others' shoes. The profundity of this scheme of justice, in which one learns experientially of one's connections with others, is that it is a form of redemptive suffering which breaks up any hard core of selfishness and cruelty. 'E.K.' comments that it is as if he saw 'through a glass, darkly' (I Corinthians 13:12) during physical life, but now sees things and himself in the light of a more comprehensive reality. Completion of the process leads to new possibilities for growth and expansion of consciousness.

'Andrew' takes up the theme and likens the process to traditional concepts of purgatory. Where the life has been definitely evil in the process is 'longer and more awful'. He comments that anger against oneself is useless, while shame and guilt 'come to be known as false attitudes due to pride'. The only solution is to accept and recognize one's full responsibility, 'stripping off all the pretensions' while working to eradicate faults and weaknesses. The final stage is said to be the emergence into consciousness of lives previous to the immediate past one, so that an overall perspective is gained; we shall return to this topic and its implications in a later chapter.

'Scott/T. E. Lawrence' speaks of the suffering caused by memories of the past which continually recur as a reminder of mistakes and crimes. On earth we rationalize them and excuse ourselves, but in the post-mortem state this is impossible: 'We can no longer ignore the point of view of the man we have injured and we have actually to experience what he felt in the matter as though we ourselves had been the sufferer.' 'Lawrence' comments that most people lack the imagination to do this, or else we might have been restrained from blindly ruthless actions. The intensity of feeling is said to depend on the fineness of one's sensitivity, so that a coarser being would not feel such pangs: a remark consistent with Barbanell's observations above. Typically, the author pushes the implications of his purgative experience to their logical conclusion when he says that this process of resonant suffering 'is really an illustration of the solidarity of mankind and proof that every deed affects the whole as well as the part'.

One poignant incident returns from the past, an incident which 'Lawrence' claims caused him infinite distress at the time, 'but the agony of realization I am enduring is in proportion to my keener powers of feeling'. During guerrilla warfare in the desert he had thought it his duty to condemn a man for conduct likely to imperil the campaign. He felt that justice demanded that he carry out the sentence himself; he murdered the man under pretext of military necessity, and bungled the job in such a way as to prolong the man's suffering. He could see no other course at the time, but now realized that he was driven to it by poverty of imagination and resource: 'Now I have to endure all that I did to him; not only the physical suffering – the smallest part of it – but I have to know his despair and remorse and the awful blow to pride and affection inflicted by my condemnation.' 'Lawrence's' mentor comments that he now realizes the full extent of sensitivity. The event was part of a train set in motion by the condemned man 'and carried on to a wrong conclusion by you'. It is a cross made by 'Lawrence' which he now has to bear. This cleansing ultimately bestowed peace and humility, 'with all pretensions to superiority, cleverness and wisdom burnt out of me': the fruit of the redemptive suffering already referred to by 'E.K.'

We can add a postscript on the effects of war, written about in the closing pages of *The Country Beyond*, which was first published in 1944. The awful deeds of war pile up an enormous amount of evil and suffering, with the net result that the purgation period is lengthened and redemption slowed up. A great deal of suffering is inflicted in wars, but the reciprocal law of resonance works just the same: 'All those who have inflicted suffering will in the after-life experience that suffering in their own being, not as a punishment but as a purgation, since in no other way can they free themselves of their own evil and pass on to a purer life.' It is important to notice the careful insistence on the word 'purgation', rather than punishment or divine vengeance imposed from outside. The deeds have in all probability been committed unwittingly and certainly in ignorance of the full range of consequences, but the moral order is not thereby evaded.

Albert Pauchard

Albert Pauchard lived his whole life in Geneva, and died in 1934. The book *The Other World* purports to be experiences and messages from him received telepathically over a two-and-a half year period after his death. One section deals explicitly with the exact mode of communication. 'Pauchard' explains that there is sometimes a time-lag between his transmitting the message and the sensitive receiving it, and that 'information which is too strange for your knowledge' is impressed on the mind in the hypnagogic stage – between sleeping and waking – when 'the exterior world has not yet had the possibility of intercepting it'. As for the mechanics, it is not the words which are given, but the ideas, for which corresponding words surge automatically to the mind of the sensitive. Moreover, if there are no available words, the message cannot be expressed. Summing up: 'I project the images of my truth into your mind – and your mind reflects them in its own way. Thus the words of my message are not from me. The message is from me – but the words are yours.'

As a postscript to this preamble on communication, it is worth noting what 'Pauchard' says about communication in the post-mortem dimension: that it is telepathic, a factor also reflected in the NDE encounters with a being of light or deceased relatives. He explains that he communes effortlessly with those in his dimension of many different nationalities: 'Conversation takes place without articulate words – by means of telepathy – don't forget this important factor; and each of the persons concerned is under the impression of hearing his own language.' This remark and other reported experiences suggest two levels of language: one implicit and direct, in which there is a direct transfer or perception of ideas and images, and the other indirect, in which communication is mediated and rendered explicit by language. In terms of Michael Polanyi, tacit communication and knowledge is made explicit, or in Bohemian terms the implication is made explicit, the images are clothed in corresponding words (see Chapter 1).

In biblical terms we are reminded of a Babel and Pentecost. Genesis tells us that 'throughout the earth men spoke the same language, with the same vocabulary'. They then make the mistake of settling down, baking bricks and building a tower, symbolic of their proud aspiration. This is too much for Yahweh, who comments that 'This is but the start of their undertakings! There will be nothing too hard for them to do.' So he decides to go down and confuse their language on the spot so that they can no longer understanding one another. The people are scattered far and wide. Now consider the account of Pentecost, with the appearance of the mighty wind and tongues of fire; those touched begin to speak in foreign languages ('speaking in tongues' is apparently not the same thing). The assembled crowd are amazed and astonished to hear what is being said each in their own language: 'How does it happen that each of us hears them in his own language?' Is it too absurd to speculate that the impression of hearing in one's own language was the explication of a communication which was in fact telepathic? We shall never know, but the intriguing possibility has been raised by this excursus into telepathic communication.

To return to 'Pauchard'. He seems to have some unusual experiences, which were at least in part a function of his own psychological make-up. Very early in the book he speaks of the burning of 'scoriae', the unacknowledged dregs in ourselves of which we are habitually unaware. The process described resembles a continuation of the Jungian individuation process in confronting and working through elements in the shadow. 'Pauchard' urges his readers to complete this process on Earth as far as is possible, probably because 'here all feelings and impressions are multiplied a hundredfold'. By being brought face to face with 'the various departments of our "I"', one is confronting the unregenerated forces of the past which will create suffering in the inevitable process of transmutation.

While walking by himself, 'Pauchard' was suddenly attacked by wasps which threatened to sting him. He was given to understand that the wasps symbolized all the irritations and thoughts of criticism which he had passively borne while on Earth. As he walked on, the sky suddenly clouded over and he was overwhelmed by feelings of desolating solitude. This time he was informed that the cloud represented passively borne depressions and despondencies. Each time the emphasis is on the 'passive hearing' of the situation, which means that he had thought the feelings justified and had therefore endowed them with life; and this thought-form now apparently has an independent existence. It can only be countered and 'exorcized' by a calm and steady contemplation which drains such feelings of the vitality with which the person had endowed them in the first place. In case this whole scenario seems too incredible to readers unversed in the dramatizations of the unconscious, one has to understand that the mental world in which 'Pauchard' finds himself is one in which the inner is manifest as the outer, a feeling of misery being outwardly represented by a desolate landscape. Swedenborg has more to say on this topic, as we will discover below. The main lesson seems to be to withdraw energy from those negative feelings and not harbour the kind of secret grudges which in any event sap our energy and lower our morale.

The next episode can be taken as an example of the creative power inherent in desire put into action. 'Pauchard' had a meeting with his parents and saw them 'as they were engraved in my memory. Scenes and conversations of the past become actual once more.' He then wondered whether it was possible to go still further into the past, and reached a time when his parents in their turn were adolescents and then children. He insists that everything was historically accurate to its minutest detail and that it was experienced in inverted chronological order, a feature occasionally noted in the NDE. His conclusion was that Earth has a memory of its own, since he entered not simply into his own past but also that of his parents. He likens the record to a cinematographical film, an image which we have frequently encountered before.

Another passage picks up on the theme of empathetic resonance. It tells the story of a woman whose purgatory consisted of feeling for herself the discomfort to which she unwittingly subjected others in her household. 'Pauchard' confirms that 'there comes a time for everyone here, when one has to become fully conscious not only for what is good and bad, but also of every joy – and every suffering – caused to another'. He makes the additional interesting observation that it is necessary to have attained a certain degree of development before one can actually pass through this kind of purgatory: 'Less developed souls are not capable of it, for they have not yet acquired the faculty to feel the necessary degree of sympathy' – a comment which goes to the heart of the matter, and implies the close link between imagination and empathy. Without imagination, it is impossible to put oneself in another's place.

This lady had been kind and good, but lacked precisely this quality of empathetic imagination. She had saved a young unmarried mother from committing suicide and found her some work; but the work was in a dark, cold and polluted room. And one of her charwomen, taken in out of kindness, was terribly overworked; the mistress failed to notice how tired she always looked, and consequently did nothing to improve her conditions. She now experienced not only the gratitude and affection of these two servants, but also the conditions in which they worked: 'At present this lady passed through a state of unconsciousness in which she personally and intensely identifies herself with the people and conditions I have spoken of.' Once more it is reiterated that although it is only those with heart and imagination who pass through their purgatory at an early stage, there invariably comes a time when the process of imaginative and empathetic identification has to be undertaken: a stage in the expansion of consciousness and compassion.

Helen Greaves/Frances Banks

Testimony of Light, published in 1969, has established itself as a classic in the field of telepathic communication between the 'living' and the 'dead'. Frances Banks was a nun, teacher and author of books on psychology, religion and psychical research. She died in 1965, and very soon made her presence felt to Helen Greaves, who transcribed the book. From the 'other side' she describes her death as a withdrawal from her worn-out body, with the immediate realization that she was the same in essence, although light and with a new sense of freedom. Her perception is more intense in the realm of thought in which she now is.

She then describes her own life-review. She starts by saying that she is beginning to realize the effects of her thoughts and to view the events that were set in motion by these thoughts and ideas. This is a 'sobering exercise', in which the mind stretches out to see all sides of a problem. Like 'Pauchard', she states that there is no compulsion to review one's past life on arrival: 'Some take a long while to tackle the problem. They dread to see the effects of mistakes and failures.' These people get 'stuck'. A case in point is a man who had been brutal and bitter to his wife and family. Having initially been tied to the places where he had exercised his cruelty and bitterness, he is now attempting to move on, 'but the film reel of his life appalled him; and he has become completely immobile'. Such people, we are told, are often overwhelmed by remorse and choose to live 'in the gloom of regret', a literal gloom on the same basis as explained by 'Pauchard': the inner state is mirrored in the environment, so that they life in 'self-darkness'. This state in turn cuts them of from 'the very Light that could illumine their minds, dissolve their guilts [forgiveness] and bring a constructive ray to bear on their problems'.

'Frances Banks' speaks of two 'blueprints' which are brought forward into her consciousness: one is 'the Perfect Idea with which my spirit went bravely into incarnation. The other is the resultant of only a partially understood Plan … in fact my life as it was actually lived.' A similar idea can be found in Plato's 'Myth of Er', when the souls choose the lives they will lead and then pass through the waters of forgetfulness. We shall return to this in Chapter 5. The first shock was the great difference between the two blueprints, so little having been achieved when one set out to do so much; all this the result of the partial understanding and clouded judgement so hard to overcome in the physical realm.

The whole cycle of her life-term began to unfold 'in a kaleidoscopic series of pictures'. She had the sense of being alone, and comments (as others have done in describing the NDE): 'Yours is the judgement. You stand at your own judgement. You make your own decisions. You take your own blame … You are the accused, the judge, the jury.' It was this searing experience which was too much for the people who got 'stuck'. It is certainly more than the panoramic memory, but it is only the first stage.

The second stage begins when the soul feels strong enough to 'take the earth life round by round', at which point the blueprints are once more brought to mind, 'only this time the start is made from the moment of departure from the body. The mind works slowly, oh! So slowly backwards through one's experiences.' This time, however, one is not alone but in the presence of a Being which she surmises may be one's own High Spirit or a Great Helper, this being gives 'strength, peace, tranquillity and [help] with constructive criticism'

45

in a way reminiscent of some of our NDE cases. The events are scrutinized for motive and result.

'Banks' also experienced a doctor's review, that of a surgeon who for years had been aware of an Inner Surgeon working with and through him. One day while under considerable domestic pressure he had cut a vein during an operation and the patient had died. He felt that he was losing his inner contact and became afraid, resorting to sleeping tablets. Eventually he had a nervous breakdown, fell ill and died. When the doctor had told 'Banks' his story, pictures of his life began to form in front of them, showing moments of stress, triumph and failure. They then visited the homes and families of those on whom the doctor had performed successful operations and saw 'the benefit to humanity, the healings, the resumption of happy, useful lives which were the result of this man's skill'. As the film wound on, the doctor saw that, in spite of his failures and weaknesses, he had carried through his blueprint. His problem had been 'a weakness in the soul's contact with the personality'.

There are many profound insights in the book which fall outside our theme, but it is worth saying a little about what 'Frances Banks' calls the Law of Progression. One of the post-mortem tasks is to shed the clutter of personality, which is accomplished in three ways: 'By self-judgement, and true assessment of experiences; by service to one's fellows; and by aspiration.' The self-judgement and resulting sense of proportion and humility have been our main focus; and we have also touched on aspiration, with 'Pauchard'. One of the laws of progress is said to be that the subjective of the Earth-plane mind becomes the objective in the new state of being: the inner content of thoughts, aspirations and desires fashions the 'outer' objective state or environment. This thought should be becoming increasingly familiar. One of its key consequences is that only by an inner life of 'meditation and contemplation and at-one-ment with Divine beauty and Truth' can one possibly aspire to the kingdom of heaven. There are no masks, no façades: the quality of the inner subjective life and light is exactly reflected; the jewel in the heart will be a radiance for all to behold.

The Significance of the Life-review

Having examined some post-mortem life-review cases in detail, I shall now adopt a broader perspective by considering the presentations of the phenomenon advanced by a number of mystical thinkers who recognize it as part of a wider pattern. Let us begin with Swedenborg, the great eighteenth-century scientist, philosopher and mystic, and then proceed to other significant figures. But we must first look briefly at two other angles.

Some of the most sophisticated mediumistic material has been published in the 'Seth' books. 'Seth' describes himself as 'An energy personality essence no longer focused in physical reality' and communicated by direct voice when the medium, Jane Roberts, is in a trance. One session was devoted to death and its immediate sequel. It begins by disabusing those who believe that they will be resting from their labours. Not only must the abilities be used beyond death, but it is furthermore necessary to face up to those not used in the previous existence. Transparent honesty is unavoidable in a world where telepathy operates without distortion and reveals innermost motives for all to see. The next process described is the examination of the fabric of the existence which has just been left: 'you learn to understand how your experiences were the result of your own thoughts and emotions and how these affected others. Until this examination is through, you are not aware of large portions of your own identity.' Once again we encounter the themes of empathetic resonance and the opening up of hidden parts of the psyche in an expansion of self-knowledge. Seth insists that self-examination is the one stage of post-mortem existence that cannot be side-stepped.

Sir Arthur Conan Doyle, remembered now far more for Sherlock Holmes than for his active spiritualism, apparently returned to give a restatement of the beliefs he had held during his lifetime. A few of his observations on values and the nature of the thought-world are relevant to our theme. The two bedrock moral criteria were, he said, 'personal responsibility and the redeeming power of love'. He went on to explain that this responsibility was not merely a question of actions, important as they are, but that one's inmost thought was crucial; the reason being that the post-mortem world is a world of thought, 'an internal state rather than an external condition'. He has found that thought is therefore more powerful than action: it creates the environment which is one's state of consciousness; and as one sows, so one shall reap.

Emanuel Swedenborg

Swedenborg was one of the great men of the eighteenth century, but has been sadly neglected by most historians of ideas. His scientific accomplishments were as wide-ranging as his interests in geology, anatomy and engineering. He also played a prominent role in Swedish political life. From 1743 until his death in 1772, he found that his spiritual senses had been opened and that he was able to enter effortlessly into the inner worlds and report back as an impartial observer; he sometimes demonstrated his remarkable abilities of ESP, but remained modest about his capacities. His most interesting book on our theme is *Heaven and Hell*, the account of his experiences in the inner worlds into which he alleged that people pass at death.

His starting-point can be simply seen from the section heading 'After death man is possessed of every sense, and of all the memory, thought, and affection that he had in the world, leaving nothing behind except his earthly body.' Some may surmise that this means that everything is left behind, but not Swedenborg. We shall first look at his ideas on memory. Swedenborg states that man has two memories, one external and natural, the other internal and spiritual. To the external memory belong the languages of the world and the objects of the senses, while the internal memory is the faculty concerned with rational thought and understanding of what he calls the universal language of the world of spirit. In the light of our previous discussion of language and telepathy it is interesting to read that this universal language is distinguished into ideas 'such as are those of thought itself' which enable instant communication. Furthermore, 'every man comes into this language immediately after death', a contention backed up by the evidence we have examined in NDEs and postmortem perception. While many events are lost to the external memory, the same cannot be said of the internal memory, since it is such that 'there are inscribed in it all the particular things, indeed the most particular, which man has at any time thought, spoken and done, nay, even those which have appeared to him as but a shadow, with the most minute details, from his earliest infancy to extreme old age'. This statement undoubtedly squares with what we have learnt about the nature of memory so far. Swedenborg is particularly insistent that nothing is lost.

This memory is taken on into the next life, where the person is 'successively brought into complete recollection of them; this is the BOOK of his LIFE, which is opened in the other life, and according to which he is judged'. His next statement has lost none of its force: 'Man can scarcely believe this, but still it is most true'; indeed it seems to be, judging from what we have observed so far. Swedenborg makes it clear that his remarks are made on the basis of 'much and daily experience' and illustrates this by citing cases in which people initially denied the crimes they had perpetrated in the world.

Confession to these felonies and misdeeds was engineered by drawing the events out of the memory for review: 'These deeds they confessed, because they were plainly set forth, with every thought, intention, pleasure and fear which occupied their minds at the time.' Those who had accepted bribes found 'every detail in regard to what and how much they had received, as well as the time, and their state of mind and intention, was brought to their recollection and made visibly clear'. One case concerned a man who had deprived a relative of an inheritance and poisoned his neighbour in secret. The relevant papers were disclosed in the first instance and the entire scene, including the person's prior thoughts, depicted in the second. Swedenborg sums up this section by stating that guilt is clearly established without any room for denial 'because all the circumstances are exhibited together' – an absolute justice unattainable even by the most perfect human legal procedure. We can gather from the above that the inner memory contains a complete record of thoughts and emotions, as well as events.

In discussing his experiences in 'Hell' Swedenborg explains that 'God never turns His face away from man, and never rejects man from Himself ... He cast no one into hell and is angry with no one', the reason being that God is Good Itself, Love Itself, and Mercy Itself. Consequently it is individuals who pass self-judgement by turning away from God, and refusing the ministry of angels. They are drawn into a sphere or state corresponding to what Swedenborg calls the 'ruling love', the essential penchant of the will. He then rejects the then-prevalent notion of God punishing human beings, and puts the onus squarely on the individual, who effectively creates a post-mortem situation.

In his exposition of the meaning of the scriptural passages referring to judgement and reward for deeds and works, Swedenborg seeks the deeper meaning, saying that the essential point is the appearance of deeds in inner form as an outcome of will and thought – in other words the underlying motivation. Externally, certain actions may appear identical, but their real worth is to be assessed according to the spirit in which they are performed. Swedenborg distinguishes various levels of inwardly good motives: they range from straight obedience to love of the good and the divine, 'for, as has been said above, deeds or works are precisely such in quality as the thought and will from which they proceed'. Nor is it enough simply to harbour good intentions: without expression in action such intentions remain 'interminate', seeds that fail to germinate.

Swedenborg's metaphysical psychology is remarkably similar in its premises to that suggested by our investigations so far: that memories are retained and reviewed, forming the basis of divine justice within the moral order of inner personal responsibility.

Rodney Collin

In his book *The Theory of Eternal Life*, Collin puts forward a theory of time cycles which he used to explain some of the characteristics of the life-review. He wonders what exactly happens between death and rebirth if one accepts the model outlined in *The Tibetan Book of the Dead*, in which there is said to be a definite interval between the two. Without entering into the intricacies of his time-scales, I can give an outline of his ideas, which are based on differences in time-speed in accordance with the three estates of death, life in the womb, and physical exist-ence. His speculation is that the period between incarnations is short, but that it contains as much experience as the whole of a physical life and must consequently be compressed and intensified accordingly.

In physical life experience and memory are sequential and successive; but if these experiences were compressed, 'innumerable connections of cause and effect' would appear. Collin goes on to cite the *Tibetan Book of the Dead*, which maintains that all the visions of the post-mortem state have to be recognized as projections of one's own mind. Combine projection with the compression of experience, and one can envisage the ecstasy or horror of a lifetime's events experienced simultaneous-ly: perceptions and feelings would, if compressed, be intensified in the way described in many of the cases we have reviewed. Collin writes:

> By the compression of time, such hates or cruelties would not only be heightened beyond bearing, but would be experienced together with all the fear, resentment and suffering to which they gave rise, and whose connection is normally hidden by the merciful oblivion of expanded time. While, on the other hand, such aspiration and devotion would become joined to the perceptions of higher laws and higher worlds to which they led. This would indeed be to ascend to heaven and descend to hell.

We thus face a situation of an expanded consciousness implying a contracted sense of time, because more earthly experience can be re-viewed simultaneously. This theory of compression and intensification is certainly thought-provoking and potentially explains the heightened emotions and empathetic resonance which we have encountered; but it fails to account adequately for the descriptions by 'Barbanell' and 'Pauchard' of a prolonged process of review which may dwell on individual incidents.

It is more like an emotional version of automatic panoramic memory. Moreover, Collin is attempting to fit his scheme into that of the *Tibetan Book of the Dead*, with its precise period of forty-nine days between incarnations. The central idea is perhaps more useful than the overall framework within which it is set.

Later in his book Collin devotes a chapter to the development of consciousness through becoming aware of the memory-film of one's life, which he speaks of as exposed but not developed. He recommends that one first bring back memories that can be recalled by association, gradually bringing to mind those most reluctantly remembered. He comments that it is our capacity to forget past weaknesses, embarrassments and failures that permits us to repeat them. Facing such memories extends our self-knowledge in a similar but less intense fashion than the life-review. From this we may come into an awareness of a kind of dual memory which sees what was and what might have been, thus providing the incentive towards reform and reconstruction of our life and character. The ultimate aim is a continual state of self-remembrance which enables death itself to be experienced consciously.

Peter Deunov/Omraam Mikhael Aivanhov

The great Bulgarian spiritual teacher Peter Deunov (1864-1944), whose sublime life and works are scarcely known in the English-speaking world, set the significance of the life-review within an overall context of spiritual evolution. The three pillars of his teaching are Love, Wisdom and Truth, also the essence of the Divine who can only be truly known in and through love. We are all destined to reach this knowledge, but some will take longer than others. After death, he says, people will see 'living images of their earthly life unwinding like a cinema film ... obliging them to relive their past in all its details. For most people this spectacle is a source of suffering and disgust.' Prolonged contemplation of these images gives rise to the desire to do the will of God from then on, at which point they may well be sent back to Earth to try again. They may once again ignore the inner voice of God, in which case the process is repeated in a compounded form. If, on the other hand, there has been progress and improvement, great joy is felt and the person begins to live a life closer to divine principles. There is a gradual process of cleansing and illumination until transparency to divine Love, Wisdom and Truth is attained. Through experiences of joy and suffering the soul slowly learns to harmonize with divine Love and maintain a constant contact with the spiritual forces of the invisible world.

Omraam Mikhael Aivanhov (1900-86) was sent to France by Peter Deunov in 1937 in order to preserve and spread his teaching in the West. There are now over 60 Aivanhov volumes in print, which compares with some 150 volumes of Peter Deunov in Bulgarian. In *Cosmic Moral Laws*, Aivanhov sets out his understanding of the moral order. It amplifies the well-known agricultural dictum that we reap what we sow, but not merely in actions: in thoughts and feelings as well. Thoughts and feelings are also seeds which grow to a harvest. Much of what he says will not be familiar to the reader: that there is a memory in nature and in ourselves which records absolutely everything, as Swedenborg maintained; that this memory is unfurled after death; and that empathetic resonance means undergoing the effects of our own thoughts, feelings and actions. This moral scheme becomes absolutely apparent and immediate only in the next world:

> All the harm we have done, we must undergo ourselves. That is what the moral law means, it is based on absolute justice. If on earth we are allowed to commit crimes with impunity, cheating, stealing, murdering, etc. … on the other side, the retribution is precise: we undergo exactly the same wrongs as we have inflicted on others. True morals are, first of all, true justice.

The consequences of being aware of such a process will be examined in more detail in a later chapter, but we can note in passing that it implies the need for much greater care and purity in our thoughts, feelings and actions.

Rudolf Steiner

Rudolf Steiner (1861-1925) developed his gifts as both seer and scientist. Decades ahead of his time, he sought to integrate his intuitive insights into a coherent scheme of spiritual science. He always insisted that others should develop their own spiritual perception, which would enable them to confirm or deny his findings. We have already seen how Steiner described the post-mortem panoramic memory. He goes on to describe the life-review as an integral part of the purging through which the I (Ego) passes in the condition of *kamaloca*, 'the place of desires'. This stage consists of a liberation from cravings and attachments to the world by 'the consuming fire of the spirit'.

Steiner tells us that during this time of purification we relive our lives backwards from death to birth and become aware of everything that did not spring from the spiritual nature of the Ego – similar to the blueprint perspective of 'Frances Banks'. Suppose, says Steiner, that at the age of forty we had an outburst of anger which caused pain to another person; we will experience the event again, but this time not with the satisfaction felt in giving vent to anger, rather 'the suffering the other person underwent through his unkindness'. The example is meant to illustrate how the painful element of this kind of experience originates in a craving to which the Ego gave way: 'In truth, by giving vent to such a craving the Ego was doing harm not only to the other human being but to itself; only the harm done to itself remained invisible during life. After death the whole world of harmful cravings becomes perceptible to the Ego.'

By the time birth is reached, all such cravings have undergone the cleansing fire and no obstacle impedes spiritual progress. Steiner stresses that the cleansing is not to be confused with karma, despite a similarity of sowing and reaping. His insight enables us to see more clearly the literal purging quality of the life-review, and the effect of yielding to negative emotions and thus inflicting harm on another human being, which eventually boomerangs back for processing by the perpetrator.

The Theosophy of Madame Blavatsky

H. P. Blavatsky's comments on the life-review follow naturally from her theory of the brain and memory. The brain is the canal between the psycho-spiritual and material worlds and is 'the registered organ of memory, but not memory itself'. Brain cells are 'receivers and conveyors of all the pictures and impressions, not their retainers', the retainer being Universal Memory which preserves everything. Indeed the word 'memory' is a misnomer in this context, outside our conceptions of space and time. Everything is present reality, from which past and future are abstracted.

At death, according to this scheme, the whole of a person's past life is marshalled 'in its minutest details':

For one short instant the personal becomes one with the individual and all-knowing Ego. But this instant is enough to show him the whole chain of causes which have been at work during his life. He sees and now understands himself as he is, unadorned by flattery or self-deception. He reads his life, remaining as a spectator looking down into the arena he is quitting; he feels and knows the justice of all the suffering that has overtaken him.

Blavatsky is here depicting an overview which enables individuals to understand their lives in a much more comprehensive fashion. The personal viewpoint is replaced by the universal and impersonal, with the widening of consciousness revealing the underside of life's tapestry.

Paul Brunton

Kenneth Ring was the first to highlight the remarkable parallels between certain elements in the NDE and the writings of Paul Brunton, a Westerner who had extensive first-hand contact with many Eastern traditions. Brunton published a series of books up to 1952, and then fell silent during the last part of his life (he died in 1981). This silence is now being amply compensated for by the issue of the notebooks he compiled during that period. They are some of the great spiritual documents of our time.

Brunton begins with the panoramic memory corresponding to a state of clairvoyance. As the person passes through death, they become aware of a secret record of 'all the multitude of ... experiences from prattling childhood to crabbed old age': nothing is lost, it all exists in picture form. Initial flashes are likely to conjure up the most intense episodes, an unwinding web of sharply focused pictures which stand out as if external to the person. Brunton agrees with Steiner's observation that the sequence runs backwards, and 'with a hitherto unknown and believable rapidity'. The whole episode, he says, highlights a backward-looking clinging to life.

The next stage, according to Brunton, is the emergence of a different consciousness, that of the Overself, the divine aspect in the overall identity. It is now the total impression of the life that is surveyed, through the revelatory perspective of the Overself which enables the person to become their own 'incorruptible judge'; the personal point of view is overlaid.

During this time he comes face to face with the consequences for other persons of his acts whilst on earth, consequences of which he was often quite unaware or in which he was often egotistically uninterested ... By this diviner light of a conscience magnified one thousandfold, he feels that whatever happened to him was a just result, was traceable in the end to his own character and his own deeds. A great remorse overwhelms him. He puts passion aside and sees this surface 'I' as the once-hidden observer sees it, without its own self-flattery and unconscious self-deception.

The common thread is once again the encounter with the consequences of one's life and the resulting feeling of remorse; also a revealing self-knowledge which redefines one's sense of identity. The new factor present in Brunton's analysis is the perceived connection between character and the events of one's life. Like Steiner, he comments on the value of this purge as a means of freeing oneself from the desires and attachments of one's past life and personality. A wider and deeper identity is discovered and experienced, to which we shall return in the next chapter. It signifies a growth beyond the concerns and limitations of our normal waking consciousness.

Pointers

In his book *Living On,* Paul Beard, one of the most experienced and level-headed investigators in the field, devotes a chapter to the topic of judgement. His concluding section clarifies various approaches to a process which he thinks is almost impossible for us to understand in our present terms. The life-review is on the one hand 'a living demonstration of moral forces in the universe playing upon and influencing a human being in order that he can learn to cooperate harmoniously with these'; then it is in the divine Will patiently helping a creature to overcome weaknesses and failings; then again it is an impersonal rendering of a balance sheet; and at yet another level it is the encounter of a person with their own creation. In each case it obliges the subject to acknowledge the truth of what is being depicted and to shift their self-evaluation accordingly.

It is now time for us to draw together the common threads of the last two chapters into a series of observations. While admitting the tentative nature of the proposals, I nevertheless feel they can give us some pointers to a likely post-mortem scenario.

1. Contrary to the expectations of the materialists, consciousness is expanded and intensified after death, with great clarity of

55

thought and acuteness of feeling. This finding is consistent with Bergson's filter theory of mind and brain, the brain shutting out most of the more subtle impressions of which we might become aware.

2. Inner and outer memory are preserved (at least in the short term); not only the events themselves, but also the associated emotions and thoughts. This memory can be accessed by sensitives through psychometry, clairvoyance and telepathy. This statement does not prejudge exactly what happens to personal memories in the long run.

3. The panoramic memory in a series of pictures 'external' to the individual and often episodic in character is one of the first post-mortem processes. It may run forwards or backwards or be surveyed as a whole. It is uncommonly vivid and flashes past at tremendous speed, which may be an effect of the compression of time.

4. The life-review is an inevitable stage but may be postponed by individuals who get 'stuck' at an initial viewing and are unable to face themselves. It requires a degree of empathy and imagination to be able to conjure up and appreciate the extent of the effects of one's life and thoughts. The review is normally experienced backwards from the moment of death.

5. The person, or deeper Overself, is the impartial judge of their lifetime. If there is an external presence, it is loving, forgiving, understanding and educative, but in no way condemnatory. The purely personal perspective of rationalizations and excuses fades away. One of the key questions is whether one can forgive oneself.

6. There is a comprehensive experience of all sides of an event in which the personal was involved, whether or not they were aware of the extent of such involvement. This means reliving both joyful and sad, creative and destructive consequences of thoughts, feelings and actions as if they were one's own. Such an emotional feedback loop suggests an underlying empathetic resonance with other human beings. There is an absolute retribution of both

good and evil, representing a personal purgation heightened by the intensification of feelings into an agony or an ecstasy.

7. The life-review is a revelation of unseen and/or repressed parts of the psyche in a way analogous to analysis procedures and the individuation process of integrating the shadow, as described in Jungian psychology. It is an encounter with the whole of oneself, an opening of the implicate into the explicate, encouraging and even compelling an honest self-assessment.

8. The life-review is also a purgation, cleansing and liberation from the past life with its attachments and cravings. The cravings are excised in the course of re-experiencing its damaging effects, as in Steiner's example of anger. The end result is pure humility.

9. The life-review is not an end in itself, but a necessary stage which enables further spiritual growth to occur on the path towards that transparency to divine Love, Wisdom, Truth, Beauty and Peace revealed in humble and devoted accomplishment of the will of God in whatever sphere one finds oneself in.

We shall now explore empathetic resonance in more detail, since it will provide connections suggesting and overall framework within which the above process of life-review can be understood: an inner interconnectedness of being, consciousness, thoughts and feelings.

CHAPTER THREE

EMPATHETIC RESONANCE AND UNITIVE CONSCIOUSNESS

Until he extends the circle of his compassion to all living things, man will not himself find peace.

ALBERT SCHWEITZER

And I have felt
A presence that disturbs me with the joy
Of elevated thoughts; a sense sublime
Of something far more deeply interfused,
Whose dwelling is the light of setting suns,
And the round ocean and the living air,
And the blue sky and in the mind of man;
A motion and a spirit that impels
All thinking things, all objects of all thought,
And rolls through all things.

WILLIAM WORDSWORTH,
TINTERN ABBEY

Man has the capacity to love, not just his own species, but life in all its shapes and forms. This empathy with the inter-knit web
of life is the highest spiritual expression I know of.

LOREN EISELEY

Introduction

At the beginning of his monumental *Golden Bough* Sir J. G. Frazer devotes a chapter to sympathetic magic. His analysis of the principles involved leads him to formulate two laws, the Law of Similarity based on the premise that like affects like, or that an effect resembles its cause; and the Law of Contact or Contagion, whereby things that have once been in contact continue to act upon each other at a distance in spite of severing of the physical contact. Both of these laws he subsumes under the Law of Sympathy since 'both assume that things act on each other at a distance through a secret sympathy.' The practice of the first type is epitomized by making models of a person and assuming that damaging the model will effectively produce the corresponding injury on the person. Larry Dossey cites a case of a man who believed that he had been hexed or cursed by a local shaman and would therefore die. He stopped eating and was wasting away towards death, a self-fulfilling behaviour pattern, until he and a colleague performed a counteracting ceremony which altered the man's belief and brought a sudden and unexpected return of appetite and health. This case is not meant to illustrate an instance of sympathetic magic, but to point out that the strength of a belief makes it possible for a hexing or curse to initiate a vicious circle: consciousness is mirrored in the physical body.

Contagious magic was supposed to work by contact, for example, the sympathy said to exist between a person and a lock of hair, so that a third party could work his will on the absent person via the lock of hair. Later in the volume, Frazer makes the point that both sympathetic magic and science presuppose an order and uniformity in Nature, although he insists that magic, is 'a spurious system of natural law' based on a misapplication of the association of ideas. But let us look a little more closely at the underlying principles as they relate to our theme.

At first sight, the empathetic resonance of directly feeling the emotions of others in the life-review seems to exemplify Frazer's Law of Similarity, with an effect resembling its cause: like producing like at a 'distance' of space and time. Perhaps, though, this model is rather crude, especially since the complex feelings experienced may arise from the multiple sources of other people's reactions. What exactly is the basis of such empathetic resonance? The very possibility presupposes an underlying web of interconnectedness and interdependence among human beings, perhaps even linking the whole of creation. Without an inner connectedness such 'co-feeling' would be impossible in principle. A moment's thought will also reveal a relation between psychometry and contagious magic: the object acts as a tuning device for the sensitive to pick up information clairvoyantly or telepathically from the owner or a cosmic memory.

We shall return to the practical implications of the principles of what Frazer calls imitative or homoeopathic magic in a later chapter. Our immediate task, however, is to make a further investigation of empathetic resonance in its various guises and in its correlation with unitive consciousness.

Empathetic Resonance with Physical Distress

One of the best-known accounts of this phenomenon was first reported in 1886. It concerns Mrs Joan Severn, who woke up one morning 'feeling I had had a hard blow on my mouth, and with a distinct sense that I had been cut, and was bleeding under my upper lip, and seized a pocket handkerchief, and held it … to the part … and when I removed it I was astonished not to see any blood'. She then realized that it was impossible for her to have been struck by anything as she lay in bed, and concluded that it must have been a dream. She noticed that it was seven o'clock and surmised, correctly, that her husband must have gone out for an early sail. At breakfast she noticed her husband furtively nursing his lip with a handkerchief, and told him that she knew he had hurt himself. He explained that he had gone out sailing and had been struck by a sudden squall, which caused the tiller to swing round abruptly and hit him on the mouth. Checking on the time established that Mrs Severn had sensed the blow at the time of the accident.

Another incident also reported by Mrs Severn concerned her mother. She had been sitting quietly with her and her aunt when the mother suddenly screamed, threw herself back on the sofa, put both her hands up to cover her ears and said 'Oh, there's water rushing fast into my ears, and I'm sure either my brother, or son James, must be drowning, or both of them.' The aunt was vexed and ashamed at her sister's behaviour, but the poor mother was quite insistent. Mrs Severn goes on to describe how her mother's feelings were unfortunately only too justified, as she looked out of the window and saw people hurrying towards the nearby bathing-place. Her uncle soon came up to the house looking white and distressed, with the news that James had indeed drowned. This case suggests a variant of the crisis apparition coinciding with the death of someone close, but this time the sensation was translated into physical terms.

One further case from the same volume was submitted by Mr F. Corder, whose wife went to London for an operation on her eyes. Her appointment was for 1.30. She had had previous experience of 'the close sympathy of our minds', he was somewhat relieved not to feel any decided sensation which he could construe as sympathetic. He went out at 2.45 to conduct a concert, and stopped in front of a watchmaker to check the time. 'At that instant I felt my eyes flooded with water, just as when a chill wind gives us a sudden cold in the eyes, though it was a hot, still summer's day.' He noticed that it was eleven minutes to three and was sure that it could not have anything to do with his wife's operation. Later on that evening he found his wife 'in a terrible state of nervous prostration' owing to the severity of an albeit successful operation. It turned out that the operation had in fact been delayed, and had started at ten minutes to three.

Other cases of spontaneous telepathy involving emotions are reported in *Phantasms of the Living*. One of the most authenticated concerns a Miss Martyn, who was sitting at home reading one evening, when at seven o'clock she experienced 'an undefined feeling of dread and horror'. She got up and paced around, but could not throw off the feeling. She then became cold and had a firm presentiment that she was dying; the episode lasted about half an hour and drained her of energy. She told a neighbour of the experience that evening, before receiving the news that a dear cousin had died at that hour. She had not associated the feeling with anyone in particular, but was simply aware that something dreadful was happening. A similar story is told by Emily Reay, who was suddenly overcome by a dreadful feeling of illness and faintness which gave her the impression that she was dying. When her husband failed to return at dinner time, it suddenly occurred to her that he had perhaps been taken ill at the time of her attack. He was brought home half an hour later in an almost unconscious state. When he was well enough to explain what had happened, he said that he had suddenly become very ill as he was leaving the office – at precisely the time that his wife had collapsed.

These five cases all have the background of strong affinity and affection – husband and wife or mother and son – which not unnaturally makes empathetic resonance through loving concern more plausible. One would hardly expect such an occurrence between complete strangers.

Few modern cases of this type seem to have been documented, but it would be surprising if this kind of empathetic resonance were not quite frequent within families; although only a proper research study could give a definite answer. One more recent case was reported by Rosalind Heywood in December 1963; she has some personal experience of similar sympathetic occurrences. Mrs D. reported that she gave birth to a son on 12 January 1963, unexpectedly early, as the baby was expected in the second half of February. She and her mother had had the sense of being in telepathic rapport on other occasions prior to this incident, but she had given her no indication that the baby might arrive early. She awoke at 2.15am on the day and immediately realized that birth was imminent, and so went to the hospital. Labour proper began at 8am and the child finally emerged at 1pm. Meanwhile her mother, in Israel at the time (two hours ahead of BST), developed stomach pains at quite frequent intervals around 11am, that is just as the baby was being born. She went to the toilet, but to no avail; the pain became almost unbearable and continued until 2.00, after which it gradually began to subside. She received news of the birth later in the day. The daughter added that at the time of birth she was 'mentally crying out for her mother', a fact which gains significance when one thinks of cases of crisis apparitions in which a third party is able to confirm that the dying person was directing their thoughts to the person who saw the apparition at the time.

We pass now to cases involving the medical profession, beginning with Dr James Rhodes Buchanan, whom I have already mentioned in connection with Psychometry (Chapter 1). In an interesting and provocative passage Buchanan recommends the development of empathetic diagnosis as part of medical training. Not that he holds out much hope for this proposal being officially adopted by a profession controlled by colleges and societies which ensure 'the maximum degree of conservative stolidity'. He joins battle with the 'dogmatic materialist' who denied (and still do!) the principles and practices of Hahnemann's homoeopathy. The customary medical assumption is that the effect produced by a drug must be in proportion to the quantity of medicine received as a result of internal contact. Buchanan went a step further than Hahnemann by conducting experiments with medicines sealed in glass phials which were then held in the hands of the subject, who was totally unaware of the contents. His results showed that between half and three-quarters of 'miscellaneous company' will feel the effects, and eighteen out of a Boston medical class of twenty. Unfortunately, however, Buchanan gives no further analysis of the results. His point is that the sensitive will pick up the effects of the dose in a manner similar to the effects conjured up in magic by a lock of hair or a letter.

In his clinical practice Dr. Buchanan claims to have had a vivid realization of his empathy with the conditions of his patients. He tells us that he suffered from depression after the visits of a patient with acute dropsy. Then, one evening, about eleven hours after his visit, he was made aware that the patient was suffering by a sensation in the head which came on quite suddenly. This happened at 10.05 pm and subsided to become a restless feeling of depression within ten minutes. Then again between 4.00 and 5.00 am Buchanan 'perceived a very restless, unpleasant and exhausted condition, which induced me to take something for its relief'. On visiting the patient at 10 o'clock he learned that the symptoms and timing corresponded. He adds that this head was particularly sensitive to such impressions.

Herbert Bland, referring to Dr. Buchanan, speaks of cases in which psychometrists are adversely affected by 'contaminated articles' associated with some mental disturbance or depressing emotion. Occasionally these effects last for some time, as happened to a sensitive who held the hands of a man who, unknown to her, was suffering from abdominal cancer. It was not long before she felt an acute pain in her own body; this continued for six weeks, until the man died. The rationale offered by Bland is that the minds of sensitive and subject are joined during the reading, and that the pain is transferred to the mind of the sensitive and becomes psychosomatically manifest in her body.

Eugene Osty has probably done more research than anyone else on what he calls supernormal cognition of the organic states of a human personality. His sensitive, Mlle de Berly, was able to enter into the organic states of his patients simply through contact with a piece of paper on which was a jotting by the patient. She had no medical knowledge and did not even know of the existence of the patient; the writing gave no abnormal indications. In one case she gave the following description (abridged):

How feeble this person ... she must have had a fever from time to time, for I am thirsty. She falls asleep suddenly but that does not last ... what a curious brain, heavy and giddy ... I should think her used up whatever her age may be ... her nervous system exhausted ... it is the blood that weakens all her organs ... she is nervous ... the bowels do not act ... the whole organism is in a bad state ... she is difficult to prescribe for because so many organs require attention ... the whole illness comes from the heart and the stomach, from digestion, and above all from impure blood.

Osty then gives the content of his own thoughts at the beginning of the séance, and confirms that the case was extraordinarily obscure and that Mlle de Berly had accurately described the symptoms. One part of the prognosis, however, contradicted Osty's own opinion: the sensitive claimed that the woman was threatened with premature death. And indeed after further medical intervention she did suddenly collapse and die.

Two more cases from Osty's book deserve mention. Mlle de D., a young war widow, came to see Mlle de Berly in 1920. Without any prompting she spoke of the lady's loss and then proceeded to describe her little boy of eight, commenting that his health seemed to give no cause for concern, 'but believe me; have the child's blood examined and put him under medical care ... his blood is affected and great trouble might arise in the future.' Mme de D. followed the advice, and it was discovered that the child was very Bordet-Wasserman positive, indicating a syphilitic taint. The other case is described by Osty as part of a discussion of imagery. Two separate diagnoses are cited: a feeling of nausea corresponding to a stomach condition; and a tiredness of the back and a painful abdomen. Mlle de Berly advised Osty to look at the patient's abdomen. In fact the women in question was four months' pregnant!

Larry Dossey has reported an interesting case: a cardiac patient of his was hospitalised in a coronary care unit. Two days previously he had suffered an extensive myocardial infarction, and he was gravely ill. His wife visited him regularly, and on the third day Dossey was summoned to deal with an emergency case of shortness of breath. But it was not his patient, but the patient's wife who was pale and clutching her chest with pain. She, too, had developed an acute myocardial infarction. Dossey comments that it is by no means rare to see sequential development of identical illnesses in spouses.

Cases of all the types considered in this section suggest an empathetic resonance to physical distress which is mediated through the consciousness and thence to the percipient's own body. The first group involved people who already had considerable empathetic rapport; the second were doctors with a devoted concern for their patients; the experience of an expert psychometrist and those of a doctor observing spouses complete the picture. It is clear that there is some kind of sensitive link in consciousness between the two people concerned in each case, the same phenomenon as that found in the life-review: a synchronistic tuning in to the state of another. For if consciousness is not actually in physical space, perhaps it makes less sense to talk about cause and effect than about direct participation in another's state. An excursus in the next station into other manifestations of empathetic resonance will take us further.

Empathetic Resonance through Emotions

In researching cases of this type I could not find an experience occasioned by a joyful incident; they all seem to herald death or disaster. A fairly recent instance was written up in March 1968 by William Freed, who had earlier had an ESP experience at the time of his elder daughter's escape from drowning. This time he awoke on 5 October 1965 with a strong feeling that something was wrong with his younger daughter. He was so depressed that he took a day's sick leave from the office. He was in New Zealand; his wife and daughter in London. In the course of the day he made a number of phone calls in an attempt to locate his wife, and eventually received a call from her telling him of his daughter's illness. In this case the daughter had felt better by the time Freed seized with the sense of anxiety, which he surmises may have originated in his wife. Prior to his first experience Freed had been a sceptic about ESP, but a telepathic dream about the near-drowning incident had changed his views.

A typical 'emotional' case would be that of a young man who had enjoyed a convivial evening with friends and was getting ready to leave just before midnight when he was overcome by 'an indescribable feeling of intense sadness' which 'heralded a complete breakdown, and I was led away from the piano in hysterics'. The following morning he received a telegram to say that is father had unexpectedly passed away in an epileptic fit just before midnight the night before. He had just been telling his sister how much he was looking forward to seeing his son the next day. In similar cases the sensitives speak of falling into altogether extraordinary states of depression and restlessness, of being 'over-whelmed with a most unusual sense of depression and melancholy', or experiencing 'a strange sadness and depression'.

Some more recent cases are less traumatic. One woman wrote of a dream she had on the night of her sister's death, in which she seemed to accompany her on her post-mortem journey. The sister announced her departure, and they were both in a sort of boat on a stream passing through an underground tunnel. They suddenly emerged into brilliant sunshine next to a river. The sister was then met and taken across the river. When she waved goodbye, the woman experienced an indescribable happiness and woke up in floods of tears. Another woman described her experience at the time of the accidental death of her husband: she had been walking on the beach when she was suddenly overcome with a tremendous sense of freedom and joy. Only later did she discover that this feeling must have coincided with her husband's death in a plane-crash. She felt that she had somehow accompanied him part of the way and returned.

Sometimes people are gripped by a strange compulsion which urges them to take an improbably and even apparently absurd course of action. For example, a friend of Dr Buchanan's, Dr Gray, was driving in New York when he had the sudden impression that he was needed by a patient. He ordered his driver to turn round and drive at full speed to her residence. As he came within a block of her house he saw her husband rushing for medical assistance. Dr Gray just made it in time to save her dying from a haemorrhage. A Mr Rowlands saved the life of a minister who had been preaching and was staying in his neighbourhood: at about 12 or 1 in the morning he felt sufficiently disturbed on his account to get dressed and go to his lodgings, where he was met by the amazed landlady, herself unaware that anything was amiss. When he went to his bedroom he found the minister in great physical distress, sweating profusely, unable to move from the side of his bed. The minister's own account of the incident reveals that he had been unable even to call the landlady – 'I could not move any further or speak'– and was convinced that he would have died without the intervention of Mr Rowlands. This particular case does not suggest a close affinity between the two parties, but Mr Rowlands was clearly somehow sensitised to act on a distress signal. It is open to questions whether we need to postulate another intervening intelligence to explain the connection.

According to Rosalind Heywood, telepathic communications between herself and her husband tend to occur when there is an emotional need and no ordinary means of communication as at hand. One case involved her leaving her notes for a BBC programme on the front doorstep. It was too late for her to go back; moreover her husband was on the golf course and unreachable. On arrival at the BBC she was going to phone home, 'only to be told that a message had already come from her husband that he was on his way with the envelope'. On his way he scribbled an account of what had happened to him: on arriving at the golf course he had been told by 'Orders' (the name they gave to apparently irrational impulses to action) to go home without playing. He was then about to enter the house by the side door when 'Orders' told him to go in at the front, at which point he noticed the envelope and hurried off to the BBC. Heywood stresses that such cases of useful telepathic interaction between them were so frequent that 'to ascribe every one of them to chance would seem to us more credulous than to accept the reality of ESP'.

One further phenomenon deserves mention in this section: the shared dream. Few modern instances are available, but there are older cases on record. One husband and wife reported frequent synchronistic dreams, some of which were quite singular, such as being charged by a bull. Another wife dreamt that she was dying and awoke to find her husband sobbing but asleep. On being roused he said that he had been dreaming that she was dying. An even more curious case concerned a woman who woke up in the middle of the night and tried to recall the first line of a Tennyson poem – was it 'Home they brought' or 'Back they brought her warrior death'? Her husband was soundly asleep but suddenly stirred, and, on being questioned, said that he had woken with the words on his lips 'Home they brought their warrior dead'. They had not been reading the poem together, and she was sure that she had not said anything out loud.

Some of the above cases are examples of needs tacitly communicated, some of shared feelings, some of synchronistic emotional responses to death or disaster; but in every case no physical communication took place. The message or impression arose in the consciousness of the other without any immediate contact. The next section brings us back to NDEs and the experience of unitive consciousness.

Cosmic Empathic Resonance in the Near-death Experience

The fourth stage of the NDE as analysed by Kenneth Ring is 'seeing the light', and usually follows the experience of emerging from a 'tunnel'.

In the letter archives of the International Association for Near-death Studies (UK) we have a number of descriptions from people who have had an NDE typical of this phase:

> I seemed to 'float' along a corridor towards, then into, all enveloping brightness and light with indefinable shades of pastel-like colours. There were what I can only describe as billions of beautiful shimmering forms, no outlines, as they were all 'cloaked' in what looked like a garment of translucent light. The most wonderful thing was the music, which I can only describe as almost a tangible joy from, yet part of an encompassing these forms, of which one appeared to be the source and somehow embraced all else.

> I found myself travelling towards this tremendous light, so bright that it would have blinded me if I'd looked at it here, but there it was different. I reached the light which was all around me ... and I felt this wonderful love enfolding me and understanding me. No matter what my faults, what I'd done or hadn't done, the light loved me unconditionally.

> A light was glowing invitingly – I was encouraged by a strong feeling to enter the light. I approached without haste as I felt the light was part of the jigsaw to which I rightfully belonged. As I entered I felt the light glow. I was peaceful, totally content and I understand why I was born on earth and knew the answer to every mystery.

> What I did have was a complete and extensive knowledge to the extent of being able to comprehend the purpose of life and Creation, because I was part of it, as when the body uses the ability to see – smell – taste and touch – hear – without prior thought.

The first two of these accounts focus on love, while the other two speak of knowledge, a different perspective on and understanding about life. The love is always described as all-encompassing, enveloping, flowing through the person so that there is no sense of separation – rather an all-pervasive unity, peace, harmony and joy. The knowledge seems literally to be an insight into the nature of reality from the unitive eye of the divine, beyond the separation inevitable in dualistic intellectual thought and perception. These experiences of love and knowledge are just glimpses, not all of which are remembered or expressible on return. We shall now look at these affective and cognitive experiences in more detail.

As the light comes closer, it becomes brighter and more all-embracing: it surrounds, encompasses and submerges the experiencer:

> I just found myself in this extremely bright light and felt absolute peace. I feel the light and the peace were one ... I had no sense of separate identity. I was in the light and one with it.

> I went forward toward the light and as I did so I had such a feeling of freedom and joy, it's beyond words to explain. I had a boundless sense of expansion.

> I came into the arc of pure golden love and light. This radiation of love entered me and instantly I was part of it and it was part of me.

> It's something which becomes you and you become it. I could say 'I was peace, I was love'. I was the brightness, it was a part of me ...

> It was just pure consciousness. And this enormously bright light seemed almost to cradle me. I just seemed to exist in it and be part of it and be nurtured by it and the feeling just became more and more ecstatic and glorious and perfect.

> In the middle of one circle was a most beautiful being ... an immense, radiant love poured from it. An incredible light shone through every single pore of its face ... I was filled with an intense feeling of joy and awe.

Although I have distinguished the affective and cognitive aspects of the experience for the purposes of analysis, no such separation is reported. It can be seen from the above extracts, moreover, that the sense of unity and non-separation is the central insight of this pure consciousness. Oneness with love, peace, joy and light implies that these qualities are at the core or centre of our being as it expands beyond its usual boundaries; and this same essential core seems present in all reports of such experiences as the source and goal of life. It is an immanent divine presence which transcends the limitations of the ego and yet represents the very fulfilment of its aspirations in the divine order. 'Knowledge is a function of being', wrote Aldous Huxley: 'When there is a change in the being of the knower, there is a corresponding change in the nature and amount of knowing'. This observation is clearly borne out in the NDE, as the following passages illustrate.

As I became one with this omnipresent light, its knowledge became my knowledge. I was in a single instant what my life had been and what had been of meaning in my life.

The second most magnificent experience ... is you realize that you are suddenly in communication with absolute, total knowledge. It's hard to describe ... you can think of a question ... and immediately know the answer to it.

You're all-knowing, and everything is a part of you ... it's just so beautiful. It was eternity.

You're engulfed by it and you begin to know a lot of things. I remember I knew that everything ... in the universe was OK, that the plan was perfect.

The unity or non-separation is the basis of this immediate knowledge, some of which cannot be recalled on return to the contracted consciousness of the body. Communication appears to be telepathic and immediate, that is it transcends language; hence, perhaps, one of the problems of recall. It is as if the knowledge is gained from the divine identification from within reality, with which the individual is momentarily fused. The first extract above resembles Jung's 1944 experience described in his autobiography: 'I consisted of my own history, and I felt with great certainty: this is what I am, "I am this bundle of what has been, and what has been accomplished" ... I was what I had been and lived.' The last quotation brings to mind Julian of Norwich's affirmation that all is and shall be well, despite appearances to the contrary. The experiencer has a momentary glimpse of the larger pattern and meaning which is hidden from normal human thought and perception.

At this point a comparison with negative NDEs is in order. They are characterized by the opposite impressions from those encountered so far. Experiencers are dominated by feelings of loneliness, fear, desolation, alienation and separation. Using the holographic image of tuning in to frequency domains, it would appear that the negative experiencers are attuning to one end of the spectrum with its fearful isolation, while the mystical merging is the reverse: an attunement 'to the primary level of reality, a dimension of order and harmony'. The first is the jangle of cosmic discord, and the second the beauty and bliss of cosmic harmony. Negative experiencers are eager to escape back into the world, while positive experiences are often reluctant to return after tasting such ecstasy. This suggests that the dynamic process of the spiritual universe is moving towards wholeness and harmony away from fragmentation and discord. The harmonic chord of cosmic empathetic resonance magnetically draws the whole of creation towards itself. The near-death experiencer is briefly in perfect empathetic attunement with this comic resonance as he or she reflects and literally dis-covers the divine qualities of peace, love, light, joy and beauty. But this is simply a foretaste of the long spiritual journey ahead.

The NDEs reported above all took place within a Western context and are typical of what is known as absorptive mysticism, where the self is absorbed into a higher or deeper order of reality. It is instructive to compare these accounts with other classical mystical texts. In speaking of the illumination of the self, the nineteenth-century scholar Récéjac comments:

The whole consciousness is flooded with light to unknown depths, under the gaze of love from which nothing escapes. In this state, intensity of vision and sureness of judgement are equal: and the things which the seer brings back with him when he returns to common life are not merely partial impressions ... they are rather truths which embrace the world, life and conduct: in a word, the whole consciousness.

The light, love, intensity and certainty are common features of the cases we have been examining. Récéjac also anticipates a theme which will be treated later in this chapter, namely the spiritual implications of the mystical encounter. The fourteenth-century Flemish mystic Jan van Ruysbroeck gives a beautiful description of mystical union:

And all those men who are raised up above their created being into a God-seeing life are one with this Divine brightness. And they are that brightness itself, and they see, feel and find, even by means of this Divine Light, that, as regards their uncreated essence, they are that same onefold ground from which the brightness without limit shines forth in the Divine way, and which, according to the simplicity of the Essence, abides eternally onefold and wayless within. And this is why inward and God-seeing men will go out in the way of contemplation, above reason and above distinction and above their created being, through an eternal intuitive gazing. By means of this inborn light they are transfigured, and made one with that same light through which they see and which they see.

This wonderfully subtle piece is hard to grasp at one reading. Ruysbroeck speaks of being the brightness itself, at one with the Light, realizing that the ground of his being is that same brightness; and that it is by this brightness or light that he sees. The ineffability is expressed by the phrases 'above reason' and 'above distinction', that is beyond duality and distinct identity. In a similar passage on spiritual marriage, Fénelon, the seventeenth-century French archbishop, talks of the soul being filled with the joy of the Holy Ghost and being given a foretaste of heaven. During the sixteenth century, Louis de Blois wrote what an exceeding great thing it is 'to be joined to God in divine light by a mystical and denuded union':

> Through the brilliancy of the divine light shining on the mind, it [the soul] loses all consideration and distinction of things and lays aside all, even the most excellent images; and all liquefied by love, and, as it were, reduced to nothing, it melts away into God. It is then united to God without any medium, and becomes one spirit with Him, as iron placed in the fire is changed into fire, without ceasing to be iron ... here the soul reposes ... sweetly experiencing the operation of God, it abounds with ineffable peace and joy.

Another exquisite rendering with a union of light and love: the light seems to enable the soul to transcend the mind, while the love melts it into unity, a divine embrace of peace and joy. These two extracts from the Christian mystical tradition display a literary finesse and sensibility which one does not expect to find in the average NDE account, and perhaps convey the essence of the experience more adequately as a result.

For the sake of contemporary comparison, we shall now look at two further accounts with common themes. The first experience took place on a bus and conveyed three distinct impressions: the first was a great brightness, the second 'was like a flash of insight during which I seemed to understand the nature of things, knew that it was good, and that all was well; and the third was a feeling that I was a vessel into which a great love was flowing from the centre of the brightness'. These comments speak for themselves.

The next account is too long to be quoted in full. It is the experience of a woman who had been ill and in a state of considerable inward distress. She was writing quietly at her desk when everything vanished from physical sight; time and space ceased to exist. Then the whole room was filled with a great golden light, and her ordinary 'I' disappeared. It was a mystical moment of union with the mysterious infinite, 'with the things, all people', a grand purgation in which the ego 'drowned in boundless being', and all fears vanished (including fear of death). She seemed to comprehend the nature of things: 'I understood that the scheme of the universe was good, it was only man that was out of harmony with it.' In observing the endless struggle towards the light, she was suffused with love and suffering and compassion, knowing that she could never again condemn any person. Here the union of empathetic resonance issues, as with the NDE, in an expression of unconditional love.

The One in the Many, the Whole in the Part

Philosophers East and West have been wrangling about the priority of the One and the Many, monism and pluralism, for almost as long as the history of the discipline. In the cases that we have been examining, the experiencer finds that the normal state of individualized waking consciousness is absorbed into a unitive consciousness which dissolves the separate sense of self both intellectually and affectively through light and love. This is what W. T. Stace calls introvertive mysticism, the dissolution of individuality into a unitary consciousness. Two of his examples come from Plotinus and Tennyson. Plotinus writes that the infinite can be grasped only 'by entering into a state in which you are your finite self no longer … when you ceased to be finite you become one with the infinite.' Tennyson's account is subtly phrased: 'All at once, out of the intensity of the consciousness of individuality, individuality itself seemed to fade away into boundless being.' The Zen scholar D. T. Suzuki puts it another way by suggesting that *satori* is an expansion of the individual into the infinite.

These examples, in the light of our earlier discussion, suggest that one useful metaphor is that of expansion and contraction. Our customary state is one of limited and contracted self-consciousness. We set up boundaries between the inside and the outside, self and other, thus tending to isolate and alienate ourselves from the oneness of reality. Da Free John (Adi Da) characterizes the ego as the activity of contraction, separation and independence, a self-contraction which is 'expressed as the differentiation of self from the Transcendental Source-Condition.' Ken Wilber takes this further when he refers to the ego as an illusory boundary which obscures the prior wholeness of the self or Atman. Fear of death in this sense amounts to fear of transcendence, fear of losing the familiar but limiting boundaries. Conversely, when transcendence is glimpsed in the mystical experience, the fear of death evaporates.

The idea of the ego as a contraction leads by analogy to modern physical field theory, which has left behind the notion of solid objects in empty space to embrace a view which regards matter as a condensation in the field – like the organism in its environment, not isolated but arising out of and interacting with it. Forms are dynamic energy patterns whose boundaries are created by velocity. Individual self-consciousness, by analogy, might be said to arise out of unitive consciousness and erect protective barriers around itself; nevertheless, as an open system, it remains semi-permeable and can interact with other individual selves as open systems. When, however, unitive consciousness is experienced, the boundaries dissolve and there dawns the realization that one's ground is the unitive consciousness field out of which other individual self-consciousnesses also arise: the many arise out of the One and are linked to each other through participation in that one.

This was the theory of the greatest Neo-Platonist, Plotinus, who expounded a version of the Great Chain of Being: Mind arises from the Supreme God and gives rise to Soul, which in turn creates all subsequent things and fills them all with life 'and since this single radiance illumines all and is reflected in each, as a single face might be reflected in many mirrors placed in a series ... the attentive observer will discover a connection of parts ... mutually linked together and without a break'. The Universal Soul is undivided, individuals being linked in a sympathy bearing witness to underlying unity behind the apparent separateness. Plotinus, in accordance with his experience described above, regards separate individuality as a limitation. In the spiritual world, he insists, Soul is undivided, and part of it is said to remain in this higher sphere, 'never wholly divided, even when animating individual lives'. Thus when awareness is focused in this higher sphere, the transcendent unity will be directly experienced. In the physical world, however, souls feel this unity less directly through *sympathia* due to their common participation in the undivided Soul: 'That sympathy exists between souls is no obstacle to my thesis. Souls are responsive to each other, because they all come from the same soul – The Soul.' In other words, empathetic resonance naturally arises between souls united in the same universal field of consciousness. The common ground of being provides the immediate conductor of such resonance, thus enabling us to enter empathetically into the experiences of other self-consciousnesses.

If we now return to the twentieth century and Paul Brunton, we can discern a similar logic in his concept and experience of the Overself, defined as the meeting-point between the World-Mind and each conscious being. Brunton points out that this World-Mind or universal intelligence cannot be encompassed by the finite self without that self merging and vanishing altogether in the experience'. The difference between the World-Mind and the Overself, he explains, is only one of scope and degree, not of kind. They are both the same 'stuff', which is ultimately indivisible, as in Plotinus. All Overselves exist in the World-Mind just as our thoughts exist in our mind. An important point flows from the indivisibility of Overselves: that 'each Overself in itself is exactly the same as and at one with another. In other words the difference is only relational and not intrinsic.' Intrinsically, essentially, we are all linked via our Overselves. The ego, in this model, is a limitation of the Overself, and owes its separate experience to loss of the 'unique and universal principle that underlies it'. The very existence of a separate ego implies a masking or forgetting of underlying unity unless this illusion is corrected through an experience of unitive consciousness. This in turn leads to a conscious realization of the interconnectedness and interdependence of all existence and therefore an empathetic resonance with all phenomena – in which the World-Mind is immanent. Loving your neighbour as yourself is loving yourself in disguise.

We are so accustomed to using categories which distinguish and divide, that it comes as something of a surprise to find physicist David Bohm saying that we are actually united by space, that a point is an abstraction from a line, the part a manifestation of the whole. In his book *Wholeness and the Implicate Order* Bohm explains that, from the point of view of physics, it is quite plausible to argue that the dynamic, flowing wholeness underlying the parts is more real than the parts as apparently separate abstractions: 'Each relatively autonomous and stable structure (e.g. an atomic particle) is to be understood not as something independently and permanently existent but rather as a product that has been formed in the whole flowing movement and that will ultimately dissolve back into this movement.'

Bohm's scheme of manifest and non-manifest, explicate (unfolded) and implicate (enfolded) means that the function of the manifest worlds is to display separate units or individuals, while bearing in mind that 'each individual manifests the consciousness of mankind.' In the manifest physical world the parts are separate but interacting, while 'in non-manifest reality it's all interpenetrating, interconnected in one.' In case there is some confusion about whether Bohm is referring to what underlies matter or to consciousness, it is necessary to clarify that the implicate order for Bohm is the ground of both. It is precisely this sense of interpenetration and interconnectedness which typifies unitive consciousness and the life-review. By definition each individual has access to the underlying cosmic totality of the implicate order, the source of compassion, love, intelligence and insight – the effective and cognitive sources respectively. The mystical, according to Bohm, goes deep into the wholeness and flowing harmony of the implicate order, but in a way which is actually more consistent with ordinary experience than might appear at first sight. If this were better understood, people would see that 'mystical experience is really a heightening, and intensification, a deepening, of something they participate in.' This penetrating assessment is entirely consistent with our finding that the sense of unity and reality is enhanced when in direct contact with the divine order. The paranormal finding that consciousness is not in space and that our senses tend to screen out more subtle communications in consciousness is taken a stage further by the discovery of an underlying unitive consciousness in which we all live and which provides the matrix of empathetic resonance.

The Near-death Experience and Transformation

Picking up the theme of the last section, we can best express continuity and development through a passage from St John of the Cross. He writes of his experience of the unity of God and the soul 'in participant transformation': 'the soul seems to be God rather than a soul, and is indeed God by participation', although he adds that its natural being, even if transformed, remains distinct from the Being of God; participation is not identity. He then goes on to say that the soul cannot reach this equality and completeness of love 'save by total transformation of her will in that of God, whereby the two wills are united after such a manner that they become one'. This last remark has much more far-reaching practical implications than a momentary melting into divine radiance: it calls for a discipline in everyday living, a centring on the stillness within, a freely chosen and devoted obedience to a higher purpose; in short, a sense of commitment and reorientation of one's life.

The NDE is clearly a traumatic turning-point for most experiences. It is usually impossible for them to return to 'business as usual', especially if they have become aware for the first time of the existence of transcendent realms of consciousness with a greater intensity of reality than the physical world. The striking changes of attitude are broadly correlated with the depth of the experiences rather than the mere fact of having been near death. For instance, little change in the fear of death is evident among those who have had no NDE but been in a life-threatening situation; while for the experiencer, this fear is overcome.

It is illuminating to compare the NDE and its transformation of values with the effects of conversion and initiation. William James devoted one of his Gifford Lectures to conversion, and quotes the spiritual quest of Tolstoy at a moment when the great writer seemed to have reached his moral death-bed. In thinking of God, 'there arose in me … glad aspirations towards life. Everything in me awoke and received a meaning.' His perception of intentionality had changed; the fullness of meaning arose within his being. James characterizes conversion as a change in what he calls 'the habitual centre of personal energy' – or 'ruling love' in Swedenborg's terminology; it is a potent emotional occasion which precipitates 'a mental rearrangement', in other words a reordering of priorities and values. Sometimes those who undergo this experience use the imagery of darkness and light, or blindness and sight: opening one's eyes to the light of truth, and being bathed in joy. The psychological results are a faith which James describes as a state of assurance with an accompanying loss of worry, a sense of inner peace and harmony; then the mysteries of life seem to make sense; and finally a sense of renewal and of the newness of experiences and phenomena. Even if the initial intensity wears off, James quotes his colleague Starbuck's conclusion that the effect of conversion is 'a changed attitude towards life, which is fairly constant and permanent, although feelings fluctuate'.

If we now turn to initiation, the parallels become even more apparent, since one of its essential features is a ritual death and rebirth, a separation from the old and an embracing of the new, 'a radical change of existential status', in the words of Mircea Eliade. Kenneth Ring and Michael Grosso have written specifically on this theme, the latter within the context of his discussion of the Archetype of Death and Enlightenment (ADE as opposed to NDE). A meeting with light symbolically means an extension of consciousness, a disclosure or opening of what was hitherto enclosed. Grosso quotes an early Greek writer, Themistios, on the specific connection between near-death and the Mysteries. Themistios states that the soul has the same experience at the point of death as those who are being initiated: 'First one is struck by a marvellous light, one is received into pure regions and meadows.' Ring has considered the Egyptian and Greek Mysteries and the way in which the ritual death and rebirth changed attitudes to death and hence to conduct in life. He points out several significant contacts with the modern NDE: that the number of candidates for initiation was small, while literally thousands of people have had NDEs; that purification and careful preparation was a prerequisite for initiation, while the near-death experience literally invades a person's life unexpectedly; that the candidate was making a conscious choice, while the NDE occurs after an accident or during illness; and finally that the Mysteries were quite secret, while the NDE is spoken of openly. One ought to add in connection with this last point that until comparatively recently the NDE was indeed a well-kept secret, as many people were reluctant to talk of it in case they were considered mentally unsound by their friends and neighbours.

As I have already hinted, the NDE is a beginning, a seed for spiritual growth rather than the flower or fruit of spiritual effort. In a discussion of secret societies, Mircea Eliade speculates that their fundamental impulse is the need for a fuller participation in the sacred. The pursuit of intensity explains the rationale for the severe ordeals to which aspirants were subjected; also the need to overcome fear and build up courage. The goal of initiatory torture in Melanesian societies was meant to be spiritual transmutation of the initiand. Eliade states that extreme suffering and certain illnesses are both an expression of initiatory death. It is certainly true that the circumstances of the NDE involve extreme suffering, although not usually during the experience itself. We find another strand in heroic and shamanic initiations where the body's abandonment by the soul during ecstasy is equivalent to a temporary death. Some traditions include a descent to hell or the underworld, the hero's journey, and many add an ascent to heaven as the stage following the descent. We have encountered both themes in our study.

We reach the heart of the matter in practices designed to change the existential status of the aspirant. In Yoga, for instance, the goal is nothing less than enlightenment, freedom from bondage, deliverance. In the Christian tradition, as Eliade points out, the believer is sanctified by baptism and eucharist. Some people even suggest that the original baptismal rite of total immersion until one nearly drowned was in fact meant to elicit an NDE and give the candidate an experiential taste of another reality. The effect of the sacraments is to separate the person from the mass of the profane and enlist them into the elect. This pattern is a good instance of the process analysed by van Gennep in his work on rights of passage. He speaks of the stages of separation, incorporation and re-integration. The separation is from one's past state, incorporation takes place when the candidate is received into a new body or society, and re-integration is the return, after *metanoia*, to one's previous habitat. One's new status, however, is different. Van Gennep's ideas were further developed by Victor Turner, who elaborated the idea of liminality, the threshold stage; Turner comments significantly that the word cunicular (being in a tunnel) might better describe the quality of that phase. In the NDE we find the tunnel at the transition between dimensions: or on the way out or, less frequently, on the return. The NDE certainly marks a separation from past perceptions and attitudes, and perhaps a temporary incorporation into the divine order; in any event the experiencer joins the invisible club of NDEers, who instantly recognize their various experiences. Reintegration is the hardest part, as is made fully clear in Phyllis Atwater's study *Coming Back to Life*. She reckons that it may take up to seven years to achieve full reintegration. At first there is an extreme reluctance even to come back into the confines of the physical world at all. Later, as we shall see, the process of reintegration is made harder for families, as the experiencer often changes values and priorities to such an extent that they are no longer the same person.

In the final chapter of *Rites and Symbols of Initiation*, Eliade widens the context of his treatment by maintaining that 'initiation lies at the core of any genuine human life', for two reasons: the first is the presence of 'profound crises, suffering, ordeals, loss and reconquest of self, "death and resurrection"'; and the second, the moment of seeing one's life as a failure, however rich and fulfilling it has proved. C. G. Jung, at the end of his life, confessed that he was 'astonished, disappointed, pleased with myself ... distressed, depressed, rapturous', likening himself to the Taoist sage who finds people around him clear, but 'I alone am clouded'. In moments of total crisis, the only way out is the hope of beginning again, of embarking on a new, regenerated life, a resurrection and transmutation. In his concluding remarks, Eliade speaks of the non-religious person's eternal longing to find a positive meaning in death, beyond the nihilism of so much modern culture: this is what we do indeed encounter in the NDE – a new myth of death, one which gives death a positive meaning but which does not simultaneously deny and devalue life. In fact it sets both life and death within a wider framework of understanding.

The initiate, then, moves through death to spiritual rebirth, transcending previous boundaries, modes of thought and existence. Part of the process is a redefinition of the sense of self through having participated directly in unitive consciousness, what Emerson called the Over-soul 'within which every man's particular being is contained and made one with all other; that common heart.' Research suggests that the three most potent factors in psychological and spiritual change after NDEs are the separation from the body with sharpened awareness and heightened feelings, the encounter with the being of light and the life-review, and meeting with deceased relatives. The first and last factors probably contribute to the conviction that consciousness survives, while the life-review and encounter with the light seem to have a dual effect: that of reinforcing the sense of the imperishability of the central core of the self, and the absorption of qualities like love, joy, peace and beauty which constitute the perennial spiritual values of the divine order.

All the major studies of the NDE confirm that a change of attitudes and values follows the experience, and all converge in their assessment of the nature of such changes. For the purposes of analysis we can break them down as follows:

1. An overcoming of the fear of death, and a conviction of the continuation of consciousness beyond physical death. This is a general finding, regardless of previous belief, background, age or sex. It is also, among people who have been very near death, specific to experiencers, and does not appear to have fallen off with time. People asked about the NDE refer to the beauty and peace they experienced, and are emphatic in their remarks.

2. An enhanced appreciation of life, and a desire to live fully in the present. In the aftermath of an NDE, life appears as a precious gift not to be squandered. There is a finer sense of beauty and a taste for silence, solitude and nature; an eye for detail and valuing of the small things in life.

3. An emphasis on unconditional life, manifesting itself in various forms: tolerance, acceptance and understanding of others; a feeling of compassion and sympathy which makes experiencers wish to help others in some constructive way and to give of themselves.

4. An expanded sensitivity and a feeling of thinner boundaries between the experiencer and other people or nature. This may feel like a greater interconnectedness or sensitivity to the emotions of others. In some cases this faculty may develop into a psychic awareness or even a new-found ability to heal.

5. A decreased adherence to conventional material values of personal ambition, fame, wealth and status, the 'having mode' described by Erich Fromm; and a corresponding concern with what Maslow terms B-values (ultimate human values) encountered in the light. An enhanced self-worth means that it is less necessary to strive so frantically for material and social ego-props.

6. A spiritual orientation whose most important feature is an inward feeling of closeness to the Divine. The stress is frequently on inner life rather than outward ritual. There is a great yearning for understanding between different traditions via the unitive consciousness.

7. A sense of purpose and meaning to life. This may derive from the experience of wider knowledge during the NDE and/or the feeling of being privileged in having been spared from death. Experiencers often speak of their conviction of having some mission to fulfil; many are told at the end of the NDE that it is not yet their time to die – they must return. Indeed some return with the specific aim of living more authentically, attempting to be more true to themselves as well as more understanding of others.

8. The wish to understand the meaning of life and death, a thirst for wisdom and spiritual understanding.

There is not space here to cite the many remarks that confirm the patterns indicated above. The reader who wishes to pursue this aspect in more depth is especially directed towards the work of Atwater and Ring. We can now discuss these patterns of changed values in a wider context. Stanislav Grof has done a great deal of work with drugs, particularly LSD, in exploring other dimensions of consciousness. In a chapter entitled 'Psychedelic Metamorphosis of Dying', Grof and Halifax discuss the after-effects of psychedelic therapy on individuals dying of cancer. After going through death and rebirth sequences the subjects' concept of death was profoundly modified, as they had had 'deep experiences of cosmic unity and of certain other transpersonal forms of consciousness' which seemed to 'render the fact of death irrelevant.' A 'new referential system' is revealed, putting life and death in a new perspective. The authors comment that striking changes in the hierarchy of life-values are directly related to the insights gleaned in perinatal and transpersonal experiences. They state that:

1. Psychological acceptance of impermanence and death awakens a realization of 'the absurdity and futility of exaggerated ambitions, attachment to money, status, fame, and power, or pursuit of other temporal values'. This corresponds to the NDE reorientation away from materialism.

2. Time orientation is typically transformed', with past and future becoming less important than the present moment: a feature related to the enhanced appreciation of life cited above. Grof and Halifax actually mention 'an increased ability to enjoy life and derive pleasure from simple things'.

3. A distinct increase in interest in religious matters 'involving spirituality of a universal nature rather than beliefs related to any specific church affiliation'. On the other hand, the authors also mention that some people found their faith 'deepened and illumined with new dimensions of meaning.'

A wider view of this question of values can be attained by looking at the work of Abraham Maslow, first in his analysis of B-values, and secondly in his discussion of the characteristics of psychological health in self-actualizing people. His generic term for the mystical experience is 'the peak experience', which covers a rather broader spectrum of phenomena. In speaking of the religious aspects of peak experiences, he says that it is quite characteristic 'that the whole universe is perceived as an integrated and unified whole ... that the universe is all of a piece and that one has one's place in it – one is part of it, one belongs to it.' Such an insight, he comments, can be so shaking and profound 'that it can change the person's character and *Weltanschauung* [world-view] forever after'. The changes, he writes, vary in intensity from that of a profound religious conversion to the lesser therapeutic effects.

As for the nature of the B-values themselves, Maslow reaches the revolutionary insight that the list of described perceptions and characteristics in peak experiences corresponds with what are generally acknowledged to be the eternal spiritual values, and indeed the very features of the self during the experience ('I was peace, I was love'): a fusion of consciousness and value, an embodiment of the value in consciousness. Accordingly, Maslow regards his list as 'either ... described attributes of reality when perceived in peak experiences, or ... the irreducible, intrinsic values of this reality'.

1. Truth, including honesty and reality.
2. Goodness, including justice and benevolence.
3. Beauty, perfection.
4. Wholeness, including unity, integration, interconnectedness, order.
5. Dichotomy transcendence.
6. Aliveness, including dynamism and energy.
7. Uniqueness, suchness.
8. Perfection.
9. Necessity (literally 'cannot be otherwise').
10. Completion, including totality and fulfilment.
11. Justice.
12. Order.
13. Simplicity, including purity.
14. Richness.
15. Effortlessness, ease.
16. Playfulness, joy.
17. Self-sufficiency.

This bare list does not actually capture the rich subtlety of Maslow's cross-reference, in which it becomes apparent that each characteristic can in fact be expressed in terms of any of the others. Language is a convenient way of dividing things up into categories, but it cannot adequately describe perceptions beyond the realm of duality. The meaning overflows the words, as Simone Well once said. Maslow's list is common to all perceptions in mystical experience, allowing for inevitable differences of emphasis. In other words, the mystical encounter in the NDE need not be set apart from the literature on mysticism.

Maslow further suggests that these values are the 'highest' in the sense that they must often come 'to the best people, in their best moments, under the best conditions': that they are definitions of the higher spiritual life, as well as being the far goals of psychotherapy and education in the broadest sense. He illustrates this thesis in his study of psychological health in self-actualizing people, loosely defined as those who have made full use and exploitation of talents, capacities, potentialities, etc. Their basic and cognitive needs, lower in Maslow's hierarchy than spiritual aspirations, have been satisfied. The subjects selected included nine of his contemporaries and nine public, historical characters including Schweitzer, Lincoln and Aldous Huxley. Their characteristics were as follows:

1. More efficient perception of reality and more comfortable relations with it than others have: a sure judgement unclouded by subjective bias. (NDE experiencers speak of being subsequently detached from events and seeing through them.)

2. Acceptance of self, others and human nature at all levels, allied to a lack of defensiveness and a distaste for artificiality and the attempt to impress others. (This correlates with our NDE item 3 on unconditional love).

3. Spontaneity, simplicity, naturalness; lack of conventionality owing to a deeper perception of true value and a pursuit of their own authenticity. (This is related to the near-death experiencer's enhanced sense of self-worth and is reflected in the previous item on artificiality).

4. Problem-centering as opposed to ego-centering: a sense of duty or mission which goes beyond personal concerns to a wider frame of reference. Unitive consciousness provides the widest possible frame and corresponds to service to a greater cause, and concern with world problems. (Specific to some NDEs are visions of the possible development of world events, which naturally encourages the experiencers to take an interest in the planetary dimension.)

5. The quality of detachment; the need for privacy. Detachment is implicit in item 1 above. (We also noticed the near-death experiencer's taste for solitude and silence.)

6. Autonomy; independence of culture and environment; will; such people have become active agents, strong enough to be independent of the good opinion of others (a feature noted in the NDE), and have serenity in the face of knocks. (One experiencer suggests that survivors come in for more knocks than might be expected, but are probably sustained by their inner faith.)

7. Continued freshness of appreciation; a richness of subjective experience in which the person may derive special pleasure from the basics of life and be grateful for them. (A similar feature was noted under NDE item 2 – an enhanced appreciation of life.)

8. The mystic experience, the peak experience occurs more frequently in self-actualizers. (This aspect is not easily related to the after-effects of the NDE, and there are no data on the issue.)

9. *Gemeinschaftsgefühl*: a deep feeling of identification, sympathy and affection for human beings in general. (This sensitivity and empathy is one of the central NDE after-effects.)

10. Interpersonal relations are deeper owing to the self-actualizer's greater capacity for love and obliteration of ego boundaries. (The depth is borne out in studies of NDEs, although, as previously mentioned, their families and friends have some difficult adjustments to make.)

11. Democratic character structure; an open friendliness to all. (Giving and opening up to people is central to NDE after-effects.)

12. Discrimination between means and ends, between good and evil. (Little data is available on this quality for NDEs.)

13. Philosophical, unhostile sense of humour. (No study has been done on this after NDEs.)

14. Creativeness. (This is reflected in the determination to use all one's capacities to the full after the NDE.)

15. Resistance to enculturation; a universality of outlook detached from a particular cultural loyalty. This feature follows from the unitive consciousness with its inclusion of all life. (It is related to the autonomy referred to in item 6 above, and is frequently found in near-death experiencers.)

Even this rather summary comparison should suffice to make it clear that the after-effects of the NDE tend to move the subject towards greater integration and psychological health. This finding can be generalized to all religious experience, as found in studies conducted by the Alister Hardy Research Centre in Oxford. Hardy himself confirmed the patterns we have been describing in NDEs and religious experience when he concluded that the principal after-effects of religious experience were a sense of purpose and meaning, a change in religious belief, and a changed attitude to others.

In an essay on field consciousness and field ethics, Renée Weber builds on the psychology of David Bohm, who urges the dissolution of the separate thinker as the highest priority for the seeker of truth. This results in the release of an energy which is not value-free but qualitatively charged: 'it is an energy unbound and flowing, characterized by wholeness, n-dimensionality, and the force of compassion'; unification of physics and ethics, of wholeness and holiness, since the 'energy itself is love'. This energy-love-peace-joy-beauty-light is the ocean in which the mystic and near-death experiencer is immersed. The experiential description is also a list of ultimate values; and the strongest impulse from such all-encompassing immersion is to become a channel for this energy, which represents total inner and outer fulfilment. The consciousness is momentarily aligned and in tune with cosmic empathy, directly experiencing the fullness of divine order. And in this divine order arise the values and goals of the moral order, which can then be translated into the human social order.

In one of her many penetrating dialogues with David Bohm, Renée Weber discusses meaning and being in a way which relates to our theme of transformation. Bohm's premise is that a change of meaning is a change of being, on the grounds that consciousness is its content and is therefore meaning: 'human consciousness is its meaning', so that if consciousness changes, so does meaning. In addition, one's meaning organizes one's categories of judgement and perception by giving them overall coherence. If one looks at this dynamically, one can express the same point by saying that meaning actively directs and shapes the use of energy. We direct our energy according to our values and priorities.

If we now apply this insight to the after-effects of peak experiences and the NDE, it becomes very clear that there has been a change of perspective, meaning, consciousness, being and values: the world no longer looks the same. It is seen as a vast interconnected web in which all life-forms are interdependent and in empathetic resonance with each other through the implicate order of unitive consciousness. The observer is inseparable from the observed; human beings are connected at a deep level which is occasionally experienced by those who transcend the boundaries and limitations of ordinary perception. The empathetic response implies an empathetic responsibility, or, as the poet Francis Thompson put it:

> When to the new heart of thee
> All things by immortal power
> Near or far,
> Hiddenly
> To each other linkèd are,
> That though canst not stir a flower
> Without the troubling of a star ...

CHAPTER FOUR

MORAL ORDER IN KARMA AND REINCARNATION

The law of Karma is not external to the individual. The judge is not without but within. The law by which virtue brings its triumph and ill-doing its retribution is the unfolding of the law of our being. The world order is a reflection of the Divine Mind.

SIR SARVEPALLI RADHAKRISHNAN

All illnesses are due to Karma, it is either the results of your own debts or the debts of others you love, Karma has to be paid off in one way or another. This is the universal law of balance. When most of the Karma has been paid off and [only after that person has received his 'lesson'] someone else can assume the remaining burden and relieve the subject from the pain.

THE MAGUS OF STROVOLOS

The universal law of karma ... is that of action and reaction, cause and effect, sowing and reaping. In the course of natural righteousness, man, by his thoughts and actions, becomes the arbiter of his destiny. Whatever energies he himself sets in motion must return to him as their activator. An understanding of karma as the law of justice underlying life's inequalities serves to free the human mind from resentment against God and man.

PARAMAHANSA YOGANANDA

Introduction

R ecent opinion polls indicate the growing popularity of the doctrine of karma and reincarnation in the West. A 1981 Gallup poll in the United States indicated that 23 per cent believed (21 per cent of men and 25 per cent of women). Young people were significantly more likely to accept the doctrine, while those who regularly attended church were less likely to do so: 29 per cent under 30 believed, while the figure for over-30s was 21 per cent; non-churchgoers scored 27 per cent, as against 17 per cent for regular attenders. Nevertheless, it is perhaps surprising to find that 21 per cent of Protestants and 25 per cent of Catholics believed, in view of the fact that it is far from being accepted Christian doctrine. In the United Kingdom, a 1979 survey showed an increase from the 1969 figure of 18 per cent to 28 per cent. Whether such people have given serious thought to the pros and cons, or have had a personal experience which has affected their views, is impossible to tell; the fact remains that it seems to be part of the world-view of a substantial minority of Westerners.

Research for this chapter has involved consulting some seventy-five books; it is therefore impossible to compress the full range of evidence and counter-evidence into a short space. I shall confine the discussion specifically to the principles of the ideas of karma and reincarnation as they affect perception of moral order in the universe. Much of the evidence and debate revolves round the nature of memory and identity: in what sense can it be said that an identity persists from one human being to another? Could veridical reproduction of other people's memories be explained by a possession hypothesis? Why are such alleged reincarnation memories so rare and elusive? Does the hypothesis of karma and reincarnation provide a satisfactory explanation of genetic and environmental inequality? Does it suggest a solution to the intractable problem of evil in the light of an omnipotent and beneficent Deity? I shall return to these questions in my concluding comments.

I shall begin with the origins of the doctrine in Hinduism, tracing it through some of the major scriptures up to its twentieth-century expression in the thought of Sir Sarvepalli Radhakrishnan, and showing how it passed into Buddhism. Then we shall look at Platonism, with its philosophical and theological offspring. Then the teachings of Theosophy and Anthroposophy, followed by a consideration of mediumistic or channelled communications and hypnotic regression. We shall look specifically at the life of the clairvoyant Edgar Cayce, whose readings throw a great deal of light on the possible relationship between disease and karma. Finally we shall delve into the metaphysical and ethical issues mentioned above and see how some Christian writers have married up the doctrine of karma with evolution.

Indian Origins

The most common expression of karma is to be found in the sentence 'As you sow, so shall you reap', a principle of agriculture and an extension of the notion of cause and effect from the physical into the moral dimension. The idea has remained powerfully ingrained in the Indian mentality since its first formulation in the Upanishads some 2,700 years ago, and has always been associated with the concomitant doctrine of rebirth. Suffering and enjoyment are the fruit or harvest springing from the actions of an individual in a previous earthly existence. While the normal version is expressed prospectively, as above, John McKenzie points out that it is also true the other way around, namely that 'whatsoever a man reaps, that must he have sowed.' The present is thus linked to both past and future through a series of lives.

The earliest Indian scriptures, however, make no mention of the doctrine of karma. The life of the individual was regarded as a one-off experience; after death the person proceeded to the land of the dead, where they enjoyed felicity or torment according to their merits, both moral and ritual. Yama, the God of the Dead, who still seems to feature in modern Indian NDEs, determined the final destiny.

Mircea Eliade explains the etymology and origins of karma as part of the structure of ritual sacrifices. The word itself means action or deed, and, in the specific context of the Brahmanas (scriptures written *c.* 1000-800 BC), it denotes ritual activity and its beneficial consequences – reaching the world of the gods after death. Eliade argues that reflection on the ritual process of cause and effect 'inevitably led to the discovery that every act, by the mere fact that it obtained a result, became an integral part of an endless series of causes and effects'. Then, once the logic of universal causality was apprehended in karma, the previous certainty about the saving effects of sacrifice was called into question: why stop at the effects of a particular kind of action? Furthermore, if the effects of the sacrifice were realized as post-existence in heaven, where were the products of all other acts to be manifest? The period of heaven was thought to be finite, and yet the Atman, the discarnate soul, must continue its existence in some realm or other: hence the necessity for rebirth into this world, reincarnation following post-existence. Thus continued existence of the soul after a sojourn in the post-mortem world leads Indian thought inescapably to the doctrine of transmigration or *samsara*, the wheel of rebirth, from which the sages seek to liberate themselves through the attainment of *moksha* or deliverance through *gnosis* or *jnana*, itself a triumph over *avidya* or ignorance.

It is worth dwelling on the exact significance of some of the key variables in the Indian moral order, since their dynamic interaction constitutes the essence of a system of metaphysics and ethics:

1. *Brahman.* A word derived from a root meaning 'to grow', Brahman represents the ultimate reality which remains identical and persists through change, the self-sufficient root of existence, the transcendent Absolute which can only be hinted at in negative terms. Radhakrishnan analyses four sides of one whole:

'the transcendental universal being anterior to any concrete reality;

the casual principle of all differentiation;

the innermost essence of the world; and

the manifest world'. He stresses that these aspects are simultaneous and not alternating sides of one Reality.

2. *Atman.* Derived from *'an'*, meaning 'to breathe', Atman is the breath of life: 'Gradually its meaning extended to cover life, soul, self or essential being of the individual' in an all-pervasive sense. It is the 'foundational reality underlying the conscious powers of the

individual, the inward ground of the human soul'. As such, this principle transcends all conditioning and limitation of individual awareness; it is pure self-consciousness and ultimate freedom.

3. Brahman as *Atman*. Early Upanishads characterize Atman as the principle of the individual consciousness and Brahman as the superpersonal ground of the cosmos, but the distinction diminishes to the point where God is both the transcendent numinous Other and the basis of human consciousness. The vital corollary of this identification is that 'Brahman, the first principle of the universe, is known through atman, the inner self of man.' And since such knowledge (*jnana*) is achieved by identification, such identification represents *moksha* or deliverance, the discovery of the central insight that 'Thou are That' (*Tat Tvam Asi*).

4. Jivatman. This is the individual self, the root of which is the pure awareness and freedom of Atman. The purpose and work of the *jivatman* is to attain the perfection inherent in its pure nature, 'the divinization of the empirical ego', the realization of the kingdom of heaven within. It is no accident that many yogic techniques involve *prana* or breathing exercises in the striving for identification with the primal breath, the return to the source, one's true nature.

5. Jnana. Derived from *jna*, meaning 'to know', *jnana* is saving spiritual wisdom which enables the aspirant to reach a true view of and identification with ultimate reality. The yogic disciplines of meditation seek to experience this unitive knowledge beyond the duality of ordinary sense consciousness.

6. Maya. Commonly rendered as illusion, the veil of apparent separateness through which we perceive, *maya* is often misunderstood in the West. Radhakrishnan is at pains to stress that it does not mean that the phenomenal world and empirical self is an illusion. The illusion, on the contrary, is to mistake the phenomenal world for ultimate reality. In this sense it could be said that materialists are caught up in *maya*. The key to understanding the concept of *maya* is that Indian metaphysics begins with the primacy of the unitive experience with ultimate reality; by comparison, everything else is secondary, relative, contingent. The unitive experience is by definition non-dual, transcending as it does the distinction between the knower and the known: 'every trace of separateness disappears; life is a seamless whole.' Ultimate reality directly experienced is one and not many; indirectly, through the senses, it appears as many. The key here is the mode of perception: a mind which looks at unity and sees diversity is seeing its own reflection, a level of experience where separateness is experienced as real. This level, however, is transcended when the *jivatman* awakens from the dream of separation into the reality of oneness.

7. *Avidya*. *Avidya* is the opposite of *vidya*, wisdom or knowledge, and thus is ignorance. *Avidya* is closely connected with *maya*, and often discussed alongside it as another expression of the deformation of true knowledge or wisdom. It is a concealment of the ultimate reality, a failure to recognize the true nature of the created world and the significance of revealed *jnana*. It is also ignorance of the consequences of acts in karma. If, as Radhakrishnan argues, the finite creation is a self-limitation of the infinite creator, then limited creatures dwell in the being of the creator without necessarily realizing it. The phenomenal world becomes, in his words, 'a passage from existence [literally to stand out] to reality'. 'Our finiteness is the condition of our awareness. Our temporality gives us a chance of knowing the eternal. Our limitation gives us the scope and opportunity to glimpse the Unlimited. The universal is seen through the particular by those with eyes to see – those not conditioned by the metaphysical blindness of *avidya*.

8. *Samsara*. This is the endless process of becoming, the Heraclitean flux, the arising and passing away of transient forms. In human terms it represents the endless and unbroken series of incarnations which continue until *moksha* is achieved.

9. *Dharma*. Derived from the root '*dhri*' meaning 'to support or hold up', *dharma* is on one level a principle of underlying order and interconnection, and on another the duty which recognizes interconnectedness and acts in the light of such an insight. The highest *dharma* is said to be *ahimsa* or non-violence, a universal love for all creation.

10. *Karma*. Karma can now be understood in the light of the order and interconnectedness implied by *dharma*, itself deriving from

the unity inherent in Atman and Brahman. The fact that karma is described as a law is a statement about the orderliness of the moral universe. Interpretations vary in their degree of sophistication from the simple results of action to the subtle interplay between will, desire, character, intention and action. It is more of an organic principle of moral homeostasis or adjustment and conservation of ethical energy than a mechanical rebound contraption, although this last expression may convey a limited facet of its operation. The homeostasis or self-regulation can also be seen as educative, impressing on the individual the underlying connectedness of human lives in particular and creation in general.

11. *Moksha. Moksha* is liberation, deliverance, salvation or illumination, the unitive experience through *jnana, bhakti* (devotion) or karma (action) by means of which the *jivatman* attains identification with the Supreme Brahman/Atman and thus moves beyond the necessity of *samsara* with its limitations and rebirth, and karma with its harvest of acts; also beyond the blinkers of *maya* and *avidya* to the realization of that inherent but elusive perfection within.

These summary classifications and definitions should clarify the dynamics of later developments in Hindu philosophy by showing the close connections of the scheme in terms of its essential terms and variables. Everything stems from the unity of the divine in Atman and Brahman, together with the proposition that Brahman is knowable through *jivatman* when it reaches *moksha* or liberation. *Jnana* and *vidya* represent the revelation of true unitive knowledge, which *avidya* and *maya* lure people into a false sense of separation which subjects them to the eternal round of karma and *samsara*. *Moksha* uncovers the insight that one's end is in one's beginning and one's beginning is in one's end. From having had the experience and missed the meaning:

> ... the end of all our exploring
> Will be to arrive where we started
> And know the place for the first time.

But such a statement is undoubtedly premature; we need to work through the ramifications of the doctrine of karma.

The Upanishads

The term 'upanishad' is normally taken to mean 'sit down near' (the teacher), but Shankara's derivation suggests that it means knowledge by which ignorance is loosened or destroyed. There are eighteen principal Upanishads, eight of which date back to the eighth or seventh centuries BC, thus predating the Buddhist era. They belong to the 're-vealed' literature, which means that they comprise insights unattainable through normal sense-perception, inference or reflection; rather, they are sayings of sages speaking 'out of the fullness of their illumined experience' and direct vision.

We find in the Upanishads the first formulation of the possibility of the release from karma and *samsara* into *moksha*: freedom from the subjection to time and concomitant karmic bondage. Herein is the meeting-point of the supreme metaphysical reality and the goal to ethics in release into universal love. It can only be attained by those free from desire of earthly things, 'whose desire is the self ... being Brahman, he goes to Brahman'. The will or desire is no longer centered on anything other than Brahman; the law of affinity therefore comes into operation and the soul naturally gravitates to Brahman.

For those still bound to the wheel of *samsara*, the law of karma applies: 'Verily one becomes good by good action, bad by bad action', a principle elaborated later in the Brihadarnayaka Upanishad:

According as one acts, according as one behaves, so does he become. The doer of good becomes good, the doer of evil becomes evil. One becomes virtuous by virtuous action, bad by bad action. Others, however, say that a person consists of desires. As is his desire, so is his will; as is his will, so is the deed he does, whatever deed he does, that he attains.

On this there is the following verse.

> The object to which the mind is attached, the subtle self goes together with the deed, being attached to it alone. Exhausting the results of whatever works he did in this world he comes again from that world, to this world for [fresh] work.

Those whose conduct has been good will have a good birth at the top of the caste system as a Brahmin, while the evil are in danger of being reborn as a hog or dog; in other words the idea of transmigration includes the possibility of rebirth as an animal, with all the problems associated with climbing back up the scale again to a human birth.

The passage quoted is a clear exposition of the doctrine in karma as understood in the Upanishads. It begins with an analysis of the results of action, proceeding to a more psychological conception of the relationship between will, desire, action and fruit. This represents a deeper and more inward level of understanding, which traces the fruit of an action back to its seed in thoughts and desires. The second verse highlights a tension in Upanishadic thought on karma by explaining that the soul must first exhaust the results of its actions in 'that world' before returning for fresh work in 'this world'. Thus the old Vedic conception of post-mortem reward and punishment survives alongside the new teaching of karma passing from one incarnation to the next – a double dose of results. McKenzie comments that 'it often requires the exercise of considerable ingenuity to get over this difficulty', although such obstacles have not prevented the doctrine of karma from exerting a powerful hold on the Indian mind for over 2,700 years.

The Bhagavad Gita

The *Bhagavad Gita*, or Song of the Lord, dates back to the fifth century BC. Radhakrishnan has described it as more of a religious classic than a philosophical treatise, while to I. C. Sharma it is 'the quintessence of Hindu culture and the sum and substance of Indian philosophical theory and practice, metaphysics and ethics, and religion, mysticism and tradition'. The starting-point of the *Gita* is the problem of action posed by the warrior Arjuna when faced with the prospect of a battle in which he thinks he will incur the karma of killing relatives fighting on the opposite side.

Arjuna's soul is 'overcome with despair and grief' at the prospect, and is upbraided by Krishna for his lifeless dejection in the hour of trial, for the battlefield is equally a moral one requiring courage and determination. Krishna explains that 'interwoven in his creation, the Spirit is beyond destruction. No one can bring to an end the Spirit which is everlasting.' Thus, 'If any man thinks he slays, and if another thinks he is slain, neither knows the ways of truth. The Eternal in man cannot kill: the Eternal in man cannot die.' 'As a man leaves an old garment and puts on one that is new, the Spirit leaves his mortal body and then puts on one that is new.' A distinction is drawn between the perishable and transient body and the imperishable eternal soul. Arjuna is implicitly reproached for focusing on the perishable and being moved by it, that is blinded by *maya* and *avidya*. This leads to the famous doctrine of the renunciation of the fruits of action but not of action itself; it is expressed in many passages of the *Gita*:

> Set thy heart upon thy work, but never on its reward. Work not for a reward, but never cease to do thy work. (II.47)

> But great is the man who, free from attachments, and with a mind ruling its powers in harmony, works on the path of Karma Yoga, the path of consecrated action. (III.7)

> He has attained liberation: he is free from all bonds, his mind has found peace in wisdom, and his work is a holy sacrifice. The work of such a man is pure. (IV.23)

> Both renunciation and holy work are a path to the Supreme; but better than surrender of work is the Yoga of Holy Work. (V.2)

> This man of harmony surrenders the reward of his work and thus attains final peace: the man of disharmony, urged by desire, is attached to his reward and thus remains in bondage. (V.12)

> Hear my truth about the surrender of works, Arjuna. Surrender, O best of men, is of three kinds.

> Works of sacrifice, gift and self-harmony should not be abandoned, but should indeed be performed: for these are works of purification.

> But even these works, Arjuna, should be done in the freedom of a pure offering, and without expectation of a reward. This is my final word. (XVIII.4-6)

The overall message of the above extracts is that it is not karma or work in itself that binds, but rather attachment to the fruits of work. Renunciation is to be applied not to action itself, but to its outcome. Thus the passive orientation of *jnana yoga* is to be supplemented by selfless action performed in a spirit of love. This reformulation is a far-reaching refinement of the doctrine in karma. All actions and their fruits are dedicated to God, a level of motivation which goes beyond external adherence to a formal code to that of symbolic sacrifice: individual action and identity are merged with cosmic action and life. Not I but Christ in me, as St Paul would say; the perfect alignment and attunement of the human to the divine will. Thus the iron fatalism of earlier ideas of karma is transcended, the relationship between *jnana yoga* and *karma yoga* redefined, while *karma yoga* itself acquires a new mystical depth.

The devotee, however, can go further than *karma marga*, the path of action, to *bhakti marga*, the path of love. *Bhakti*, derived from the Sanskrit root *bhaj* meaning 'to adore', 'connotes "an affection fixed upon the Lord", the *Bhagavat* or Adorable One'. This is the supreme creative God who incarnates from time to time as an *avatara* (literally 'descent') for the salvation of mankind. The individual soul is thought to be an emanation from the Adorable One; it has separate conscious existence and is indestructible, but is bound to the wheel of *samsara* until saved by *bhakti*. Brandon points out that *bhakti* is a sort of profound personal trust in the grace of the Adorable One akin to St Paul's faith in Christ. The main Christian departure from the views expounded in the Upanishads is the postulation of a personal god of love and grace, to whom one can relate through devoted service. The Supreme is no abstract concept, but has 'a concrete individual existence', thus enabling loving communion to occur. The following verses fill out the attitude of *bhakti* and show its relation to the true *jnana* or *vidya* of perceiving unity rather than diversity at the heart of things:

When one sees Eternity in things that pass away and Infinity in finite things, then one has pure knowledge.

But if one merely sees the diversity of things, with their divisions and limitations, then one has impure knowledge. (XVIII.20-21)

The Yogi who pure from sin ever prays in this harmony of soul soon feels the joy of Eternity, infinite joy of union with God.

He sees himself in the heart of all beings and sees all beings in his heart. This is the vision of the Yogi of harmony, a vision which is ever one.

And when he sees me in all and he sees all in me, then I never leave him and he never leaves me. He who is in the oneness of love, loves me in whatever he sees, wherever this man may live, in truth this man lives in me.

And he is the greatest Yogi whose vision is ever one: when the pleasure and pain of others is his own pleasure and pain. (VI.28-32)

These passages could be summed up as follows.

1. Perception of eternity, infinity and unity in temporal, finite and diverse forms of life is true perception.

2. In union with God resulting in unitive vision, all forms of life are perceived as manifestations of the divine and as such worthy of love.

3. This unitive state of consciousness automatically sets up an empathetic resonance between the Yogi and other people, such that he experiences others' emotions as his own.

The metaphysical basis of this scheme is the same as the reciprocity implied in the Christian parable of the division of the sheep from the goats. The sheep implicitly recognised Christ in all people and are ready to alleviate their distress. The *Gita* version, however, does not spell out specific actions in the same way. The ethical implications of the metaphysic of unity are made crystal clear later in the text: 'And when a man sees that the God in himself is the same God in all that is, he hurts not himself by hurting others: then he goes indeed to the highest Path' (XIII.28). It is precisely this implication which was illustrated in our cases of life-review: experiencers found that they received back what others had experienced of an event in which they had participated. An underlying unity of being implies empathetic resonance, and empathetic resonance implies an underlying unity of being.

Bhakti marga emerges as even more essential than *karma marga*, but is expressed in devoted and selfless action. In other words love takes precedence over action in a similar fashion to St Paul's faith over works, with the reservation that such faith naturally bears fruit in loving action. Krishna states that 'only by love can men see me, and know me, and come unto me' (XI.54). Hence 'He who works for me, who loves me, whose End Supreme I am, free from attachment to all things, and with love for all creation, he in truth comes unto me' (XI.55). The principle here is an exact parallel of the love we met in *jnana* in the Upanishads: 'Being Brahman he goes to Brahman' by the law of attraction, affinity and identification. The *bhakti* Yogi has the powers of the soul in harmony, with the same loving mind for all, therefore finding joy in the good of all beings. The moral order of the *Gita* is rooted in the metaphysical order, itself anchored in the divine order; the ethics of *bhakti* reflect the nature of God; spiritual values stem from the experience of union with him, that is from Peace, Love, Light, Wisdom and Joy.

Buddhism – The Dhammapada

Within the scope of this study it is not possible to do justice to the full development of different schools of Buddhist ethics. I shall therefore confine my observations to the teaching of the Buddha himself and in particular his remarks about the nature of *karma*, *samsara* and *nirvana*. In common with earlier thinkers, the Buddha regarded earthly individual existence as an undesirable state dependent for its maintenance on *tanha* or thirst/desire, the inevitable outcome of which was *dukkha* or suffering. Perhaps the Buddha's central insight was that of impermanence, which he applied not only to the phenomena of the world, but also to the individual self with his doctrine of *anatta*, or no self. What we take to be the self, he explained, is actually an aggregate of *skandhas* or assemblages. Impermanence here is translated into non-substantiality, in contrast with the Upanishadic teaching of the imperishable Atman as the principle consciousness; if the accent of the Atman is on static being, that of *anatta* and impermanence is on the flux of becoming. This tendency is even reflected in meditative techniques.

Ninian Smart characterizes the Buddha's understanding of karma as a psychological force arising from attitudes and desires. The process of rebirth is likened to the carrying on of a flame, whereby one lamp is lit from another, providing, that is, that the flame of wrong attitudes and desires is still alight. If it is not, then *nirvana*, the extinction of the flame, is attained. Thus it is the karma which transmigrates rather than the self or *skandhas*, which simply dissolve: 'the karmas of a temporary aggregation, called a particular individual, pass on to another temporary aggregation, which is a different individual.' Bhattacharya comments that since karma rather than soul migrates, this should enhance our sense of responsibility, 'seeing that by our action we are laying the foundation of happiness or misery of another individual.' Unscrupulous people might heave a sigh of relief if their burdens are in fact to be shouldered by someone else; indeed just this criticism is levelled against the doctrine by brahaminical philosophers, who regard it as a double injustice: not only does the agent fail to reap the fruits of his own actions, but another person suffers the consequences into the bargain! As mentioned in the introduction, there is a considerable controversy about the nature of what it is which might reincarnate in any event. The Buddha is formulating the polarity of discontinuity, while the Upanishads lay more emphasis on continuity.

There is nevertheless an ambiguity in the doctrine of *anatta* as it relates to rebirth. Eliade mentions an incident in which the Buddha refused to give a direct answer to questions concerning the existence of non-existence of the Atman, not wishing to founder on the Scylla heresy of permanence and the Charybdis of annihilation at death. In his own case, the Buddha is reputed to have been able to remember past existences, an indication of some continuity. A complete denial of the self or Atman leads to the paradox of the existence of suffering without a sufferer, of acts without an actor; and the observation that the person who reaps the fruits of an act is not the performer, 'but he is not another'.

Eknath Easwaran provides us with analogies which may enable us to extricate ourselves from this existential maze. His understanding of the Buddhist universe is that the universe is like a vast sea where a stone thrown raises ripples among billions of other ripples: we can choose to pursue our self-interest and add to the 'sea of selfish behaviour in which we too live', thus guaranteeing a return of the consequences. The karma is stored in the mind, while personality actually consists of karma, 'for it is the accumulation of everything we have done and said and thought.' It is this last idea which features in the opening lines of the *Dhammapada* (The Path of Duty), translated by Easwaran as follows: 'Our life is shaped by our mind; we become what we think. Suffering follows an evil thought as the wheels of a cart follow the oxen that draw it ... joy follows a pure thought like a shadow that never leaves' (I.102). The first phrase is translated by Radhakrishnan as 'The mental natures are the result of what we have thought, are chieftained by our thoughts, are made up of our thoughts'; while Mascaró renders it 'What we are today comes from our thoughts of yesterday, and our present thoughts build our life of tomorrow: our life is the creation of our mind.' While Easwaran's translation is the elegant one, it is clarified by the other renderings. The main point is the importance of mental acts as acts, something which is denied by, for instance, the Jains, with their more literal approach. Returning to Easwaran's discussion of personality, he draws on analogies of modern physics by likening personality to a field of forces which can be talked about meaningfully, but which is not separate from the rest of life. He cannot avoid referring to the 'I-consciousness' or self, however: he claims that he chose the context of rebirth – albeit nonconsciously – since it is the sum of our previous actions and desires. He uses the analogy of an acorn propagating itself and growing into another oak: it has inherited some of the characteristics of its parent, and draws the rest of its substance from the immediate environment. It is a moot point whether the analogy of the flame passing on is really parallel to the growth of an acorn. It is undoubtedly more in keeping with the organic images of the late twentieth century, but perhaps out of phase with flames; the death of the acorn is the birth of the tree, but what of the extinction of the flame?

In spite of these philosophical arguments and subtleties, the Buddhist universe is profoundly moral, and becomes even more so with the emergence of the ethic of the Bodhisattva in the Mahayana school. The radical themes are those of impermanence with its non-substantiality of the self, and the key role attributed to thoughts and desires in a psychological understanding of the doctrine of karma.

Platonism

Although I shall touch on Plato's thought in Chapter 5, it is appropriate to state some of the themes of his philosophy and influence within the context of karma, especially since Christian eschatology took on board the idea of the immortality of the soul without its concomitant doctrine of metempsychosis. The soul of the Orphic-Pythagorean tradition is divine and immortal, and undergoes purification through a series of incarnations until release is obtained. Plato thought of virtue or goodness as its own reward, and therefore did not think that good conduct should be based on an assessment of likely rewards; as least not for the philosopher.

Radhakrishnan points out how alien Platonic thought is to the tradition which preceded it, and argues for the possibility of some Indian influence: 'The essential unity of the human and the divine spirit, the immortality of the human soul, the escape from the restless wheel of the troublesome journey, the phenomenality of the world, the contempt for the body, the distinction between knowledge and opinion contradict every single idea of Greek popular religion.'

Translated into Sanskrit terminology, we find the doctrine of the Atman with its identifying of the human soul with the divine, the possibility of liberation from the round of *samsara*, the doctrine of *maya*, and the distinction between *jnana* or *vidya* and *avidya*; Brandon explains that continued transmigration 'resulted from the soul's ignorance of its true nature and its willing involvement with matter', that is the *maya* of taking the sensory world as ultimate, and the *avidya* of failing to recognize the nature of the soul.

For further illumination of the distinction between knowledge and opinion, we can turn to the simile of the divided line and the cave in *The Republic*. Plato distinguishes between what he calls the goodness of the philosopher and popular goodness: the former is the outcome of direct personal apprehension of what he calls the form of the good, the source of reality and truth is well as ethics; while the latter is based on acceptance and practice of time-honoured traditions, not on personal insight. The divided line further elaborates the differences between first-hand knowledge and second-hand opinion. The simile of the cave does the same thing in graphic form: most people are prisoners in a cave, unable to turn their heads, and enjoying only the shadows cast on the wall in front of them by a fire behind. Occasionally, however, a prisoner escapes from this restricted mode of perception into broad daylight, a far more intense form of reality which puts cave-perception literally in a new light. The shadows of *maya* would no longer be the whole truth for the intrepid troglodyte who had ventured out of the cave. He would return convinced that he had been 'nearer reality and seeing more correctly'.

In the *Bhagavad Gita*, Krishna in his divine form appears to Arjuna as 'brighter than a thousand suns'; in the NDE we find an incredibly bright light 'which does not hurt the eyes', and in Plato we encounter the simile of the sun as a parallel to the form of the good; after unitive knowledge of the One, the many are apprehended as relative and transient, in a word less real. Returning now to the issue of knowledge and ignorance, we find ignorance defined in the *Protagoras* as 'having a false opinion and being mistaken on matters of great moment'. On the grounds that 'no one willingly goes to meet evil or what he thinks as evil', it is obviously that wrong actions done without knowledge (in this higher sense) are done in ignorance. Plato arrives at the conclusion that no one willingly does evil; but if they do, they must by definition by metaphysically ignorant, that is have no direct experience of the form of the good. This may strike the modern reader as curiously naïve, but the key to understanding Plato's notion is his distinction between knowledge and opinion. He is not referring to intellectual assent which might or might not be reflected in the will and thence in actions, but to a direct apprehension of the good which makes it impossible for the person not to perceive correctly and act virtuously. Such people are less burdened with 'a load of forgetfulness and wrongdoing', having 'seen the most of Being', and thus being 'seekers after wisdom and beauty' in attempting to recapture the dim memory of the primordial vision.

In the above comments on knowledge if the form of the good relate the metaphysical to the moral order in Plato, a moral order is also implied in the survival by the soul of bodily death. If death means annihilation, there can be no bearing of the metaphysical on the moral order of physical life. If, however, as Socrates is convinced, the soul survives, then we neglect it at our peril. The only escape or security from evil, therefore, is to become as good and as wise as possible; only education and training can be taken into the next world. Rewards and punishments, he supposes, are meted out according to deserts. Those guilty of 'curable' sins are cast into Tartarus for a year, while the 'incurable' are annihilated.

In his last dialogue, *The Laws*, Plato is concerned to prove the justice of the gods to upstart youths who doubt the moral coherence of the world; he explains that company is selected on the basis of affinity, and that the lad 'will be done by according to the standards that birds of a feather apply to each other'. The sentence is inescapable; no one can hope to evade the proper penalty; apparent injustices of impious and wicked people living in prosperity will be corrected. The youth is urged not to trust appearances, to which the law of karma pays no heed. This level of morality appeals to expediency and self-interest, while the philosopher, at the other end of the spectrum, is virtuous for virtue's sake, for love of the good. The former pragmatic carrot and stick consideration reappears in the philosophy of Kant, who postulates immortality as one of the necessities of a morally coherent universe.

It would be hopeless to try to trace the moral influence of Plato's philosophy in the subsequent history of ideas in this chapter; I shall therefore restrict myself to a brief discussion of the greatest Neoplatonic philosopher, Plotinus, who in his turn influenced Porphyry, Iamblichus and Proclus; then came the Neoplatonic revival in the Italian renaissance, and the Cambridge Platonists of the seventeenth century; and in the twentieth century and Cambridge philosopher McTaggart was one of the foremost exponents of a theory of reincarnation. Much of the history of Platonism was described by Dean Inge, whose two volumes of Gifford Lectures are devoted to the philosophy of Plotinus.

The basis of Plotinus' metaphysics is characteristically Indian in that 'unity is the source of highest character and true existence, separation the very sign of imperfection and defect of reality'. Soul has two aspects, a higher which is sinless and a lower, 'the image of the Soul', which can sin and be punished. After death the lower soul goes to where it longed to be in accordance with its desires; only if it is illuminated by the higher can it accompany it to the blessed realms in liberation. Otherwise the lower soul is reincarnated at the appropriate level of being, whether human, animal or plant. Circumstances are precisely ordered according to *adrasteia* (inevitable retribution), a principle of reason not chance. No mistakes are possible; 'It is not an accident that makes a man a slave. No one is a prisoner by chance; every bodily outrage has its cause. The man once did what he now suffers. A man that murders his mother will become a woman and be murdered by a son; a man who wrongs a woman will become a woman and be wronged.' Such a cast-iron interpretation enjoins acceptance of the present and acts as a deterrent for the future. There is no mitigating grace of *bhakti*, no karma yoga of selfless devotion. The fact that Plotinus dwells on punishment is partly accounted for by his conviction that good should be done for its own sake, not with a reward in view.

Channelled Teachings

Practically all the books of channelled material (purporting to be from people in a post-mortem world) published since the middle of the last century have embraced some theory of karma and reincarnation, usually on the grounds of cosmic justice and the possibility of expiation of misdeeds and continuing moral improvement in the school of experience called Earth. We shall concentrate here on a number of recurrent themes in such books which shed light on karma and reincarnation: the question of repeated psychological patterns in different incarnations; the life preview in relation to the life-review; so-called group souls; personal karmic relationships; and knotty metaphysical problems like physical and mental handicaps.

In reflecting on his own experiences 'T.E. Lawrence' delves into the law of karma as manifest in the cycles of growth in incarnations; he likens the post-mortem phase to a mopping-up operation after the real work on Earth: 'each succeeding life presents the same kind of problems and offers fresh opportunities to solve them.' He explains that an individual has built into their being certain tendencies which are likely to show up as typical patterns. These patterns will be mirrored in similar crises which will tend to elicit built-in responses unless the weakness or blind spot is overcome or transcended. This idea is extended to cover recapitulation of previous life-patterns like the re-enactment of human evolution into embryogenesis. Giving a concrete illustration, 'Lawrence' refers to a person who had repeatedly been killed in battle in his youth through not recognizing and therefore failing to control aggressive impulses; it is suggested that the next incarnation must be female in order to minimize the risk factor.

An intriguing scheme is put forward to account for this continuity of psychological patterns. As the individual moves from one cycle to the next, the tendencies of previous lives are stored in 'layers' in the unconscious, so that there is a progressive complication of the life-pattern and a greater number of recapitulations to work through; the scheme presumably presupposes a limited number of incarnations; otherwise one would be in danger of spending a whole life on recapitulations ... The diagram deals only with five. An interesting extension of this idea is Jung's archetypes of the collective unconscious, which are also likened to innate tendencies or instincts – chreodes in the biological domain, or habits according to Rupert Sheldrake's morphic resonance theory. Research done in hypnosis (see below) indicates that specific memories are available via or from the unconscious, while Jung's patients come out with mythical patterns in their dreams which are quite unfamiliar to the conscious mind. Jung himself wrote of the psyche in terms of psychological resonance from past lives one might propose a layer of the unconscious as it were between the personal and the collective unconscious which is personal in one sense and collective in another. Within this framework reclamation of the unconscious tendencies of past lives would correspond to the Jungian process of individuation.

Preview and choice of life is discussed in a number of books. We will see how in Chapter 5 Er mused over the forces impelling souls to choose particular lives in Plato's myth; and we touched upon the subject when looking at the life-review experiences reported by Helen Greaves in *Testimony of Light* (Chapter 2). The immediate implications of choice and preview are the ability to make a 'decision' about a pattern of experience, and a degree of foreknowledge or apparent predestination. Near-death experiencers occasionally glimpse episodes of supposed past existences as well as future personal and even global events, but they all emphasize the 'free will' factor, at least in response to events if not in shaping the events themselves. The scenario of a pre-life-review or choice entails a self-imposed pattern, which is of the essence of the law of karma anyway; but it removes the element of arbitrary external compulsion, whatever the reaction of the personality when the event occurs. How much of the jigsaw is it possible to see from the purely physical angle?

In a section on karma, 'H. A.', communicating through Tony Neate, stresses that each soul chooses its own path before incarnation, but once reborn one is subject to the laws and pressures of the environment and world conditions. There is no such thing as luck, he insists, but only hidden design. He interprets the biblical passage about an eye for an eye and a tooth for a tooth as an expression of karmic law which metes out exact repayment and warns against harbouring thoughts of resentment, ill-will, contempt and hatred, which tie one to the individual against whom such emotions are directed. Before incarnation the soul sees the broad outline of the life ahead, with its overall pattern but without much detail. Difficult lives may be chosen either in atonement for past misdeeds or as a means of learning. This operation, if true, highlights the importance of accepting and coming to terms with one's life 'because one's own inner self has chosen it and it is our own record you will have to review when you leave it'.

'Frances Banks', through Helen Greaves, became increasingly aware of a pattern and plan as her consciousness expanded: a blueprint which indicates that 'a definite line of advance is voluntarily accepted by the soul before incarnation'. The necessity of incarnations is explained by the need for the soul to project 'some part of itself back into the denser environment of earth in repeated attempts to master the trials and stresses of those vibrations'. This passage suggests that the soul is a composite being containing and transcending the individual incarnating personalities. It is interesting to compare this remark with 'Maurice Barbanell's observation in his post-mortem report that in reincarnated souls a part is in the physical realm and a 'residue' of the former personality is left in the spiritual realm; it is not the whole that returns. 'Banks' continued that a portion of the soul may wish to reincarnate for enlargement of experience, seeking a grail of strength, an emotional compensation or some other particular circumstances. It therefore fixes its own coming events because they will afford the necessary experience and will fit in with the overall pattern of development.

'Gildas', through Ruth White, also comments on the process whereby the higher self decides upon or chooses the situation into which the soul will reincarnate. The situation is chosen 'specifically' to give the soul certain opportunities for repaying and redeeming karmic debts'. One's life situation is thus predetermined to a certain extent, perhaps in terms of one's family circumstances; but the emphasis falls on the word 'opportunity', which may or may not be used, depending on the exercise of free will. 'Gildas' says that actual crises and their outcome are not determined, although the guidance of the higher self is intuitively available. It follows that a close connection with the higher self, a feature of overall spiritual integration, will present the most favourable opportunities for learning. At a later state in his exposition, 'Gildas' suggests that at one level the entire pattern of life is foreknown, but that it is not preordained. Here we are back with the intractable problem of divine omniscience, pre-destination and free will; but the essential point is how the present personality relates to the higher self, a message also highlighted by 'Frances Banks'.

These three explanations open up an unfamiliar metaphysical scheme of an expanded part of our consciousness choosing the circumstances of our lives on Earth without the meaning necessarily becoming apparent to us. However, when one considers the reactions of those fellow human beings who have found meaning and inner resources in the face of seemingly overwhelming odds – for instance Victor Frankl in Auschwitz – one can begin to wonder about our narrowly based assumptions of a chance universe devoid of intrinsic moral and metaphysical order.

St Paul speaks of the Church as the body of Christ and of the way in which we are members one of another, while Swedenborg describes the appearance of heaven as a 'Grand Man', the macrocosm of the microcosm, a spiritual hologram in which the whole is present in the parts. This leads us to a consideration of the relation of an individual soul to a group, or soul groups which unite to constitute a group soul. Our two sources here will be 'Frances Banks' and 'F. W. H. Myers'.

'Banks' prefaces her remarks by observing that the idea of group souls may not be all that palatable to a society that prizes individualism. The basic conception is akin to a series of ever-larger Chinese boxes, a nested hierarchy of holons. The smallest group, the family (perhaps expanded to the tribe), is contained within the wider groups of interest extending beyond family boundaries. The next stage of groups is likened to advance classes at university, wise beings who study the laws of the divine process and participate in the creative divine imagination, perhaps looking after and inspiring 'cell-like clusters of souls' which they in a sense contain. Beyond these groups are postulated further more inclusive and unified groups researching up to the infinite and transcendent Godhead, 'the Great Soul Being in which we live and move and have our being'. This breathtaking vista indicates a gradual widening of consciousness and identity until one reaches the cosmic awareness of one's essential and intrinsic unity with the universe, the *jivatman* realizing *Tat Tvam Asi*. Life is within Life, so that we progress towards unity through expansion of awareness and sympathy, hence of freedom; but the expansion is not simply *towards* unity, it is also *through* unity, by means of unity, from the unity and affinity of two souls in love progressing to the ultimate all-embracing unity of the Divine Light of Love.

'Myers' starts by saying that, as far as he can make out, souls normally only reincarnate up to six or eight times, during which incarnations they can do little more than touch the fringes of the total possibilities of human experience. The same impression can be gained by travelling either in person or vicariously on television: the range of human circumstances is so diverse that it is scarcely credible that such different lives can be lived on the same planet. This limitation can be overcome, according to 'Myers', by participating in the life of the group soul. This entails entering into 'every act and emotion in their past chronicles' in a way identical to that depicted in the life-review; the experiences are then assimilated and awareness correspondingly enlarged. The soul 'perceives ... all the consequences of acts, moods, thoughts in detail in this life of a kindred soul, and so it may ... in this communal group-state, win knowledge of all typical earth existences'. Empathetic resonance increases one's experience and might easily be mistaken for a case of straight reincarnation. Swedenborg counsels against this when he insists that apparent reincarnation experiences may be the reliving by another soul of its own life through the memory of a soul on Earth in such a way that the incarnate soul mistakes it for its own. Yet such an interpretation need not be inconsistent with the idea of a group soul, as the incarnate soul may well learn from the experience.

'Myers' briefly refers to another group relationship in which a 'young' soul may take on the karma of an 'older' soul through entry into the group memory or assuming a pattern created by this older soul. It should be noted that this is not so much vicarious atonement as the working out of an affinity which may afford constructive learning opportunities for the individual soul as well as the group. The overall picture is one of mutual coinherence and empathetic resonance expanding, like the universe itself, into ever-wider circles of understanding.

In his satirical portrayal of human foibles in *Erewhon*, Samuel Butler explains the mythology of pre-existence, whereby incarnating into the world is a criminal offence. The soul was well provided for in the kingdom of the unborn, having no cause for discontent, but 'he did of his own wanton depravity and restlessness conceive a desire to enter into this present world.' Then 'he did with malice aforethought set himself to plague and pester two unfortunate people who had never wronged him, and who were quite contented and happy until he conceived this base design against their peace.' According to this view the child is responsible for the choice of parents; the normal view would be just the opposite, except that there is no sense in which a particular child is chosen. The parents usually choose to have a child, whom they are inclined to regard as their own creation. This question takes on a different hue when we consider the soul in relation to the body. Various possibilities suggest themselves.

1. The denial of any principle beyond the physical; hence the parents are the creators of the child.

2. The soul, immortal after death, is created simultaneously with the body, and has therefore no influence on its circumstances and constitution; there can be no question of a life preview.

3. The soul pre-exists and in some way chooses its material circumstances, and thus probably its parents, with whom there may be previous connections.

The first view is orthodox materialism; the second orthodox Christianity (with the qualification that the soul is created by God); and the third is the system consistent with a theory of karma and rebirth.

This analysis extends the idea of the previous section on group souls and affinities existing within the group. I shall look at the topic of karmic relationships in more detail in the following sections. For the present I will confine myself to comments made by 'Gildas'. A relationship in a previous life may well have created attachments in one of two ways: through the binding force of either love or hatred, with corresponding positive or negative thoughts, emotions and actions. The affinity will tend to draw souls together for mutual comfort on the one hand and karmic adjustment on the other: 'As you proceed through your lives, you meet again the same souls in different circumstances, and receive the opportunity to repay old debts, to learn again lessons which were not understood before.' The obvious problem is lack of memory of connections and circumstances, but 'Gildas' suggests that many a difficult and trying life situation or relationship is likely to be karmic. He adds that the identity of subsequent incarnations is clearly not the same in every sense, but that 'these different personalities or aspects are like tiny flowerets which compose one main flower on one stem, and the stem may be likened to the higher self, the guiding light of the soul.' This is similar to Christ's vine and branches image, which we can better understand by relating it to Frances Banks' ever-widening enveloping circles of being. Resolution of negative ties cannot arise from further enmity and recrimination, but must begin with tolerance, forgiveness and understanding. When Christ encouraged his followers to forgive their enemies, he was uttering a profound truth in terms of the dissolution of negative karmic ties: a reaction of bitterness and hatred simply perpetuates and prolongs the vicious cycle. 'Gildas' speaks directly of the choice of parents by the higher selves, with all that this implies for family relationships and individual autonomy.

Coming now to Gordian knots which need unravelling if the mystery of the human condition is to be penetrated, we can ask ourselves questions like those that Voltaire asked in the wake of the Lisbon earthquake: why did 55,000 people perish? How does this fit into the cosmic scheme of physical and moral evil? As well as natural disasters, what about inequality of circumstances and apparently innocent suffering, a source of such anguish to Dostoevsky and Camus? Further treatment of these issues will be found in the concluding chapter, but it is worth sketching in some responses at this stage.

Any explanation of the tragedies of starvation and famine is going to sound callous to some degree, whether we go for chance, the inscrutable God, or karma. 'Gildas' suggests three possible categories of soul whose higher selves might choose such a poor, nasty, brutish and short incarnation: those taking a really steep path up the mountain of knowledge and experience; those repaying old karmic debts – in all probability not personal ones; and those who might give themselves to such suffering 'for the sake of world karma, in an attempt to awaken in mankind a greater compassion'. (A more general proposition is that much world karma is now being rapidly paid off in preparation for the advent of a new civilization; but pursuit of this line would take us too far off course at present.)

'Myers' and 'Gildas' have suggestions on the subject of handicaps. For 'Myers', as for 'Gildas', the basic purpose of karma is learning, so that tyrants and inquisitors are apparently reborn as idiots or imbeciles in order to 'learn to sympathize with and understand the sufferings of their victims'. These sufferings may be so appalling that the 'perpetrator's centre of imagination becomes disorganized and he is doomed to exist throughout his next incarnation in a state of mental disequilibrium'. Empathetic resonance invades the mind of the criminal and pulls him through a hell of his own making.

'Gildas' takes a broader view, although including retribution for ill-treatment of others. He offers three other scenarios: the soul may choose such a route in order to help a relative learn the lesson of compassion; a soul may take on the karma of the group; or a soul emerging from the stage of animal evolution may take on an imperfect body in its human incarnation. In general terms he shuns the use of the categories of sin and punishment, preferring instead to speak of cause and effect, learning and progress. From all this it follows that constructive acceptance and work within one's circumstances is the creative path of development. Furthermore, one must be especially cautious in applying superficial and unsympathetic strictures to the misfortunes of others: 'judge not'; indeed a hard-hearted refusal to help others on the grounds that they deserve their misfortunes can only serve to entangle ourselves in the karmic web. The purest path is indicated in both Christianity and the *Bhagavad Gita*: selfless and devoted service to others, the ethical mysticism of Albert Schweitzer.

Hypnotic Regression

Interest in hypnotic regression has burgeoned over the past ten years or so. Some regard it as a significant phenomenon, while others dismiss it as a fabrication of the unconscious. Much attention has been focused on ostensible memories. Many are unverifiable or else turn out to be quite extraordinary cases of hidden memory or cryptomnesia, the events in question perhaps deriving from the reading of a long-forgotten novel with appropriate modifications (see Chapter 1). Here we are less concerned with the correctness or otherwise of the memories than with the psychological conditions said to be connected with karma, which are released through a form of 'past-life therapy'. From a pragmatic point of view, as indicated in an article by Dr Ronald Wong Jue, it is less important whether one accepts the metaphysics of karma and reincarnation; the crucial finding is that people have been helped by such methods and enabled to overcome allergies, phobias and other psychological or psychosomatic disorders. For my part, I can say only that the evidence is consistent with the operation of karma across time.

Many of the themes already treated recur in the literature on hypnotic regression: we will investigate the NDE and life-review, the life preview, recapitulating patterns of experience, karma as an educational opportunity, karmic ties with close friends and relatives; then we will look further at the psychological significance along lines suggested by the readings of Edgar Cayce.

Many subjects taken back to a previous death report a sensation of floating out of their bodies. One speaks of the body expanding to fill the whole room, and then being flooded with a euphoria which was accompanied by an insight into the meaning and justice of the cosmic process. Another woman whose interlife period and subsequent life were fraught with difficulties also described blissful feelings at death. She found herself floating in an all-embracing golden light and able to see in all directions; there was no sense of separation and division. Her next experience, after a despairing suicide by drowning, was to see the karmic script or blueprint which would have been played out had she made the required effort. We shall return to Heather's case in looking at the life preview.

Dr Joel Whitton's subjects found themselves faced with a 'board of judgement', archetypal figures in loose white garments who radiated a healing energy in the presence of any remorse felt by the soul. Empathetic resonance is said to occur in precisely the way we encountered in the NDE life-review: 'any emotional suffering that was inflicted on others is felt as keenly as if it were inflicted on oneself'; and the time for reparations is past – hence the remorse. Yet these beings, like the being of light, do not condemn the soul but rather encourage it to learn and benefit from past mistakes. Subjects use similar phrasing to those reporting NDEs, saying that the review is a total recalling and reliving, which happens in an instant. Particular episodes are reviewed and discussed, and eventually an understanding is reached within the context of life-patterns running from one existence to the next.

The board is then supposed to assist in the planning of the next life, not so much according to wants as needs, in the light of karmic debts and lessons. Less-developed personalities must apparently have a more detailed blueprint, while more 'evolved' souls can make do with a general outline. The choosing of obstacles acts as a spur to development, while life purposes may include the overcoming of emotional difficulties. One especially interesting case concerned a person who planned 'a tragic event which would cause me to change my entire soul complexion during my thirties'. This statement suggests that the higher self may even engineer an NDE for transformative purposes, in other words that the NDE is written into the 'karmic script'.

Helen Wambach's subjects were divided about willingness to be reborn, although the majority, 81 per cent, said they did choose birth, however reluctantly; once again the tension between impersonal needs and personal wants. The outcome of Heather's review was a 'dismal conglomerate of frustration and tears', but she emerged with a determination to grapple with the repercussions of the profligate artistic life of the previous personality, Isobel. She was horrified at the prospect of being born to her mother, but reassured to see her grandmother, whom she claimed to recognize from an earlier, happier incarnation. Heather herself was subject to massive allergic reactions including headaches, chest and throat congestion and skin rashes, which were compounded by attacks of pneumonia and bronchitis. After reliving a traumatic car accident which had happened to her previous identity Isobel in 1931, Heather experienced a horrific three days of sleeplessness, nausea and sobbing which left her prostrated; but when she awoke after finally managing to sleep, she found that her habitual allergic reactions had vanished – the headache, ringing ears, chest congestion; and persistent skin problems began to clear up. They had apparently been released from the psychosomatic circuit.

Our findings on personality patterns and tendencies in channelled teachings are reflected in the data of hypnotic regression. They can be illustrated by the case of Steve Logan, who rarely visited his sick father in a nursing home because of appalling treatment in childhood. On one occasion, however, he noticed during a visit that his father was having difficulty breathing because the respirator had become dislodged. There was a moment when he could have done nothing and allowed his father to die. But instead he called for the nurse. A few years later he had a bad bicycle accident in which he was lucky not to have been killed himself. In an altered state of consciousness it became clear to him that the incident with his father was an important test which hinged on Steve's ability to forgive his father for transgressions 'which appeared to extend over several lifetimes'; and as a result of passing this test he was not killed in the accident and moved on to an agenda in his scheme of development which had not been scheduled for this lifetime. Again we see how forgiveness may hold the key to the breaking of a pattern.

Whitton and Fisher use the image of a cosmic classroom to expound their version of karma. They distinguish three stages, starting with strict retribution, moving on to compensation and finally the 'school of hard knocks', in which knowledge is acquired through repeated trial and error. Acquisition of this knowledge presupposes acquaintance with and acceptance of the theory of karma, if the feeling of being victimized in this lifetime is to be understood well enough to allow the individual to assume a constructive attitude towards people and circumstances. It is much easier to give in to bitterness, resentment or vengefulness if one is quite ignorant of the dynamic implications of karma; whereas if one can see a situation in this light, it may help one to come to terms with it and cultivate acceptance and forgiveness in order to move on and release a pattern of thought or behaviour. Karma is spoken of as a means of progressive refinement of one's nature, a phrase reminiscent of the purification through incarnations in the Orphic and Platonic traditions.

Among the examples given by Whitton and Fisher is the case of a man with a tendency to kill those who treated him badly; with knowledge of karma in his current incarnation the urge was held in check even under extreme provocation. A woman underwent the trials of bereavement because she had sentenced people to death in a previous life. A surgeon learned that he was compensating for his past cruelty and persecution; he now mended bodies as he had broken them himself in a former life, and was on the receiving end of persecution.

Eighty-seven per cent of Wambach's birth regression subjects stated that they had known parents, friends or other relatives in different guises from other lives. The relationship is not constant but there is some connection, some positive and some negative. Negative connections include coming back to correct a relationship with one's own murderer; positive ones include close friends or siblings becoming marriage partners. There is invariably unfinished business to sort out, which may involve the necessity for forgiveness along the lines already mentioned.

We have already encountered the disappearance of allergic symptoms in Heather. Other researchers like Dr. Edith Fiore have noted a wide spectrum of associated conditions which have been cleared up by regression therapy: chronic weight excess and cravings traceable to horrifying incidents that occurred during sleep in previous lives; chronic headaches related to head injuries or executions and abdominal pains to being run through with a deadly weapon. Wambach mentions violent death as a particularly strong cause of phobias, citing instances of fear of horses going back to being killed by a horse; and, related to the theme, a fear of drowning turning into a terror of water. All these effects seem to operate by a kind of empathetic resonance across time, and can be discharged when the experiences are relived and integrated into the psyche.

From the last two sections we can see a consistent picture emerging, one of a moral order operating in the universe in a subtle and comprehensive way. It points towards a thorough-going responsibility for who and where we are, even if the choosing was carried out at a level normally inaccessible to the conscious personality. The data make sense in psychological and spiritual and, if one can accept it, in metaphysical terms: psychologically, we see the alleviation of mental and emotional distress; spiritually, we encounter the urge to forgive our enemies and accept our lot; while metaphysically we can begin to discern a pattern and meaning behind apparently unjust or arbitrary situations.

The Metaphysics of Edgar Cayce

Born in 1877, Edgar Cayce was one of the most extraordinary clairvoyants of the early twentieth century. He started out by giving readings under hypnosis for people with chronic health problems, but soon found himself embroiled in metaphysical as well as physical analysis. The records in Palm Beach contain transcripts of some 14,000 readings given to over 6,000 people over a period of forty-three years. One of Cayce's early successes in medical clairvoyance was a case of a girl who had unaccountably lost her reason. Cayce's diagnosis under hypnosis revealed that the girl had an impacted wisdom tooth which was impinging on a nerve in the brain. Dental investigation led to the discovery of an unsuspected impaction, which, when removed, led to the girl's complete return to sanity. The two books which deal most fully with Cayce's readings are both by Gina Cerminara, and I shall draw on them considerably here. One further introductory point: as an evangelical Christian, Cayce was at first dismayed to find that he had referred to reincarnation in his readings under hypnosis, but long experience and reflection convinced him of the truth of the doctrine.

I.C. Sharma, an authority on Indian ethical systems, made a special study of Cayce and compared his metaphysics with that of the Upanishads and *Bhagavad Gita*. He quotes Cayce: 'Know that thy body, thy mind, thy soul, is a manifestation of God in the earth – as is every other soul; and that thy body is indeed the temple of the living God. All the good, then, all the God ... that ye may know, is manifested in and through thyself – and not what somebody else thinks, not what somebody else does!' The purpose of life is summed up as follows: 'That it, the entity, may know itself to be itself yet one with the purposes of the First Cause that called it, the entity, into being, into the awareness, into the consciousness of itself. That is the purpose, that is the cause of being.'

It follows that 'sin', 'missing the mark', is rooted in ignorance of the basic oneness and wholeness of life, leading to selfishness and separativeness, a denial of the truth which is unity. Equally it follows that love is the fulfilment of the law of unity in harmony and peace. Other premises of Cayce's world-view are: the purposefulness and continuity of life; the operation of life under the law of karma and reincarnation; the view that the will creates destiny; that the mind has formative power; and that the answer to all problems is within the self. The ultimate remedy for suffering is the love of God, both given and received.

Cayce elaborates quite a sophisticated scheme of karma. Karmic records were accessible through the unconscious and communicate by Cayce under hypnosis. (We noted hypnotic diagnosis practised by Eugene Osty in Chapter 3). Two basic categories of karma are outlined: continuitive and retributive, each with various aspects.

Continuitive karma is a principle of conservation and accumulation. It is said to operate in talents and skills as well as characteristics, interests and attitudes. There is some evidence in the work of Ian Stevenson of the transmission of skills and interests. He cites cases in which precocious skills in sewing, in fishing and in dealing with engines manifested in three individuals who claimed to be reincarnations of people who had exhibited decided talents in those directions. Such continuity also makes sense of precocious musical or artistic ability, but we shall find this simple equation challenged by Steiner below.

Retributive karma metes out an effect appropriate to and proportionate with the original harm done to another manifestation of life; it can manifest either in the physical or in the psychological realm, and may even arise from excessive mockery or criticism of others. Three kinds of retributive karma are distinguished by Cerminara:

1. Boomerang. A person who blinded others in the past or laughed at cripples may find themselves blind or crippled in the present. Infidelity may be reciprocated.

2. Organismic. A glutton in one life may suffer from a digestive weakness in the next; the causal factor is misuse of the organism.

3. Symbolic; A psychosomatic condition may be symbolically transferred. For example one may be deaf owing to having turned a deaf ear, anaemic from having 'bled' a country; frequently such health problems prove to be particularly intractable.

Not all such karma necessarily appears in the immediately following life; it may be suspended for various reasons, such as the inability to handle the consequences or the need to repay the debt in association with other entities. It is significant that none of Cayce's cases suggested that a present affliction had been initiated by a victim of the perpetrator. The karma operates directly on the person concerned either psychologically or psychophysically; Cerminara claims that the reversal or reaction is more exact in psychological than in physical terms.

Sharma considers Cayce's theory of reincarnation and karma in the light of Hindu teaching; he calls karma the 'law of the conservation of ethical energy' by means of *samskaras*, traits or tendencies crystallized into karmic traces which persist in the unconscious mind. There are three kinds of karma: accumulated karma which is manifest in the future, fructifying karma which ripens in the present incarnation, and voluntary karma which is generated in this life and which will be carried forward. According to Sri Ramana Maharshi, the personal god Iswara selects suitable karma from the subconscious warehouse to suit the soul's spiritual evolution at the time; the root of karma can be cut off only by loving surrender of the ego to God and the consequent realization that there is no doer other than the divine will. Sharma considers karma in relation to grace by saying that karma is the effort and grace the prize, thus suggesting that the categories need not be regarded as mutually exclusive. He then shows how the Sermon on the Mount (Matthew 4), with its basis of loving one's enemy, is a reversal of karma, a point which we have already noted in our discussion of the value of forgiveness.

With the obvious responsibility implied within the moral order as envisioned by Cayce comes his insistence on the creative force of the will and the formative power of the mind. If we have created the present in some sense through our thoughts and actions, it follows that the future will be a crystallization of the actions and thoughts of the present. Few people realize just how powerful the human mind is.

The Anthroposophy of Rudolf Steiner

Rudolf Steiner's Anthroposophy sprang out of the Theosophical movement inaugurated by H. P. Blavatsky in the mid-1870s. Theosophy can be largely credited with the promotion of the metaphysics of karma and reincarnation in the West, and indeed, through Gandhi and others, for reawakening some Hindus to the jewels of their own religion. Madame Blavatsky herself likened karma to a thread which people weave around themselves, putting the creative initiative firmly in the human realm by saying 'It is man who plans and creates causes, and Karmic law adjusts the effects.' She adds that the adjustment is not so much an act as universal harmony – a kind of moral self-regulation or homeostasis; we therefore reward or punish ourselves, while karma is merely the means. She argues that karma explains the origin of evil and ennobles our idea of divine immutable Justice 'instead of degrading the unknown and unknowable Deity by making it the whimsical, cruel tyrant, which we call Providence'.

Steiner's voluminous writings on karma and reincarnation include five volumes on karmic relationships, as well as other shorter works. These conceptions were central to his philosophy, and he anticipated that the doctrines would eventually achieve more widespread acceptance than they enjoyed in his day. His starting-point is the familiar proposition that the human soul is the architect of its own fate. He illustrates the thinking required to make a link of similes of waking and sleeping – in a sense one reincarnates every day – and travel to a foreign country. A change of scene of action from Europe to America puts the person in new surroundings, but life in America depends on the previous life in Europe in the sense that a mechanic or a bank clerk will find themselves in different environments in accordance with their professional leanings and skills; a particular environment is likely to attract some people but not others, in accordance with their nature and experience. Similarly the soul (or Spirit-self in Steiner's terminology) 'inevitably surrounds itself in a new life with that to which it is related from previous lives'. A new life is thus a 'self-created destiny' in which the soul is liable to be interacting with those known in the past because 'actions which have taken place between them must have their consequences'.

In addressing the question of what comes over, karmically, from previous lives on Earth, Steiner's answer is blunt: it is we ourselves that come over, 'for, in the last resort, we ourselves are our karma'. To wipe out our karma would be to wipe out ourselves, the root or source of the karma. This is exactly Ramana Maharshi's point (referred to in the previous section) that the ego and karma are ultimately one, so that to transcend the law of karma is to transcend the ego and to transcend the ego is self-realization, identification with the divine Atman within and thus liberation from the wheel of *samsara*. Steiner makes the philosophical observation that freedom requires the ground of necessity, that is karma, which arises out of our selves in previous lives. Hence we reach the paradoxical conclusion that freedom and necessity both arise from within ourselves: the necessity from connections with actions, thoughts and feelings come from previous lives, and the freedom to act, or at least to think and feel, within this self-created circle of necessity. For Steiner, immediate consciousness of freedom is in thought: even the thoughts of a prisoner cannot be put in chains; he is always free to think a new and therefore creative way which will form future patterns different from the past. We thus embody both freedom and necessity.

Steiner placed reincarnation firmly within an evolutionary context. He argued that if evolutionists were to explain the present in terms of the past, then this method must also be legitimate when applied to the soul; furthermore, he rejected the idea that things pertaining to the soul can arise other than from the soul. In other words there is a heredity of the soul as well as of the body. Agreeing with Cayce, he shows how it is possible to meet with *a priori* rejection from reductionist wielders of Occam's hatchet on the grounds that hypotheses were being multiplied unnecessarily. Steiner's logic is that one's environment is invariably connected with one's karma, and that this environment includes genetic factors. Through the principle of affinity or attraction the soul gravitates towards those parents who can provide the corresponding physical heredity. Steiner's example concerns a soul wishing to develop moral courage, who searches out the family which will enable the unfolding of this quality. Moreover, as we have already indicated, he maintains that souls may be drawn together because they have been connected in previous lives. Both Cayce and Steiner therefore argue that spiritual heredity is the primary force, and that it acts in conjunction with physical heredity through the principles of affinity and correspondence.

We now come to Steiner's conception of continuitive karma, whereby the talents and skills of one life are reflected in the next. He states that this may well be the case, but that it is easy to be deceived by appearances and that the overall dynamic of human existence is to develop into an 'all-comprehensive being by passing through the most manifold life activities'. Continuity, he argues, will be most apparent if the talent was unable to come to full fruition in a previous life. For instance, a mathematician who died young will be born with a talent for mathematics in the next incarnation, but if the same mathematician had lived to a great age the talent might have spent itself; in the next life the person might show no aptitude at all, but the talent might be translated into another quality, capacity or force.

A more general statement of this principle is to be found in the connections between action, destiny or karma. Steiner maintains that during the interlife state a soul sees itself mirrored in surrounding souls according to the good or evil performed; all the feelings return from the soul that was helped or harmed. The previous lives, but particularly the immediately preceding one, are laid out 'as though in a far and widespread reflector'; and the feeling of 'I' is modified by this spectacle. The next stage is the formation of the astral (feeling) body through an internalization or absorption of these pictures; the process gives us impulses which attract or repel us to certain souls in incarnation.

A sublime aspect of this mirroring is the way in which love poured out to other souls is returned in a stream of joy and gladness. The opposite holds: deeds performed from a motivation of cold antipathy and hatred are likewise mirrored and turn into the opposite of joy, that is pain, distress and unhappiness; this, Steiner says, may then manifest in a subsequent life as mental dullness. Thus his general scheme is that love leads to joy and an open heart, while the sequence for hatred or antipathy is suffering and stupidity. In another example of the negative process Steiner attributes a grudging disposition to intense hatred felt in a previous life. Forgiveness and love are the only way out of such a straitjacket.

Another philosophical minefield is the significance of chance. Steiner claims that it is legitimate to speak of chance within the physical world where things may outwardly meet which are inwardly connected. However, in the case of a brick injuring some undeserving person by chance, the karmic adjustment will now be set in motion for the future. Thus it is possible for Steiner to say that there is no chance if all the worlds, past and future, are taken into account. This kind of analysis might be extended to explain connections of what Jung calls synchronicity (meaning coincidences) and significant correlations arising in sophisticated astrology.

The implication of a minimal role for chance in life is that freedom and responsibility are enhanced. Insight into the nature of karma can hasten the development of such qualities. Steiner rightly observes that 'insight into and knowledge of karma only gains real value when it flows into our will for the future.' He sees human evolution as moving towards ever-greater freedom and consciousness, hence responsibility, and bases his educational system on such a premise. The time has perhaps now come for human beings to develop inner strength and corresponding inward conception of religion, which relies less on external forms and support. The person who has truly assimilated the moral element in karma and reincarnation knows that 'According to what I was in life, I shall have an effect upon everything that takes place in the future, upon the whole civilization of the future!' The limited degree of responsibility we are aware of is extended beyond birth and death by such knowledge and will be intensified 'to a degree that was formerly impossible'. The ethical and metaphysical horizon will be widened, with corresponding changes in ideas and conduct, in education and psychology, in politics and religion. It will be part of my present task to begin to penetrate such implications in the final chapter.

Karmic Moral Order and Spiritual Evolution

> The next stage of evolution is not in man's physique but in his psyche, in his mind and spirit, in the emergence of a larger understanding and awareness, in the development of a new integration of character adequate to the new age.

> SIR SARVEPELLI RADHAKRISHNAN

Radhakrishnan was one of the foremost exponents of Indian thought and culture. He produced classic editions of some of the great Indian religious texts, many of which we have consulted in previous sections. The larger understanding he refers to can be seen in two lights: externally as a greater tolerance and co-operation among nations within the context of global ecological balance, a transcendence of narrow nationalism; and internally as an appreciation of the oneness of life and consciousness, expressed in the workings of karma in individual lives. The larger awareness will also be more mature, acknowledging the responsibilities of interdependence. Along similar lines, Paul

Brunton distinguishes three stages of the connections between ethics and metaphysics in the West. The first involves 'uncertain fears of a probably existent God', leading to no restraint. The ethics of the future, he surmises, will be based on 'rational understanding of the power of karma, the law of personal responsibility'. This, he maintains, will lead to right restraint on conduct. At first, however, people might only conform through fear, but moral development will lead eventually to the selfless service of love.

Theories of karma and reincarnation, while varying in detail and depth as we have seen, are sufficiently consistent for a coherent moral order to be deduced from them. They incorporate a view of the divine order, a metaphysical order, and a moral order within the context of the first two orders. We shall consider these orders in turn.

The divine order embodies the qualities that are found at the core of all religious traditions, notably Love, Wisdom, Energy and Unity. It is this Unity that underlies both the metaphysics and the ethics which derive from it. It is immanent within creation as mind or consciousness and as life or energy, and yet it transcends the whole creation, holding it in an all-embracing love, which can be experienced through human consciousness. Wisdom – *vidya* or *jnana* – is manifest in the aspiration to and the achievement of at-one-ment with God; also in the perception of the underlying unity of creation as real, as opposed to attributing ultimate reality to the sensory world and falling into the clutches of *maya*.

The metaphysical order is in a sense the explicit structure of the divine order. All souls are manifestations or aspects – droplets or sparks – of the divine Oneness, and are thus integrally connected at the core of their being. Brunton makes this point nicely when he says that Overselves are separate but not distinct. Souls undergo a process of involution or condensation into individual forms, and then have the yearning to recapture the unity from which they sprang. This process takes place through a series of rebirths, which represent a progressive refinement of the human soul until it achieves transparency to the Divine, expressed in love and service towards all life-forms. The end (*telos*) is liberation or salvation for all beings.

The lynchpin of this moral order is the law or principle of karma, elsewhere characterized as the conservation of ethical energy, the law of cause and effect applied to the moral realm, or a moral homeostatic self-regulation of balance and harmony. In my discussions I have distinguished various forms and modes of operation of karma: the continuitive and the retributive aspects; compensations from the past and in the future; physical and psychological effects in terms of health and mental or emotional disturbance. I have also alluded to the issue of heredity and the power of karma as an explanatory principle for apparent inequality and injustice. Before spelling out the implications, it is worth considering the objections to the theory on grounds of memory and identity.

One of the most common protests is that people have no memory of previous incarnations. We have seen, however, that it is possible to recover lost memories of the present life through hypnosis, and that there is some suggestive evidence that memories of previous incarnations are recoverable as well. Although the hypotheses of possession if not fabrication are advanced to explain the phenomenon, they are not very plausible in some instances. Possession may not be totally wide of the mark, but it would be reasonable to suppose that an individual might in a sense be possessed by a previous identity and have access to their memories; or, by Myers's theory, this might represent the experience of another member of the group soul. If, as has been suggested, memories of previous incarnations are accessible in the unconscious (leaving aside the question of who they 'belong' to), then it can be surmised that they might exert a psychological influence. We saw earlier how some patients were relieved of their phobias or allergies through reliving and integrating inner experiences ostensibly emanating from the memory stream of a deceased individual. Relief of such symptoms makes the fabrication hypothesis look rather thin, especially in view of the intensity and pain of the re-enactment, and the fact that the symptoms had often proved intractable to any other form of treatment.

Whose memories are they, then? In other words, what is the relationship of the present individuality to the experiencer of the life situations 'relived'? Memory is a crucial variable in identity, and yet we cannot consciously recall much of our experience in the last week, let alone in the past year. We do, however, recognize memories of events in which we have participated. According to people who have had regressions and who at the same time are able to tune in to the memories of other people through psychometry, they can easily distinguish a memory 'of their own' from other experienced by another person. This may be thoroughly unconvincing to the sceptical reader, but it is a similar phenomenon to the cases of those who have had NDEs who tell us that the experience is not like a dream. We are free to disbelieve them, but have no *a priori* reason for doing so if we ourselves have had no similar experience and consider the person concerned psychologically balanced in other respects. The subjective impression, then, is that they were directly involved in the past situation; they may well add that the other protagonists are related to them in this life, and that the situation throws some light on their relationships. In one case, for instance, a person found themselves provoked beyond control and had seized a weapon with which to murder their partner; then, suddenly, a vision flashed up that this situation had played itself out in a previous incarnation and marriage. The insight was enough to prevent a fatal repetition. The person concerned was inwardly convinced of psychological continuity with a previously existing personality.

Without some degree of psychological continuity, karma as an explanation for apparent inequality and injustice would be scarcely different form the arbitrary lottery of chance: as it is, people may feel that they are not to blame for their life situation, owing to a lack of memory of the possible connecting threads.

A second criticism is levelled by John Hick, that karma does not provide an ultimate explanation for present inequalities: if there is no first life, the problem is endlessly postponed in an infinite regress of previous lives; and if there is a first life, then the problem arises at the moment of initial creation. Furthermore, the creator is then implicated in the inequalities of his creation. For some reason, Hick does not see fit to apply the Christian criterion of free will to this issue: God gave his creatures a degree of free will which involves the risk of making mistakes; differences and inequalities can then be referred back to previous misuse of free will, and karma provides the opportunity of learning to apply the law of love. In this respect, orthodox Christianity, with its doctrine of one life, has a good deal more explaining to do when confronted with inequalities which impair the exercise of free will and render spiritual progress difficult if not impossible. It is hard to understand the cosmic justice involved in a metaphysics which allows one life of ten days in Ethiopia and assumes that the rest of that soul's development will take place in the beyond. This issue is further discussed in Chapter 8.

We can now return to the implications of the karmic moral order, bearing in mind that there is at least some suggestive evidence of psychological continuity and consistency. The logical problem of extrapolating from the particular to the general remains, however; but this is a hazard of postulating any comprehensive moral and metaphysical order. We cannot pretend to discern more than a part of the pattern from within the limitations of the physical order. Our picture is bound to be incomplete.

I began by reiterating the inner interdependence metaphysically implied by the karmic moral order: the interconnectedness of all souls within the all-embracing divine Being, and the particular empathetic resonances between individuals in the present and some identities in the past. This interdependence implies responsibility, since we are all parts of the same Whole and are therefore able to affect other parts through the resonance of our common coincidence: the balance of the organism can be upset by the malfunctioning of a single organ, and regains equilibrium and harmony only when that organ is healed and is once more dynamically and constructively interacting with the whole. Using the metaphor of the symphony orchestra, there is an overall discord even when one member is out of tune. In terms of the karmic moral order, application of the law of love is harmonious attunement, while failure to apply this law is a discord which will require the instrument to be returned.

The freedom implied by responsibility has both a retrospective and a prospective aspect within the karmic moral order. Retrospectively it means acceptance that one's present situation is the outcome of one's past thoughts, feelings and actions, for which one was responsible. This is not predestination, as I pointed out in discussing Steiner, since it is assumed that one was exercising free choice oneself in the past, albeit under the influence of various *samskaras* and external factors; predestination, on the other hand, implies the sovereign decree of an omnipotent God who simply places you in a situation over which you have no control. We have also seen how a sense of retrospective responsibility leads to an acceptance of one's position, and frequently to a perception that forgiveness is the only constructive response to negative recapitulations, the way out of the vicious circuit of continuing bitterness and recriminations. Sometimes critics of the theory claim that it induces too great a degree of fatalism, or that it encourages spiritual procrastination, but this ignores the prospective aspect.

Prospective responsibility looks forward from the present, insisting on the creative power and dynamism of mind and will: our life is the creation of our mind, as the *Dhammapada* puts it. Mind determines our reaction to circumstances, while will translates thoughts and feelings into acts, which become habits, then character, then 'destiny", influencing the choice and pattern of future existences. The influence of the past through the unconscious makes our present freedom only partial; we are impelled by strong drives which may be a critical factor in decision-making, throwing up consequences which provide material for further tests and instruction. We move gradually towards deeper knowledge, wider freedom and greater love. If each of us is following the curriculum of a self-designed course of education, the goal nevertheless remains the same: to penetrate and express the love and wisdom of God. Karma is a form of continuous assessment giving us as many opportunities as we need in learning to apply the law of love, leading at last to harmony, joy and peace in our own consciousness, and radiating such qualities in our interaction with others. Grace and forgiveness are ever-present in the love of God, but the key question is whether we are able to forgive each other and ourselves, releasing the past patterns that bind us and obscure the luminosity of our own potential transparency to the divine order.

CHAPTER FIVE

THE EMERGENCE OF POST-MORTEM JUDGEMENT

—————=🙰🙰🙰=—————

As the moon dieth and cometh to life again, so we also, having to die, will rise again.

JUAN CAPASTRINO INDIANS OF CALIFORNIA

Introduction

We shall now retrace our steps in order to explore the gradual moralization of human concepts of the afterlife, the establishment of a moral order within the metaphysical context of survival by the soul or conscious self of bodily death. The existence of a post-mortem state is rarely, if ever, denied by preliterate societies, whether historically in the past or anthropologically in the present. In the African religious heritage, for example, 'death represents a transition from corporeal to incorporeal life … and the incorporeal life is taken to be as real as the corporeal'. This view is related to an understanding of death as the separation of the immaterial part of the human being from the physical body.

If death represents the separation of soul from body, it also means the end of a person's physical participation in the community. Continuity is assured, however, through 'prayers, libations, offerings, and the observation of other religious rites'; and the dead, in return, protect the living, intervening on their behalf. There is thus a sense in which the social order extends into the afterlife, without the sharp demarcations usually found in Western thinking. Nor does the same eschatological time-structure predominate, with beginnings and endings of history. African concepts are more cyclical than linear.

Social continuity may mean that one's status in the next world often remains unaltered: the basic criterion is rank rather than moral quality, so that the privileged may continue to enjoy an enhanced prestige. Frazer mentions a Fijian society in which it is believed that the ferryman of the River of Souls asks the would-be passengers whether they were ordinary or cabin passengers, 'for … the ghosts of chiefs kept strictly to themselves at one end of the canoe, and the ghosts of commoners huddled together at the other end.'

Lévy-Bruhl contrasts the universal belief in an afterlife with the vague and indefinite conceptions entertained by many of the preliterate societies he investigated. Opoku also remarks on the absence of clear-cut notions of heaven and hell, adding that this does not rule out the idea among some tribes that people have to give an account of their earthly lives. We find individual morality developed in some, but by no means all of these societies. The equivalent of salvation is to take one's place among the ancestors, to be incorporated in the group or clan. Such a belief ensures the subservience of the individual to group identity, with the damnation of exclusion looming as the ultimate penalty.

During earthly life, the men of many preliterate societies undergo initiation as a ritual incorporation into the group. They are then expected to marry and produce male heirs to continue the traditions. Failure to produce sons, in one tribe from the Fiji Islands, would make the man afraid to die 'and face the forebears of their race, who would be enraged with the wretch who had failed to supply posterity for the continuance of the family worship'. From this ordeal, it can be inferred that one's reception in the next world is a momentous event. Lévy-Bruhl cites various determining factors such as rank, manner of death, number of descendants and funeral honours: the danger lurks that the soul may be ostracized by the group; childless men occupy the lowest status in the social order. The point of recounting these details is to illustrate that status in the next world is more often a function of rank than of moral attainment. The continuity of social structure is intimately bound up with the welfare of the whole society, which includes both the living and the 'dead'.

Crimes and Punishments

Preliterate societies are noted for their emphasis on social cohesion, necessary in order to assure their survival. Obedience to authority is the keynote. Virtue is defined in terms of behaviour which promotes or strengthens this cohesion, while vice is conduct which weakens or undermines the group social order. Moral order is based on obedience to an authority which, although apparently social, is legitimated by religion. There is no real separation between what we would recognize as the authority of society or the state, and that of the Church; in the same way, no clear distinction is drawn between custom or convention and the law.

By its very nature, law describes and/or prescribes a certain order. The law of gravity describes an order in which bodies are attracted to each other, while a law against murder prescribes a form of social order, or at least attempts to do so. If the latter kind of law is not obeyed, a sanction is imposed on the offender. Sanctions are implicit in any social law. They aim to prevent a certain act, to deter others by the example of the punishment of a transgressor, and ultimately, to reform the offender. By its edicts the law prescribes a social duty; and if this duty is not carried out or if a crime is committed, then the sanction will come into force.

Because the distinction between civil and religious authority is blurred, sins are treated as crimes and crimes as sins; at a later stage in a society's development, sin is defined as a violation of the law of God, while crimes are infringements of human law. Some crimes/sins are common to nearly every known society, such as murder, theft, adultery, incest and lying; some, like sorcery, considered anti-social through the inflicting of death and suffering on members of the tribe, are peculiar to the tribal outlook; while others, like neglect or contempt of worship and ritual, are more strictly religious offences. Taboo is the unifying and pervasive principle of regulation. Freud points out that the word means both sacred or consecrated, and dangerous or forbidden: what is sacred is unapproachable and forbidden. The psychology and motivation is to inspire fear and dread so as to inhibit anti-social behaviour. Prohibitions are expressed as negative restrictions on individual behaviour: thou shalt not ... The entire scheme of taboos induces conformity to the established norms and therefore contributes towards social stability.

One should also mention that there is one standard for 'insiders', those belonging to the tribe, and another for 'outsiders', who may be murdered or pillaged as the chiefs think fit. Sympathy and identification do not yet extend very far. One moral seed which is planted in the field of taboo is a sense of guilt when the person is literally consumed by the knowledge, a sort of nocebo effect or self-hypnosis by means of which the mere thought of the sanction is sufficient to make it real. Those touching the king on pain of death have been known to waste away in the knowledge that death follows violation of that particular taboo.

Social punishment or retribution originates in personal revenge, the action taken by one individual against another who has done him a wrong or who has encroached upon his rights or interests. It starts as a reflex action of self-defence, for instance in striking back, and is a primitive form of deterrence. It shows the aggressor that he cannot attack with impunity, and therefore suggests that it is in his best interests to steer clear of trouble. If he does not, he can expect to pay for his action: an eye for an eye and a tooth for a tooth, the *lex talionis* of proportionate compensation. Such a personal arrangement, however, is nothing if not anarchic in social terms, as the individuals are laws unto themselves, and thus is soon followed in any society by the establishment of public authority and justice, perhaps through the power and prestige of the chief who comes to act as a judge. Private revenge is regulated through a more official system of compensations, which represent a kind of public or collective revenge with a view to the society's own self-preservation. Such a developing system mirrors tribal sympathy and indignation on behalf of the victim; and the degree of punishment demanded itself reflects the extent of this common sense of outrage. Even now emotional arguments for capital punishment are based on satisfying public indignation at a crime which calls out for a measured retribution. Punishment along the lines of 'an eye for an eye' is the underlying principle of the early codes of law, and was considered to be the most fitting proportionate compensation. It meted out an equivalent amount of physical pain to the criminal. It paid scant regard to differing motivation, regarding the act itself as a sufficient measure. It therefore treated all criminal action on an external basis. Mitigating circumstances and psychological disorder have no role to play in deciding the severity of the sentence.

Given the fact that no distinction was drawn between crimes and sins, it is quite logical that divine punishment for the infringement of a taboo should not necessarily be confined to this lifetime. The idea of survival when taken in tandem with divine sanction leads to the possibility of revenge or punishment taking place after the death of the individual, either instead of punishment in this life or indeed in addition to it. Thus the moral order of society was extended into the hereafter.

Ordeals

As a last resort in the primitive judicial process, the accused might be obliged to undergo an ordeal, a physical test fraught with danger. The result was considered to be 'the immediate judgement of Deity' on the case. Ordeals took various forms, such as poison, immersion of a limb in boiling liquid, licking a hot iron, combat (which persisted in the chivalric duelling tradition), being held under water, walking on fire, or simply drawing lots. The classes of heat ordeal were judged on the extent of the injury incurred: the more serious the harm, the more guilty the accused. It is interesting to note a psychosomatic factor observed in instances where the consciousness of innocence appears to have had an immunizing effect on the victim. One could draw a parallel here with modern firewalking experiments, in which the aim is to attain a state of mind in which you are convinced that red-hot coals are not actually going to burn the soles of your feet. Out of the primitive ordeal have developed practices of torture and divination, as well as wagers and the use of oaths in court.

The ordeal is clearly a form of assessment of individual guilt, however crude, aiming to establish whether or not the accused is responsible for the action, and therefore what kind of punishment, if any, should be administered. The idea of individual post-mortem retribution presupposes the development of a sense of individual identity along with a feeling of moral responsibility for one's actions. The individual is no longer simply a function of the group but has a degree of dignity, autonomy and value. In his discussion of the emergence of a belief in a desirable immortality, John Hicks points out that the notion 'desirable' implies not only a value accorded to the individual, but also the higher value of the Divine and its goodness. Desirable union with the Divine is, then, achieved through the cultivation of goodness by the individual. Duty is no longer subsumed under the collective tribal identity. We shall see below how crucial this transition was in the development of Hebrew ethics.

When conceptions of post-mortem reward and punishment are encountered in preliterate societies, it is always hard to know whether the ideas were original, or have been borrowed from a more advanced religion through missionary activity. Rarely, however, do preliterate narratives show their beliefs to be entirely ethical. In them the soul is frequently able to escape the clutches of some post-mortem guardian of the gate through a display of courage, skill or cunning. One might concede that this kind of courage was a virtue, but the same hardly applies to cunning. Frazer describes the beliefs of the Gilbert Islanders about the soul's journey of ordeals in spirit-land. The guardian of the gate, Nakaa, spends his time making nets with his back turned to the path leading to the entrance through which the soul must pass. The souls try to sneak past, but Nakaa knows of their approach, stretches out his hand and entangles the soul in the strands of his knitting. He then lays it across his knees and examines the heart for evil. If he finds traces of incest, thievishness or cowardice, the soul is either cast into a place of everlasting nightmare, impaled on a stake, or flung into a writhing mass of entangled forebears. Although most Islanders believed this judgement to be unavoidable, the soul might cunningly escape past Nakaa's left hand and fail to be caught in the net. In other words it was seen to be possible, exceptionally, to evade this moral assessment by means of amoral skill.

With the advance of ideas about the moral accountability of the individual, the role played by skill and cunning in post-mortem ordeals diminished. The next three themes, those of 'the Bridge', the 'Weighing of the Soul' and the recordings in the Book of Fate can be regarded as ordeals, the standards of which become increasingly impersonal as societies progress, and thus better aligned with the impartiality of divine justice. They are powerful images which have been adopted by more sophisticated religious systems.

The Bridge

In the eighteenth century Benjamin Franklin, the inventor of the lightning conductor, was criticized by some of the contemporary clergy for attempting to divert the judgement of God on sinners whose houses were struck in thunderstorms. A similar psychology underlies man's early attitude to bridges. Rivers were looked upon as natural frontiers set up by the gods, each with its tutelary divinity. To bridge the stream was a Promethean act of daring against divine ordinance amounting to a sacrilege; a compensating sacrifice was therefore required, often in the form of a human immolation in order to appease and placate the river spirit. In ancient Rome bridges were regarded as an insult to the river-god since they deprived him of the food which he would normally have acquired in the form of hapless travellers unsuccessfully trying to ford the stream and drowning in the process. The annual sacrifice originally consisted of living citizens, but these were later replaced by stuffed effigies of old men.

Some awesome associations with bridges were transferred to the idea of the Bridge of Judgement in the after-death state. The earliest images of the crossing of this frontier bridge between one world and the next depict, not surprisingly, an ordeal of skill rather than morality. The Ponapean soul must cross the *kan kaper* or Dancing Bridge, guarded by hideous fiends. On arrival the soul must begin to dance in an effort to distract the fiends by a dazzling show of antics, so that they forget their duty as the wily dancer slips by. It follows that the best dancer has the greatest chance of success, while those who are unable to dance, like Molière's pretentiously absurd Bourgeois Gentilhomme, would be doomed in advance. The Todas must cross a ravine by a thread: a different image with a similar meaning. Bad people, including the selfish, jealous, grudging and 'all offenders against the sacred diary' (the meaning of which remains tantalizingly evasive!) fall into the river and are bitten by leeches. They are then helped out by people on the banks, with whom they remain for a period related to the extent of their badness, before continuing the journey. Although the above criteria are moral, the inhabitants of certain districts are apparently able to cross with impunity, however licentious their earthly life. Once again we find an exception to the impartial workings of the moral assessment.

In the Iranian tradition the bridge is called Cinvat, variously rendered as the bridge of Separation, of Decision, and of the Requiter. The ordeal was originally related to knowledge of the correct password, and was adapted by Zoroaster (sixth century BC) 'as a test of a person's allegiance to the supreme Deity', Ahura Mazda. Such allegiance would imply an alignment with the good against the evil forces of Ahriman, but the exact moral content of such a stance is unspecified; the emphasis 'is essentially on correct faith, not on moral conduct'. The bridge was nine spears' lengths wide for the righteous, but a razor's width for the wicked, who plunge headlong into hell.

The Bridge Test, over al-Sirat, was adopted by Islam from Iran. Laid directly above hell, the bridge was sharper than the edge of a sword and finer than a hair, with briars and hooked thorns on either side. The ease of the crossing depended on the quality of one's faith, and associated practice. The righteous scampered across, while those labouring under a burden of guilt, or sceptics who had scoffed at the message of the prophet, lost their footing and slid into the gaping chasm beneath.

As a postscript to our discussion on the Bridge Test, it is interesting to look at the origin of the word pontifex, now applied to the pope in his capacity as pontiff. The term is derived from the Latin 'pons' meaning bridge and 'facio', to make: thus pontifex is the bridge-builder. Its original connotation was that of priest-engineer, who was concurrently a servant of religion and a civil engineer. Given the sacred nature of bridges referred to above, and the fact that the river-god had to be placated for the infringement on his sovereignty, it was natural that this priest-engineer should perform the appropriate rites of appeasement. This class of people held the keys of both scientific and religious knowledge, thus investing them with a good deal of power. In Rome Father Tiber was the object of an annual sacrifice, as we have seen. The title of Pontifex Maximus was conferred on the Emperor Augustus in 13 BC, passing to subsequent pagan and Christian emperors. The date of its transfer to the bishop of Rome is impossible to ascertain, but in this new context it came to signify the bridge-builder or boundary-crosser between Earth and heaven or hell, 'between the material and the spiritual, between the human and the divine'.

The Weighing of the Soul

The idea of the weighing of the soul as a form of assessment is an obvious image to those concerned with measuring and fair exchange. In Greek it came to be called *psychostasia,* a literal translation of the idea. Our modern bathroom scales would of course be of no use in such a judicial process, as the essential point is to be able to weigh one thing against another, in this instance good deeds against evil. The opposition of these two kinds of deed reflects the prevailing dualism, with its notions of the fight of good against evil, a theme to which we shall return below when discussing the important role of the archangel Michael in medieval representations of the *psychostasia.*

The earliest known reference to weighing in the balance is to be found in the Egyptian Coffin Texts dating from the Middle Kingdom (*c.* 2160-1580 BC). A person's deeds were originally heaped up in two piles for the comparison which would decide their fate; the idea of weighing the deeds was introduced subsequently. *The Tibetan Book of the Dead* refers to the counting of good deeds as white and evil deeds as black pebbles. Such a process is intimidating for the soul, who attempts to protest innocence in terms similar to those of Chapter 125 of *The Egyptian Book of the Dead,* to which we now turn.

The Egyptian Book of the Dead contains two apparently conflicting accounts of post-mortem judgement. In Chapter 125 the soul recites a long declaration of innocence in which both ritual and moral misdemeanours are denied. Some scholars argue that these declarations are a magical spell aimed at subverting divine justice, while Brandon contends that the declarations of innocence occur prior to the weighing, which actually establishes the truth. Thoth presides over the weighing; the heart is balanced against the symbol of *Maat* or truth, and an impersonal verdict is obtained. The fact that *Maat* also signifies conscience means that judgement is passed not simply on the actions of the soul, but also on its motivation: a much more searching test, and one which goes beyond externals to penetrate into the inner moral life.

In the Iranian tradition it is Rashnu who weighs the deeds of the soul in his spiritual scales: 'not a hair's breadth will he diverge, for he is no respecter [of persons]. He deals out impartial justice both to kings and princes and to the meanest of men.' Islam envisages that 'Just balances will be set up on the day of the resurrection, neither shall any soul be wronged in aught, though, were a work but the weight of a grain of mustard seed, we would bring it forth to be weighed: and our reckoning will suffice.' 'Then as to him whose balances are heavy – his shall be a life that shall please him well: And as to him whose balances are light – his dwelling-place shall be the pit.' The emphasis here lies in the exactness of the measurement and the irrevocable outcome of the weighing.

The Old Testament contains several references to weighing on scales in this life. Job reflects that God will see his innocence 'if he weighs me on honest scales'. Proverbs 16:2 observes that 'a man's conduct may strike him as pure, Yahweh, however, weighs the motives'. Daniel tells Nebuchadnezzar that he has 'been weighed in the balance and found wanting'. It appears that the Christian tradition of the weighing of souls can be traced back to the Egyptian beliefs described above. In the Testament of Abraham, an apocryphal text, the just deeds and sins are weighed by the archangel Dokiel 'according to the justice of

God'. Although the judgement described here occurs immediately after death, the great medieval depictions have transferred the event to the day of the Second Coming and the Last Judgement, so graphically portrayed above the doors of many Gothic cathedrals. The pilgrims arriving at Chartres, for instance, would enter by the south doors, between which stands the welcoming figure of Christ, but should their gaze travel upwards they will see Christ seated in majesty and presiding over the Last Judgement, with Michael exercising his function as just weigher of souls. His presence is explained not by any scriptural authority or by his natural supplanting of the role of Dokiel, but he appears rather as the defender of souls against the devil at the moment of death. Thus at Autun Michael counters the action of a demon who is doing his best to tip the scales in his direction. As the centuries go on, he gradually emerges as man's champion against the devil, and the weighing of the soul degenerates from being an impartial assessment of moral worth to a straight contest between Michael and the forces of evil. The implications of such a change of significance point to a greater reliance on faith than on works, which might be regarded as a morally retrogressive step, sapping individual responsibility and promoting independence on ecclesiastical guarantees and directives.

The Book of Fate

As we have seen in the panorama of the life-review, the events of our lives seem to be indelibly recorded in our inner memories. Likewise, the book of fate is traditionally supposed to contain a record of the person's life, which is opened and examined at death in order to assign the soul to its right place. The Old Testament book of Life or Remembrance contains the names of Yahweh's people. Sinners are in danger of having their names blotted out; so what began as a straight record becomes a roll of the righteous, and in the New Testament an index of those whose names are written in heaven. Psalm 139 is a meditation on the omniscience of Yahweh symbolized by the book: 'you had scrutinized my every action, all were recorded in your book.' The psalmist's thoughts are read from far away, every detail of his conduct is known; nowhere can he escape the presence of Yahweh. He asks for his heart to be examined and his thoughts probed so that pernicious ways are avoided and he is guided 'in the way that is everlasting'.

The task of filling out the book may be delegated by Yahweh to a recording angel, as described in Ezekiel: 'the man in white with a scribe's ink horn on his belt'. He is ordered to go through Jerusalem setting a cross on the foreheads 'of all who deplore and disapprove of the filth practised in it'. Others are then called and told to kill all people without the distinguishing mark. This imagery recurs in Revelation, where those with the seal of God on their forehead are spared. The culmination of the dire events of the 'last days' is the opening of the book of life and of 'other books' which were a record of what the souls had done in their lives. The relevant passage is somewhat obscure: it states that those whose names were not found written in the book of life were thrown into the burning lake, while a judgement according to deeds is also implied. It is not clear whether everyone is judged according to deeds, or only those not inscribed in the book of life. In any event, judgement is passed according to the way in which the people had lived, thus making each responsible for his own actions. There is no hint here of sins having been blotted out by the sacrifice of Christ.

The Koran claims that when heaven is cleaved asunder, the stars dispersed, the seas commingled and the graves turned upside down, 'each soul shall recognize its earliest and its latest actions'. Guardians, called 'illustrious recorders', have been set over every soul and are 'cognisant' of its actions. On the day of resurrection a book is proffered wide open to the soul, who is ordered to read it, for 'there needeth none by thyself to make out an account against thee on this day'. The manner of presentation of the book is critical: should it be given into the right hand, the soul 'shall be reckoned with an easy reckoning'. If, on the other hand, the book is presented into the left hand behind the back, he will wish that his book had never been given to him and that death had made an end of him. His wealth and power is now of no avail. Because 'he believed not in God, the Great, and was careful not to feed the poor' he is tied in a chain of seventy cubits' length and thrust into hell-fire. The consequences of faith and conduct are inescapable.

A development of the image of the book can be found in *The Tibetan Book of the Dead*. If the soul tries to deny that it has committed any evil deed while the black pebbles are being counted, the Lord of Death retorts that he will consult 'The Mirror of Karma … wherein every good and evil act is vividly reflected. Lying will be of no avail.' Evans-Wentz interprets the mirror as memory and the judge as 'conscience itself in its stern aspect of impartiality and love of righteousness'. There ensues a dialogue between the advancing of excuses and justifications against the penetrating and objective evaluation of motives. There is equally no escape from the fruits of karma.

From Homer to Plato

I have discussed many variations on Greek thought about soul, body and death elsewhere, and so shall confine this section to questions relating directly to individual morality and post-mortem judgement. The earliest recorded speculations occur in Homer, who describes the melancholy and gloomy conditions of the inhabitants of Hades in Book 12 of the *Odyssey*. Because death marks the shattering of the integrity of the personality, subsequent existence is a mere shadow of the fullness of Earth life, an insipid and joyless continuation which is the common lot of all, regardless of moral worth. The only initial exceptions were men like Tantalus and Sisyphus, whose crimes against the gods merited the respective eternal penalties of ceaseless hunger and thirst on the one hand, and fruitless and frustrating hard labour on the other.

Emotionally speaking, the Homeric prospect inspired no hope and scarcely any fear, but something more akin to resignation. A few lucky favourites and relations of the gods like Menelaos, however, were fortunate enough to escape the subterranean cavern by direct translation to the Islands of the Blessed. This operation is carried out by the might and will of the gods, quite independently of any moral considerations. The erstwhile human being achieves divine status and thus a desirable immortality, not merely an undesirable continuation of existence. Others may make the grade by eating delectable ambrosia and quaffing fragrant nectar, thus assuring themselves of immortality by magical means. These ideas were supplements to rather than contradictions of the prevailing Homeric view of a common fate; they do nevertheless contain the germs of some separation of souls after death, even if the criteria applied amount to nepotism or magic.

The Eleusinian Mysteries held out the prospect to worshippers of a rosier life than was graphically depicted by Homer. Stories and poetry had fed the imagination and the desire for something fuller, and the Mysteries were able to provide people with some assurances in this respect. No restriction was imposed on access apart from for murderers; the only kind of purity demanded was ritual. Those initiated were not taught that the soul was immortal in its own right, but were simply assured that their post-mortem existence would be livelier and more fulfilling. Nor was there any question of a moral influence or demands for a reformed life. By definition, initiates now belonged to a special class and were assured of better treatment for this reason alone: the ultimate significance of these mysteries was magical and not moral.

The spiritual superiority conferred by initiation continued to play a prominent role in the Orphic tradition, which also drew on and refined elements of the Bacchic practice. Dionysian orgies induced a state of 'ecstasy' in which worshippers felt that they were participating in the divine, that the human element had been temporarily laid aside. From this Bacchic insight the orphics drew the conclusion that the soul was immortal and therefore divine, and 'so doing they replaced *orgia* by *katharsis,* the technique of purification taught by Apollo'. The divinity and immortality of the soul came to be sharply contrasted with the mortality of the body, which was considered to be the tomb of the soul, from which it must strive to escape by means of such *katharsis*. Why, wondered the Orphics, had it been necessary for the soul to 'descend' into the body in the first place? They conjectured that it had committed some unspecified sin before birth and had been obliged to expiate the error through a spell on Earth in a physical body; the soul was held individually responsible for its pre-natal sin, so that at the end of the pilgrimage it claimed to have 'paid the penalty for deeds unjust' as a result of which it could now seek entry into 'the abodes of the pious'.

The purification process, however, might require more than one lifetime to accomplish. The primordial sin condemned the soul to 'The Wheel of Birth', from which the only escape was initiation into the Orphic Mysteries and practice of the Orphic way of life. The intermediate state between Earth-lives was a period of punishment and purgation for the reprobate; and furthermore 'for the deeds of the past life [the soul] is recompensed in the next life that it lives, and each man must now suffer exactly what he has done to another'. The good are rewarded with lives of increasing happiness, while the malefactor condemns himself to another round of misery. The cyclic pattern was repeated endlessly by the uninitiated soul: birth, death and an intermediary stretch of reward and punishment. No definite end to the temporal process was envisaged, as in the Judaeo-Christian conception of a last judgement at the end of time.

This Orphic strand of Greek thought reaches its culmination in Plato's *Phaedrus* and *Republic*. It is important to stress that Plato does not make post-mortem rewards and punishments the basis of his ethical ideas. At first he establishes that virtue or goodness is its own reward, regardless of the consequences. He speaks of it as 'the health of the soul … or ordered harmony of our nature', through which we can achieve happiness as well as the highest good, in so far as we come to resemble goodness itself or God. Only then does he go on to discuss transmigration and judgement. His teaching is presented allegorically through the myth of an Armenian soldier, Er, who has been left for dead on a battlefield. His twelve-day sojourn in the other world enables him to recount some details of his observations in the intermediate stage between lives; this stage apparently lasts a thousand years, before a new Earth-life is chosen.

After arriving in 'a wonderfully strange place', Er sees two chasms in the sky, and two in the Earth, between which sit the judges. Having received judgement on their lives, the souls have the evidence fastened to them, proceeding either by the right-hand road up into the sky, or else taking the left-hand path into the Earth. Other souls then come into view, who have completed the thousand-year intermediate period: they either look bedraggled and travel-weary or 'pure and clean', depending on where they have spent the time. They are now ready to choose their next Earth-lives. The system of judgement operates on a payback ratio of ten to one. Thus 'for every wrong he has done to anyone a man must pay the penalty in turn, ten times for each, that is to say, once every hundred years, this being reckoned as the span of a man's life. He pays, therefore, a tenfold retribution for each crime.' The good are rewarded in the same proportion. Thus rewards and punishments are not simply the equivalent repayments which we saw in tribal legal systems, but the interest payment exceeds the capital sum by a long way; the return on the investment is compounded, the sowing of a wind reaps a whirlwind. The moral order is firmly placed within the metaphysical context of reincarnation, which we discussed in great detail in Chapter 4.

In his concluding remarks on the influence of the Orphic tradition, Radhakrishnan observes that 'it gave rise in Christianity to the consciousness of sin and the need for redemption, rewards and punishments after death, the latter both purgatorial and punitive, initiation by sacraments as a passport to a happy life hereafter, the necessity for moral as well as ceremonial purity'. All of this is a far cry from wily dancers slipping across the bridge and cunning souls escaping entanglement. We shall see how the themes outlined above by Radhakrishnan develop in Christianity, with its Hebrew background providing another stream of influence. Meanwhile Plato had made the individual firmly responsible for his actions, leaving him without recourse to magic or skill in a desperate attempt to tip the scales of justice in his favour.

CHAPTER SIX

ESCHATOLOGY AND THE CHRISTIAN MORAL ORDER

———————⟶ɔ⊕ɕ⟵———————

I am the origin and also the dissolution of the entire universe.

BHAGAVAD GITA VIII:6

I am Alpha and Omega, the beginning and the end, the first and the last.

REVELATION 22:13

I n the closing years of the twentieth century we became quite familiar with apocalyptic pronouncements and prophecies foretelling the end of the age, if not of the world. They lend a certain sense of urgency and missionary fervour to those who promulgate them, and leave the rest of us with a vaguely uneasy feeling that there may be some truth in their warnings, and that we should perhaps pay them some heed; especially if we are fully aware of the extent of environmental degradation and instability. That such forecasts of imminent destruction have a long history is perhaps less well known, and this will constitute the focus of this chapter on the relationship between eschatology and moral order. Eschatology, derived from the Greek 'eschaton', is the study of the 'last things' in traditional Christian doctrine: death, judgement, heaven and hell. More specifically, we shall be concerned with the question of moral order as it relates to individual destiny and ethics. We shall see that the moral order in the Old Testament is initially situated within the physical and social order: in other words no idea of an afterlife (the metaphysical order) intervenes in the overall scheme. Justice is thought to be meted out in this lifetime, requiring no otherworldly compensation. As this view came under increasing pressure with the evident prosperity of the wicked and scandalous misfortunes of the good, so the metaphysical order was brought into play in order to balance the scales of divine justice. It is also invoked as a moral force in the apocalyptic pictures of divine wrath on the day of the Lord, sweeping away evil and establishing peace and justice.

The Contexts of Old Testament Moral Dynamics

The Old Testament begins with creation, coming into being, but by the time of Jesus the focus had shifted to the end, to the anticipated culmination of history through divine intervention. Throughout, however, flows the legal analysis of act and consequence, of moral cause and moral effect. The following chronological scheme is an attempt to outline the major dynamic moral factors and structures operating within the Hebrew context over that period.

1. The divine order is established in creation: it is in equilibrium and harmony based on obedience to divine ordinance, but has built into it the potentially destablizing factors of free will and an independent power of reason that can be led astray.

2. Temptation is followed by violation of the divine command. This can be variously categorized as a misdeed, a sin, an introduction of dis-equilibrium, or an eruption of disorder into the preordained harmony.

3. The consequences of the disobedient act: punishment by means of death, toil and suffering.

4. Repentance and contrition for the act committed, the change of mind or *metanoia*.

5. Forgiveness of the transgression; ultimately deliverance and salvation, the vindication and re-establishment of divine harmony, the reconciliation of the sinner with God by means of a new covenant.

More generally, human beings are thought to be capable of exercising their free will and reason in accordance with or against divine ordinance; in the Old Testament those in the former category would be classed as righteous while the rest were 'fools' ('the fool has said in his heart, there is no God'), and the righteous would prosper in this life while the fools suffered. When notions of post-mortem judgement became more distinct, the justice of God would reward the righteous, while his wrath would descend on the heads of the fools, in the afterlife. This is a post-mortem vindication of divine justice, an application of sanctions, the distribution of the fruits of actions.

Eden and Beyond

In common with the metaphysical ideas of other near-east civilizations such as Egypt, the creation act is not seen as simply the bringing into existence of the physical world: it is also the establishment of a moral order. As indicated above, human beings are expected to act in accordance with this order, in the context of a system of rewards and punishments: "Righteousness" for humans is thus not fundamentally a stance of piety but a pattern of behaviour which supports rather than subverts the cosmic and moral order.' Adam and Eve are expected to obey the divine injunction not to eat of the fruit of the tree in the middle of the garden. The first fall is thus an act of disobedience, while the second, represented by the murder of Abel by Cain, is a violation of the sanctity of life.

The fall represents the advent of moral evil in a world which was primordially good. God created the world good, but humanity introduced evil through misuse of free will: humanity is therefore accountable for the occurrence of evil. Some, like Jung, would argue that the evil is ultimately the responsibility of the creator who formed creatures capable of perpetrating evil, but this line will not be pursued here. Things go from bad to worse, with mankind rapidly sliding into such a lamentable state of corruption that Yahweh intervenes with the flood, voicing his regret at ever having made man on the Earth. Noah, 'a good man, a man of integrity among his contemporaries who walked with God', is to be spared. After the flood a new world order is established for Noah and his descendant. Subsequently Yahweh makes a covenant with Abraham, 'A Covenant in perpetuity, to be your God and the God of your descendants after you'. This ethnic covenant is a central pillar of the Old Testament moral order, allied as it is with notions of the justice and goodness of Yahweh. His justice is encoded in the Law, of which Yahweh himself is the guarantor; thus no doubt the workings of the Law is to doubt the very justice and goodness of Yahweh. The Hebrew experience of reality was constantly measured against this background of divine moral order, giving rise to various tensions, as we shall see.

The Hebrew picture of the human being as a psychophysical unity of soul and body leads to the conclusion that death is the shattering of this unity. There are initially no distinctions of status in the metaphysical order of Sheol (literally 'pit'), into which all descend without exception. There is therefore no direct bearing of the metaphysical order on the moral order through subsequent reward and punishment for earthly conduct. Logically, then, all scores must be settled in the physical world in spite of apparent discrepancies between goodness and fate.

Von Rad makes the valuable point that individual conduct is less directly affected by the norms set out in the Decalogue and the Sermon on the Mount than by the expectations and examples of community life, i.e. by the existing social order in which the person has a role to play. In the early history of the Hebrews, goodness and worldly goods were thought to be closely connected. Thus the good man, who is acquainted with the constructive quality of good and the destructiveness of evil, will wisely follow these patterns, leading a constructive and hardworking life. In turn (so the theory goes) he will be rewarded with prosperity, health, longevity and plentiful offspring. The wicked man, on the other hand, will run into poverty and illness before succumbing to an early death. Nor is this all: the consequences of the fathers' acts will be visited on their families down the generations so that blessings and curses reverberate across time. Not only does the individual reap the fruits of his own actions, but he also reaps those of his forebears; and in turn he imposes the consequences of his actions on his descendants. The moral responsibility is communal.

Natural disasters like the flood were not simply considered as unfortunate accidents. They were attributed a cause and a meaning: the cause was Yahweh and the meaning divine displeasure, notions foreign to the modern mind except perhaps during perusal of insurance policies under the section 'Acts of God'. The creator controls his creation and is able to use natural events to secure justice. The standard display of power involves the sword (war), famine and plague in return for rebellion and/or abandonment of Yahweh by Israel, or else their sins against his dictates. The agents of the sword are belligerent neighbours used by Yahweh as rods of punishment. The prophets speak of Yahweh intending to vent his fury on Israel in this way, that Israel is being chastised for some transgression committed. It is clear that the sanctions work on both individual and collective levels. There is ultimately no distinction other than scale to be drawn between personal and communal prosperity or adversity, supposed to originate respectively from good or evil actions.

Justice and the Individual

This version of moral order was soon apparently at variance with experience. The good did not always prosper, while the evil did not inevitably come to a swift and sticky end. Jeremiah is ready to debate the point of justice: 'Why is it that the wicked live so prosperously? Why do scoundrels enjoy peace?' Why indeed, if events are within divine power and guidance? One possible answer to this, pressed in Job, is that disasters strike those who are outwardly upright but inwardly corrupt. Israel found it very hard to abandon this original link between goodness and prosperity. The prophets were especially insistent that people (or their families) are only punished in proportion to their sins. This analysis applied *a fortiori* to national disasters, which automatically raise the 'retrospective question of corresponding guilt'. The guilt in turn called for repentance and a new life of obedience and love. At a national level, the act-consequence relationship underlay prophetic proclamations of disaster. The prophets could see that Israel's corruption would anger Yahweh, who would then unleash famines and plagues to bring them to their knees, unless they were prepared to repent before it was too late. They hoped that their dire warnings would act as a moral catalyst.

Jeremiah and Ezekiel, living at the time of the fall of Jerusalem and subsequent Jewish exile at the beginning of the sixth century, were inclined to view this catastrophe as a divine judgement on the wickedness of Israel. But this was not wholly convincing: for a start the king had recently introduced some reforms in accordance with Yahwist policy; and then the scale of the disaster was altogether too overwhelming for the thesis of divine vengeance to remain entirely credible. People

147

asked what sin they had committed, and even went as far as complaining about Yahweh's injustice, thus attacking the very foundations of the existing moral order of communal responsibility expressed in the adage: 'The fathers have eaten unripe grapes; and the children's teeth are set on edge.' It was because individuals had been uprooted from their old social context that 'the suffering of the innocent came to be a burning issue'.

The answer proffered by Jeremiah and Ezekiel was to lay the emphasis on individual responsibility and retribution; 'But each is to die for his own sin. Every man who eats unripe grapes is to have his own teeth set on edge' or 'The man who has sinned, he is the one who shall die.' The net result, therefore, of the response to national exile was the individualization of religion and the moral order. The individual became the subject of divine judgement, a feature which may also correspond to a growing awareness of the value of the individual in his or her own right, not simply as cog in the community wheel. There is also the chance of individual repentance by renunciation of sins and subsequently living an honest and law-abiding life. The sins will be forgotten and the person will survive and prosper.

If the doctrine of communal responsibility was fraught with difficulties, this turned out to be equally true of the doctrine of personal responsibility when rewards and punishments are limited to this life. The evasive action of the prophets entailed them leaping out of the fire into a frying pan which gradually heated up until it was really sizzling in the books of Job and Ecclesiastes: 'If the sufferings of the individual were no longer to be explained as due to "sins of the fathers", how were they to be accounted for when the person concerned obviously did not deserve the misfortunes which befell him? We need to remember at this point that there is no redress in Sheol for undeserved suffering on Earth; in addition, Yahweh is characterized as just and omnipotent. Something has to give: either justice or omnipotence. In the event, there was considerable reluctance to relinquish either of these attributes. A third solution suggested itself, namely that the designs of Yahweh are unfathomable and simply have to be accepted as a limitation on human understanding of justice. We return to these themes below.

It would, however, be misleading to assume that the fate of the nation as a whole no longer mattered. So far, we have focused on the threatening aspect of the prophetic message, without mentioning hope and consolation. Divine judgement had been executed on Israel with the fall of Jerusalem and the Babylonian exile. Was Yahweh simply to abandon his people at this point? Ezekiel and Deutero-Isaiah felt not. In Ezekiel 37 the prophet has a vision of a valley full of dry bones and is asked by Yahweh whether these bones can live. He answers humbly by saying that only Yahweh himself knows. The bones are indeed alive; Yahweh covers them with flesh and an immense army stands up. This is interpreted as the dry bones of the house of Israel who have lost hope in being led back to their homeland. They are not to despair; the power of Yahweh will be manifest in allowing them to return home; this in turn will rekindle their faith.

Isaiah 40-55 is a self-contained book written by an anonymous author towards the end of the period of exile; it is known as the Book of the Consolation of Israel, and seeks to formulate a new interpretation of their sufferings. Previously, the only available hypothesis had been the sins of the fathers being visited on the children. The Deutero-Isaiah viewpoint is not a complete departure from this, as it also implies the vicarious sufferings of one individual or an elite for the transgressions of others. But the new element is vital: the figure of the suffering servant of Yahweh deliberately and consciously assuming the burden of sin; as such he prefigures the messianic role of Jesus in the New Testament. Israel is urged to trust in Yahweh, to lean on him, and in return 'I will make you the light of nations so that my salvation may reach the ends of the earth.' This sentence shows a widening of the jurisdiction of Yahweh beyond the bounds of the nation, casting the chosen people in the role of mediator between Yahweh and the heathen.

It is then possible for Israel's sufferings (or at any rate those of the elite) to acquire a new meaning, which emerges most fully in the fourth song of the servant of Yahweh. The man of sorrows, familiar with suffering, is despised by the people, 'and yet ours were the sufferings he bore, ours the sorrows he carried. But we, we thought of him as someone punished, struck by God, and brought low. Yet he was pierced for our faults, crushed for our sins. On him lies the punishment that brings us peace, and through his wounds we are healed.' The point is that appearances were deceptive: the first impressions were of a man struck down more or less on his own account, while a deeper understanding revealed that he had humbly offered his life in atonement; and by taking the faults of others on himself he justifies many, i.e. releases them from the burden of their sins. This act is seen as part of divine activity itself, the servant being Yahweh's representative and thus the instrument of divine grace and reconciliation. Despite this moral and religious advance, though, it is clear that the servant is finally rewarded in the conventional this-worldly sense by seeing his heirs and enjoying a long life. The traditional moral order of compensation and rewards remains thoroughly embedded in the social and physical orders.

The issue of individual retribution and innocent suffering is most acutely and dramatically portrayed in the book of Job. In the prose prologue, written by a different author from that of the main body of poetic drama, Yahweh is depicted in conversation with the Satan (literally 'adversary') about his servant Job, apparently the paragon of patience in adversity. He is characterized as 'a sound and honest man who fears God and shuns evil', although the subsequent portrait in the main body of the text is rather less humble. The job of Satan is investigation of earthly affairs, and in this instance to test the faith of Job, whose wealth corresponds with his goodness, a logical state of affairs under the old moral order. Satan suspects that his piety may be superficial, that he would abandon Yahweh if his possessions were destroyed. Yahweh takes up the gauntlet thrown down by Satan and, relying on Job's faith, gives permission for Job's worldly goods to be destroyed. This is accomplished with consummate thoroughness: his oxen and camels are carried away by raiders, his sheep are consumed by lightening, while his sons, daughters and all of his servants, bar the inevitable messengers of woe, are killed. Job still worships Yahweh, according him the right to take away what he has given.

Satan returns to Yahweh, complaining that Job's life is as blameless as ever and seeking to harm him physically in order to test him further. Once again, permission is granted, and Job finds himself covered with ulcers and sores. This is too much for his wife, who urges him to curse God and die. Job stands firm, though, answering that he must accept both happiness and sorrow from the hand of God. At this point three friends hear of Job's misfortunes and come to offer him sympathy and consolation.

The dramatic role of Job's friends is to represent the traditional ideas of moral order: that a disaster, especially one on this scale, must indicate a sin on the part of Job. To them it is logically inconceivable that Yahweh can do anything unjust, so that Job must somehow take the blame of what has transpired. No one is sinless and pure before God. Job should therefore repent 'and acknowledge his suffering as a beneficial, judicious action on the part of God'. If he resists, he will be broken by divine power. Job refuses to apply this correspondence of guilt and punishment to his own case and continues to protest his innocence: 'I hold fast to my righteousness and will not relinquish it, my conscience disparages none of my days.' He insists that it is Yahweh, not him, who has broken the relationship and demands an explanation of the vagaries of cosmic justice as they apply to him. His sufferings appear to be meaningless by virtue of their disproportion.

We should remember at this point that no possible future compensation is envisaged. All accounts must be settled within the physical order. At length Job encounters Yahweh, who speaks to him out of the tempest, asserting that it is his turn to ask questions: 'Where were you when I laid the Earth's foundations? Tell me, since you are so well-informed!' He displays the extent of his knowledge and power in comparison to Job's, asking him whether his arm is as strong or his voice as thunderous. Finally, Job has to admit 'I have been holding forth on matters I cannot understand, on marvels beyond me and my knowledge ... I retract all I have said, and in dust and ashes I repent.' His repentance is more for his seeming arrogance in questioning divine wisdom than for any transgressions committed before the disasters supervened. It does, however, herald a new relationship with Yahweh.

The poem itself ends at this point, without any vindication of the old moral order of just deserts in this life: there is no neat answer to the question of suffering and theodicy. The epilogue, however, strives to defend the old moral code by doubling the quantity of his possessions (for instance he comes to own the incredible number of fourteen thousand sheep). Yet even such largesse is ultimately inadequate: Job's sons and daughters are not replaceable as individuals, in spite of the renown of his new family. The old moral order is stretched beyond credibility to breaking point.

In Ecclesiastes we see the collapse of the old moral order of individual retribution confined to the physical order, although one should note that the book was probably not very widely diffused and represented the views of a small, sophisticated and world-weary minority. The preacher still assumed the power of Yahweh to determine events, but fundamentally questioned his justice, and therefore the logic of trusting faith. He had seen the good man perish and the godless man prosper: 'the good, I mean, receive the treatment the wicked deserve; and the wicked the treatment the good deserve.' All is vanity; no meaning, pattern or purpose can be discerned behind it all. Furthermore, death makes an end of man and beast alike, all being of the dust and returning again to dust. The preacher does not have any direct encounter with Yahweh which might make him change his point of view, as was the case with Job. The impenetrability and inexplicability remain in full force, and without any possibility of post-mortem redress, since the concept of resurrection had yet to be developed. All that remained in the meantime was the happiness and pleasure to be experienced while still alive, and the hope that no arbitrary misfortune would supervene.

The Day of the Lord

The day of the Lord, or the day of Yahweh, is an important traditional idea for an understanding of the background of Old Testament apocalyptic eschatology. In the physical order it corresponds to a display of power evident in catastrophic upheavals in nature. From a political angle, the day originally signified the fulfilment of the covenant with God through the destruction of Israel's enemies: Israel would be avenged of the wrongs inflicted on it, but without any notion of individual ethical compensation. At this stage there is no clear idea of this divine intervention representing the end of history; it was rather a decisive military victory.

Although the theme of retribution against Israel's enemies persisted, the emphasis of the day gradually shifted towards a focus on the vindication of the moral order, the ultimate triumph of righteousness over evil at the consummation of history; thereafter ideal social conditions would prevail. This dualist philosophy of history has its intellectual roots in the Zoroastrian conflict of Ormuzd and Ahriman, the latter evil principle being finally vanquished by the forces of light.

Amos was the first prophet to turn the logic of the day of the Lord against Israel itself by introducing a moral criterion to which he would be subject. He was writing in the eighth century BC, well before the fall of Jerusalem, which was retrospectively regarded as the day of the Lord. He warns: 'Trouble for those who are waiting so longingly for the Day of Yahweh! What will this day of Yahweh mean to you? It will mean darkness not light, as when a man escapes a lion's mouth only to meet a bear.' The people are exhorted to seek good, not evil, so that they may prosper. The covenant is conditional on obedience to the Law, and as such imposes a great responsibility on Israel. Nor can they plead ignorance of the divine will; judgement on them is therefore correspondingly more severe.

Zephaniah graphically depicts the traditional imagery of the 'day of ruin and devastation, a day of darkness and gloom, a day of cloud and blackness', sweeping away men and beasts, and sending the wicked staggering. The conclusion is a call to repent, to seek integrity and humility, so that shelter may perhaps be found 'on the day of the anger of Yahweh'. A humble remnant will be left after the removal of the 'proud boasters'; people who do no wrong and tell no lies: the judgement is to fall on the wicked, and the oppressors of Israel will be vanquished. The threats are accompanied by a corresponding hope. Having said as much, there remains a problem for individual retribution, if the day of Yahweh fails to arrive within their lifetime. Descent into Sheol provides no redress, as we have seen. The survivors of the day are the prototype of a righteous remnant, an idea which eventually evolves into the resurrection of the dead.

Joel's vision of the day elaborates the traditional imagery of the earth quaking, the skies trembling and sun and moon growing dark. The people are called upon to repent, and the prophet then dwells upon an era of abundance and plenty, a new age in which the spirit is poured out on mankind, while portents announce the impending judgement of nations and the restoration of the fortunes of Israel. This time, owing to the repentance of Israel, the judgement descends on their foes, whose lands are ravaged and laid waste.

Old Testament Apocalyptic Eschatology

We have now reached a critical point in the development of Hebrew thought about moral order in relation to the afterlife. We have seen how the thinking of Jeremiah and Ezekiel highlighted the doctrine of individual retribution, and how this doctrine faced almost insuperable difficulties in the life experience of Job, even if he was supposedly compensated in the end. Furthermore, we have looked at the genesis of the Day of the Lord, the day on which the moral order will be vindicated; but we have noted that the day may come too late for many already resident in gloomy Sheol. It became increasingly clear that the demands of a just moral order could not be settled within the compass of one physical lifetime; hence the pressure towards formulating some kind of post-mortem redress whereby the scales would be balanced.

The earliest formulations of the resurrection are, however, of a more purely spiritual nature. In Isaiah the upright man speaks of his intense longing for Yahweh, 'my spirit in me seeks for you'; in Sheol this communication with Yahweh would be cut off. While the sinner is annihilated, the righteous dead will come to life, their corpses will rise and communion will be re-established with Yahweh and the other faithful; this communion will be consummated with the advent of the kingdom of God. In Ezekiel we have a somewhat different picture, in his vision of the valley of dry bones. It is as much an allegory for the restoration of Israel as it is a statement of the mechanics of resurrection through the inbreathing of life and the reclothing of the skeletons; it is nevertheless consistent with the notion of the person as a psycho-physical organism which must be restored in its integrity for a full life to be possible.

The problem of post-mortem justice is placed in even sharper relief by the fate of those sacrificing their lives for the cause of Israel. Their only possible redress is in the afterlife. Historically, the first definite reference to the resurrection occurs in II Maccabees, although its best-known presentation occurs in the book of Daniel. Daniel speaks of a time of great distress preceding the resurrection, a time which comes to be known as the Messianic Woes, when evil attains unprecedented force and intensity. Then, 'of those who lie sleeping in the dust of the earth many will awake, some to everlasting life, some to shame and everlasting disgrace'. Here, as Charles indicates, 'there is an absolute transformation of the resurrection doctrine. Heretofore it was the sole prerogative of the righteous Israelite; now it is extended to the pre-eminently good and bad in Israel.' The original significance, as noted above, was the restoration of the communion of the righteous with Yahweh. The importance of the development of the doctrine of resurrection and judgement can scarcely be exaggerated. It signifies the eclipse of the old moral order whereby rewards and punishments were applicable only to the physical life, and the advent of the teaching that eternal life depends on one's earthly conduct: the stakes are that much higher. At first the perspective of this new doctrine was more national than individual, but attention was focused on individual fate in some of the later books of the Old Testament.

The dynamic driving force behind the apocalyptic visions of the end of the age followed by judgement and resurrection stems directly from the prophetic tradition of threat and consolation: threat if the voice of Yahweh is not heeded, and consolation in the deliverance following repentance. As such, the appeal is essentially ethical, as is the final intervention which settles the scores and heralds the era of righteousness after the vindication of the moral order. Although we can discern this close connection between prophecy and apocalyptic, the latter becomes much more universal in scope as the jurisdiction and intervention of Yahweh is extended to all the peoples of the Earth and becomes a comprehensive philosophy of history with a clear moral structure. This will become more apparent when we reach the New Testament.

Elsewhere I have discussed the compartmentalization of the hitherto undifferentiated souls in Sheol into four categories ranging from the righteous to sinners; also the other-worldly outlook of the Wisdom of Solomon. In Enoch we encounter the first division of judgement into immediate post-mortem and the final reckoning and assignment at the great assize, a conception which we shall see elaborated in Christianity. In Wisdom the picture of judgement is quite elaborate. The godless view of life as a matter of chance and death as the end of the individual, with its concomitant ethic of might-is-right, is regarded as gravely mistaken: 'Their malice makes them blind. They do not know the hidden things of God, they have no hope that holiness will be rewarded ... yet God did make man imperishable.' Long life is no longer seen as an indication of divine favour; rather, it is possible for understanding to be interpreted as grey hairs, and untarnished life as ripe old age. In other words quality, not quantity, is the ultimate measure; the Lord has taken the just man to safety, away from the wickedness which surrounded him. The godless 'will come trembling to the reckoning of their sins, and their crimes, confronting them, will accuse them. Then the virtuous man stands up boldly to face those who have oppressed him ... and they, at the sight of him, will shake with cowards' fear, amazed that he should be saved so unexpectedly.' The jungle values of the world are inverted, a warning to those who oppress the righteous. The moral order is balanced in the distributive and retributive justice of the afterlife.

In a sense, the preoccupation with individual fate in Wisdom is not typical of the Hebrew tradition as a whole, owing to its Hellenistic roots which are reminiscent of the Orphic/Platonic stream. The centre of Hebrew preoccupation remained the fate of the nation right up to the sack of Jerusalem in AD 70, Thereafter, in a similar way to the reaction to the disaster of 587 BC, thoughts turned more exclusively towards individual destiny. But this occurred after the coming of Christianity.

Ethics and Eschatology in the Synoptic Gospels

We are told in Matthew's gospel that Jesus began his preaching with the message 'Repent, for the kingdom of heaven is close at hand.' From these words unfolds the kernel of his message to his contemporaries. The injunction to repent, to rethink (as in 'repenser' in French), to change one's mind and consciousness as implied in the Greek *metanoia* is reinforced by the urgency of the imminent coming of the Kingdom – the fulfilment of the promises of God to deliver the righteous among his people at the time of final reckoning. Scholars such as Schweitzer at the beginning of the century argued that the entire ethic of Jesus was to be understood in interim terms, and that an apocalyptic view of imminent upheaval formed the essence of his ethical message. This view has been modified by subsequent scholarship which, while not discounting the insights of Schweitzer, has taken issue with the primacy of eschatology over ethics by pointing out that the Kingdom is spoken of both in present and future terms, as something which already exists *and* as something to be anticipated in the near future. It is not entirely clear, however, whether this emphasis on the presence of the Kingdom was an adjustment in the light of its delayed arrival; the most explicit references are to be found in Luke.

Many of Jesus' central ethical principles are stated in the Sermon on the Mount in Chapters 5 to 7 of Matthew. It is thought that the work was composed in about AD 50, a compilation of sayings attributed to Jesus reworked and rearranged to conform to a typical format. The teachings are essentially those of traditional Judaism with its theology of continuous creation; the authority lies in the interpretation in opposition to the pharisaic conventional and literal reading. It is noteworthy that messianic ideas of salvation are absent from the discourse.

The Lord's Prayer emphasizes the fatherly relationship of God to his children and the importance of mutual forgiveness; the people are enjoined to trust in providence, while the true disciple is the person who does the will of the heavenly Father, not the hypocrite who ostentatiously fasts, prays and gives alms. Virtue must run deeper than that of the scribes and Pharisees; it is the inner disposition which really counts. It is not sufficient simply to refrain from killing; one must not be angry with one's brother. It is not sufficient to refrain from adultery; one must not even entertain the adulterous thoughts which are the necessary prelude to action. Nor is it sufficient to apply the *lex talionis* of an eye for an eye and a tooth for a tooth, or to love your neighbour and hate your enemy; rather, one must go as far as offering the wicked man no resistance and loving one's enemies, praying for one's persecutors. These last two injunctions in particular were great inspirations to Tolstoy and later to Gandhi, forming one root from which emerged their doctrine of non-resistance to evil, of *ahimsa* and non-violence.

Reciprocity is another key theme: forgiving in order to be forgiven, 'if you forgive others their failings, your heavenly Father will forgive yours; but if you do not forgive others, your Father will not forgive your failings either.' Similarly 'Do not judge, and you will not be judged; because the judgements you give are the judgements you will get, and the amount you measure out is the amount you will be given.' In other words you will be subject to your own criteria, so that the work starts with oneself, not with criticism of others – first taking the plank out of your own eye. These examples of reciprocity culminate in the golden rule: 'Always treat others as you would like them to treat you.' As you treat others, so they will treat you, and so your heavenly Father will treat you likewise. As indicated above, the emphasis throughout the Sermon on the Mount is on personal response and responsibility.

Some of the parables about the kingdom of heaven point towards the scene of the last judgement depicted in Matthew 24-5 and Mark 13, for instance the stories about the tares and the dragnet. The tares and wheat are to be left to grow together until the harvest, the end of the world; at that point the tares are gathered up and burnt in the fire, while the wheat, the virtuous, 'will shine like the sun in the kingdom of their Father'. Likewise, the fishermen will collect the good fish into a basket and throw away those that are no use: 'This is how it will be at the end of time: the angels will appear and separate the wicked from the just to throw them into the blazing furnace where there will be weeping and grinding of teeth.' Such emphatic imagery is typical of Matthew.

The so-called eschatological discourse is immediately preceded by the sevenfold indictment of the vanity and hypocrisy of the scribes and Pharisees who are characterized as serpents and broods of vipers destined for hell. It has been argued that the Great Refusal on the part of the Jews exercised an influence on the doctrine of the Last Things. As the attitude of the Pharisees towards the preaching of the Kingdom became increasingly hostile, so the character of the preaching itself changed: 'It was no longer the glad tidings of a great opportunity, but a stern rebuke for an opportunity lost, and a warning of impending and retributive wrath.' It should also be noted that the strongest passages about future punishment are to be found in Matthew, who has added some graphic details to the more restrained account to be found in Mark. We also find traditional apocalyptic features already familiar from the Old Testament scenarios of the day of Yahweh, for instance the darkening of sun and moon, earthquakes, wars, etc.

The framework of the discourse, written around AD 80 and reflecting the ideas current in the Greek-speaking Jewish Christian community, also incorporates a prophecy about the destruction of the temple in Jerusalem, which took place in AD 70 and which greatly intensified the anticipation of the impending return of the Son of Man to judge the disintegrating world. Although the coming of the Son of Man 'on the clouds of heaven with power and great glory' will be evident to all, the exact timing is known only to the Father. It is to happen before the passing away of the generation listening, but people are told to be on the alert, to stay awake – like the wise virgins. They are also encouraged to make the most of their talents, and not to bury them in the ground like the good-for-nothing servant who was thrown out into the dark.

Finally, we arrive at the scene of the Last Judgement itself, the judgement at the end of time which definitively decides individual destinies. All the nations are assembled at the great assize before the throne of the King, whose task it is to separate the sheep from the goats. The sheep are those who loved their neighbours as themselves, who gave food to the hungry, drink to the thirsty, hospitality to the stranger, clothes to the naked, consolation to the sick and imprisoned. Like the Good Samaritan they responded to the needs of their brothers and sisters, each of whom was Christ in disguise. Such was the philosophy adopted by the monastic tradition enshrined in the Rule of St Benedict, and such is the inspiration behind the work of Mother Teresa of Calcutta in our own time. The neighbour is Christ in disguise. Those who neglected these duties and opportunities in life have no second chance: they are cast into the 'aeonian' fire.

A number of points arise from the above. The criterion of reciprocity enunciated in the Sermon on the Mount is applied at the last judgement: the measure and treatment meted out to others return to oneself; the merciful and loving receive love and mercy, while the callous and unthinking are punished accordingly. It is no longer nations who are judged as a whole, but individuals according to their actions; there is 'nothing said about the death of Christ as effecting salvation'; justice is absolute and unrelenting. The dualism of the classification of good and evil is stark in the extreme: there are no mitigating circumstances or borderline cases – one is either a sheep or a goat. This scenario reflects Matthew's tendency to legalism and his wish to give such clear directives that there is no room for subtle qualification.

The greatest commandments of love of God and love of one's neighbour as oneself underpin the moral order of act and consequence, cause and effect. Application or neglect of the law of love leads unerringly to the moral consequences of salvation or damnation. The metaphysical order of heaven or hell provides the ultimate vindication and sanction of the moral order. Human beings are considered free and rational agents capable of making up their minds about life and its moral priorities and therefore liable to the outcome of their decisions and patterns of behaviour. Justice will be seen to be done: no gratuitous forgiveness interferes with its course. The original message of Jesus to 'repent, for the kingdom of heaven is at hand' now comes full circle in its logical development. The moral exhortation to repent is reinforced by the eschatological perspective of the imminence of the Kingdom. Here the arrival of the Kingdom is depicted, and the moral message triumphantly proclaimed in the salvation of the righteous and the perdition of the wicked.

In Luke's gospel we find a somewhat different emphasis on the nature of post-mortem judgement. It is perhaps instructive to begin by observing that the Beatitudes are countered by respective curses. Thus:

> How happy are you who are poor: yours in the kingdom of God. Happy are you who are hungry now: you shall be satisfied. Happy are you who weep now: you shall laugh.

Then:

> But alas for you who are rich: you are having your consolation now. Alas for you who have your fill now: you shall go hungry.

> Alas for you who laugh now: you shall mourn and weep.

Luke also accounts those happy who are persecuted for their allegiance to the Son of Man, for in the day of his coming, alluded to in Chapter 21, 'your reward will be great in heaven'. In other words their present tribulations will be compensated in the next world. We can see throughout this gospel a tendency to identify with the poor and outcast, not just with the poor in spirit.

The same logic underlies the parable of Dives and Lazarus, but with one crucial ethical difference: the disciples are rewarded for the sufferings endured for the cause of Jesus, while Lazarus is compensated simply because of the sufferings of his poverty in his earthly life. There is no indication that Lazarus was a particularly good man. The opening lines describe the contrast between Dives with his purple and fine linen and Lazarus, covered with sores, who lay at his gate. Both men then die. The rich man suffers the torments of Hades, while Lazarus rests in Abraham's bosom. When the right man asks Abraham for some relief, he is informed that 'during his life good things came your way, just as bad things came the way of Lazarus. Now he is being comforted here while you are in agony.' It would be plausible to suppose that the rich man had not lived up to the standards indicated in the last judgement scene in Matthew, and that he should therefore suffer on that account. But this is not the picture presented by Luke: the rich man suffers because he had his consolation in earthly life, while the poor man is compensated for his physical sufferings, not because of any loving on his part. The moral order featured here is one of reversal and compensation, depending on the nature of earthly circumstances.

A further point raised by this parable is the contradiction or tension between immediate and final judgement. Immediate judgement, as in the case of Dives and Lazarus, occurs at or just after death; while the last judgement takes place at the end of time. If an immediate judgement has taken place, what then is the function of the last judgement other than as a confirmation of the initial sentence? In practice these traditions continued side by side. Another story of immediate judgement comes with the story of the penitent thief, also unique to Luke. In Matthew and Mark we are told that even those who were crucified with him taunted him, while Luke describes one mocking thief and the other who realizes that Jesus is innocent and begs to be remembered in his kingdom. It is a case of deathbed repentance, and an effective one, judging from Jesus' reply that the thief will be with him in paradise that very day. Perhaps the true message here, however, is the continuing capacity of God to forgive. But taken at face value, the thief's final gesture outweighs his disreputable life. It is clear that once again we have a different idea of moral order to that of Matthew: no mention is made of the thief's moral qualities prior to that time. And, unlike Lazarus, he is not being compensated for his sufferings, but rewarded for his recognition of Jesus' innocence or divinity, and for the plea that Jesus should remember him.

The Gospel, Letters and Revelation of John

In the fourth gospel there is no dramatic assize, no external act of judgement on the deeds of individuals. The process, rather, is an inner and continuous one of self-judgement implied in the rejection and refusal of the Light. The last judgement, in so far as it features, simply reveals the outcome of this inner process. God loved the world so much that he gave his only Son, so that those who believe in him might have eternal life, 'For God sent his Son into the world not to condemn the world, but so that through him the world might be saved. No one who believes in him will be condemned; but whoever refuses to believe is condemned already.' Similarly in Chapter 12 Jesus asserts that he has not come to condemn the world, but to save the world, and 'he who rejects me and refuses my words has his judge already'. Rejection and refusal demonstrate that men prefer darkness to light 'because their deeds were evil'. The wrongdoer hates and avoids the light which might expose his actions. It is in this sense that the words of Chapter 9, verse 39, become comprehensible, when Jesus states that he has indeed come into the world for judgement, 'so that those without sight may see and those with sight turn blind'. Such judgement is a discriminating process, whereby people have the opportunity to measure and judge themselves in their response to the Light. The Son does the will of the Father, so that he entrusts all judgement to the Son; he is appointed supreme judge, so that when the dead leave their graves at the sound of his voice 'those who did good will rise again to life; and those who did evil to condemnation'. The moral order here stems from the justice of a self-imposed judgement arising from the individual response in faith and works to the call of Christ. The spiritual condition or character is made manifest at the last day, resulting in eternal life or condemnation.

In his exquisite first letter John sets out the mature fruit of a lifetime of spiritual experience. He states the conditions of the truly Christian life: breaking with sin, keeping the commandments, especially that of love, being detached from the world, and being on guard against the enemies of Christ. Acknowledgement of sins brings forth forgiveness and purification from God, 'but if anyone should sin, we have an advocate with the Father, Jesus Christ, who is just'. Jesus is the sacrifice that takes the sins of the world away. The role of Jesus in this context is that of saviour rather than judge; he mediates and intercedes on behalf of sinners, who are nevertheless expected to show genuine repentance and live a Christ-like life to the best of their ability. Loving one's brother is living in the Light, while hating one's brother is life in the dark. Detachment from the world is recommended partly owing to its transitory nature and expected imminent demise; John is quite convinced that he is living in the last days.

His mysticism reaches a sublime height in the discourse on love in Chapter 4, where he tells us that 'God is love and anyone who lives in love lives in God, and God lives in him ... as long as we love one another God will live in us and his love will be complete in us.' The perfection of love will be clear when we can face the day of judgement without fear, for 'in love there can be no fear, but fear is driven out by perfect love: because to fear is to expect punishment, and anyone who is afraid is still imperfect in love.' The moral order is fulfilled in the perfection of love of God in us casting out fear and separation from him. If there is no separation from God in life while living in his love, there cannot possibly be any separation after death at judgement.

This chapter would be incomplete without a further reference to the Apocalypse of John, from which many Christian representations of the last judgement derive. The martyrs come to life at the first resurrection and reign with Christ for a thousand years. Then at the final assize the books of life containing the record of the deeds of the dead are opened, and the dead judged according to the way in which they have lived. The legacy for the wicked is the second death in the burning lake of sulphur. Then comes the descent of the New Jerusalem, the new creation following judgement and destruction, the re-establishment of the moral order on Earth. The imminence of the second coming is almost perennial, and has always stirred people into an urgent sense of moral reform, not always from the highest of motives. The cycle of creation/corruption/destruction/re-creation runs right through the Bible from the Genesis flood and the new covenant with Noah to the destruction of Babylon and the subsequent millennium. The apocalyptic consciousness has continued to dominate human thought, and can be paralleled in the Hindu cycle of Yugas. Just as many Christians consider that we are now living through the proverbial last days, so Hindus would maintain that we are experiencing the corruption and nadir of the Kali Yuga before the establishment of a golden age following cataclysmic upheavals. We shall return to this theme in the final chapter.

CHAPTER SEVEN

FAITH AND WORKS, HEAVEN AND HELL

He who wants to do good knocks at the gate; he who loves finds the gate open.

RABINDRANATH TAGORE

The scribes and Pharisees occupy the chair of Moses. You must therefore do what they tell you and listen to what they say; but do not be guided by what they do: since they do not practise what they preach.

MATTHEW 23:2-4

He who is too busy doing good finds no time to be good.

RABINDRANATH TAGORE

Introduction

I n this chapter we shall focus on the issue of faith and works as they relate to one's fate in the afterlife. Is faith itself a sufficient guarantee? What exactly does it mean or imply? How is it intrinsically connected to works? Why might good works in themselves be deemed insufficient for entry to heaven? What is the relationship between the grace of the atonement and the moral responsibility of free will? How is emphasis on the primacy of faith connected with an acute sense of sin and a low estimate of the potential of human nature? Since the answers to such questions reflect deep-seated temperamental differences, as analysed by Jung, it will not be surprising to find lively argument over the relative importance of grace and free will right down through Christian history. My treatment will be both historical and thematic.

The Early Church at Jerusalem

Before considering the teachings of Paul, we shall put them in context by looking at the doctrines of the Church of Jerusalem, which was essentially a version of Christianity which remained loyal to its Hebrew roots, and which, according to Brandon, 'must have represented the original tradition about Jesus, and yet it was so vehemently repudiated by Paul'. The fact that Paul's version was eventually established as orthodoxy owes a great deal to the destruction of Jerusalem in AD 70, with the accompanying obliteration of its Christian community.

Brandon identified the fundamental cause of divergence between the two views as the interpretation of the person and mission of Jesus. The Jerusalem Christians saw the mission of Jesus as messiah of Israel within the context of Judaism, therefore repudiating any universal validity of his message unless the converts first obeyed the Jewish customs and Law. For contemporary Judaism the messiah did not have divine status commensurate with Yajweh; he was seen as the vindicator of Israel, and would certainly not be expected to die in order to achieve national salvation. Still more alien would be the notion that such a messiah might die 'to bring spiritual salvation to the hated Gentiles'. The crucifixion, therefore, was, as Paul observed, a stumbling-block for those whose expectations had been conditioned by the figure of a triumphant vindicator 'who would blast his adversaries by the breath of his mouth'. Put bluntly, the crucifixion was in direct contradiction

to the traditional ideas about the role of the messiah, and was therefore an event requiring delicate explanation.

The explanation which provided some kind of rationale came from
the figure of the suffering servant of Yahweh in Chapters 40 to 55 of
Isaiah. In Chapter 12, Matthew characterizes Jesus as the servant of
Yahweh, while Luke makes the connection with the crucifixion even
clearer when Jesus says that the words of Isaiah 'He let himself be taken
for a criminal' had to be fulfilled in him. The reference to Isaiah makes
the parallels even clearer when it speaks of the servant offering his life
in atonement, his sufferings justifying many, and his bearing the faults
of many. 'Hence', argues Brandon, 'the view emerged that the crucifixion was an unfortunate accident, brought about in ignorance by the
prophets and did in fact confirm the Messiahship of Jesus.' Thus Peter,
in explaining the healing of a man in the name of Jesus, states that it
is faith in the name of Jesus, the same Jesus you handed over and then
disowned in the presence of Pilate', which restored the man to health.
He then goes on to say: 'Now I know, brothers, that neither you nor your
leaders had any idea of what you were really doing; this is the way God
carried out what he had foretold when he said through all his prophets
that his Christ would suffer. Now you must repent and turn to God, so
that your sins may be wiped out'. Peter very explicitly leaves the door
open for the Jews to repent of the 'error', which was nevertheless part
of the divine scheme. Even so, the use of the suffering servant analogy
is only part of the picture, and is not intended to eclipse the majestic
return of Jesus at the second coming 'to fulfil the role of the Messiah
and save Israel from the oppression of its enemies'. In other words, the
victorious, conquering messiah-figure was not altogether dispensed
with, but simply translated ahead in time to the expectation of the
second coming and last judgement on the day of the Lord. It can readily be appreciated how great a gulf lies between the mission of Jesus a
messiah of the Jews and as saviour of both Gentile and Jew.

Paul – Justification by Divine Grace

An understanding of Paul's teaching is impossible without some knowledge of his background and the overwhelming experience on the road
to Damascus. His own description of his background appears in Phi-
lippians. He was born a Hebrew of Hebrew parents and was duly circumcised; he was a Pharisee and early persecutor of the Church; 'as far
as the Law can make you perfect, I was faultless. But because of Christ,

I have come to consider all these advantages I had as disadvantages.' In the light of his later convictions it is important to note that he saw circumcision and the following of the Law as insufficient for salvation. He goes on to explain that he is no longer trying for perfection by his own efforts – the perfection which comes from the Law – but yearns only for the perfection that comes through faith in Christ. In Romans he speaks of himself as a prisoner of the law of sin so that 'I fail to carry out the things I want to do, and I find myself doing the very things I hate ... I know of nothing good living in me – living, that is in my unspiritual self ... my body follows a different law that battles against the law which my reason dictates.'

While Saul 'was still breathing threats to slaughter the Lord's disciplines'. He made the fateful journey to Damascus, during which he was struck by a light from heaven. The voice of Jesus asked him why he persisted in persecution, and ordered him to continue into the city. This extraordinary encounter could only be paralleled in numinous terms by the experience of the disciples at the transfiguration. His sight was restored by Ananias, who was informed by Jesus that Paul was his chosen instrument to spread his name both to pagans and to the people of Israel. The conversion is a dramatic intervention in Paul's life through no initiative of his own, an intervention which completely changes the course of his life. The amazement of his hearers can only have been matched by Paul's own astonishment at the turn of his fortunes and later at the magnitude of the mission with which he had been entrusted.

Although the details of Paul's eschatological thinking develop in a number of stages, it is nevertheless possible to outline the principal elements of his theology of salvation as they bear on the questions of moral order and the *parousia* or second coming.

1. The major premise about the human condition is that 'All have turned aside, tainted all alike; there is not one good man left, not a single one.' This is elaborated as follows:

    (a) God is angry with the pagans on account of their impiety and depravity; not only do they indulge in all kinds of wicked practices, but they even encourage others to follow their example.

    (b) The Jews are no better off: 'In judging others you condemn yourself, since you behave no differently from those you

166

judge.' Their stubborn refusal to repent will only further exacerbate God's anger. God has no favourites and does not give preferential treatment.

(c) 'No one can be justified [i.e. forgiven and achieve salvation] in the sight of God by keeping the Law: all that the Law does is to tell us what is sinful.' This is a more extreme proposition than that put forward earlier in the chapter that 'it is not listening to the Law but keeping it that will make people holy in the sight of God.' The second proposition puts the accent on observation, while the first is a preparation for the insistence that only faith in Christ can justify the sinner.

(d) Circumcision will not in itself save those who are circumcised, who must also keep the Law; indeed it is more valuable to keep the Law even if one is not circumcised than to fail to observe it if one is: 'The real Jew is the one who is inwardly a Jew, and the real circumcision is in the heart – something not of the letter but of the spirit.'

2. Since mankind is in a fallen condition and quite incapable of saving itself through personal efforts and works, the only hope is justification through faith in Christ, or, more fully, 'justification by grace alone, for Christ's sake, through faith active in good works'.

(a) Sin entered the world through one man, Adam, and through sin death. One man's fall brought universal condemnation from which there was no escape. The wages of sin are death.

(b) Symmetrically, 'the good act of one man brings everyone life and makes them justified'; 'Death came through one man and in the same way the resurrection of the dead has come through one man. Just as all men die in Adam, so all men will be brought to life in Christ.'

(c) 'If it is certain that through one man's fall so many died, it is even more certain that divine grace, coming through one man, Jesus Christ, came to so many as an abundant free gift.' The grace and forgiveness are entirely undeserved, the free gift of the love of God through Christ. The initiative is God's, quite independently of the merits of man.

(d) The gift of grace is offered to all alike, pagan and Jew, through faith in Christ. No other or prior allegiance or commitment is expected. Both Jew and pagan are sinners, and all are justified through 'the free gift of his grace by being redeemed in Christ Jesus'.

3. The means of justification is through the sacrifice of Jesus on the cross, 'to the Jews an obstacle that they cannot get over [as analysed above], to the pagans madness'.

(a) Far from explaining the crucifixion away as an awkward anomaly, Paul makes it central to his whole theology: 'Redemption is brought about by a gratuitous gift of God, namely, the death and resurrection of Jesus Christ.'

(b) 'We were still helpless when at his appointed moment Christ died for sinful men.' Again, the love of God is proved by the fact that 'Christ died for us while we were still sinners. Having died to make us righteous, is it likely that he would now fall to save us from God's anger?' The phrase 'appointed moment' makes it clear that the death and resurrection of Christ was part of a grand divine plan of salvation, and not merely an unfortunate accident.

(c) The aim of Christ's death was reconciliation of God and man. Previously we were still the enemies of God, but we were reconciled through the actions of God in Christ: 'It was God who reconciled us to himself through Christ and gave us the work of handing on this reconciliation. In other words, God in Christ was reconciling the world to himself, not holding men's faults against them.' The crucifixion transforms judgement with a verdict of condemnation into grace with a verdict of acquittal. The debit column is erased.

(d) Baptism is death to sin and to the old self; and, imitating Christ's death, the Christian also imitates the resurrection through mystical identification. The former self is crucified and freed from the slavery of sin, so that the new self can be put on 'created in God's way, in the goodness and holiness of the truth'. The presumption here is that the Christian will remain sinless until the second coming, something which became increasingly difficult as this event was delayed.

4. There is a certain tension between the efficacy of faith and works. I observed above that justification by grace assumed faith active in good works as a result of the inner spiritual revolution. In other words good works are the manifestation or point of inner transformation.

    (a) Paul asserts that the remnant of Israel is chosen by grace: 'By grace, you notice, nothing therefore to do with good deeds, or grace would not be grace at all'. Then in Romans 4 he quotes David as saying that a man is happy if God considers him righteous, irrespective of good deeds. The point which Paul is at pains to stress is the primacy of grace over works, and therefore the primacy of God's initiative over man's own efforts. If good works alone were sufficient, grace would be superfluous and faith unnecessary: the Christian claim for the uniqueness of Christ and his redemptive mission would lose all its force and appeal; Christ could only be held up as an uninspiring example, not hailed as the saviour of the world. We shall return to this critical issue below.

    (b) On the other hand, speaking of the Jews, he says of the day of anger when the just judgements of God shall be known: 'He will repay each one as his works deserve. For those who sought renown and honour and immortality by always doing good there will be eternal life; for the unsubmissive who refused to take truth for their guide and took depravity instead, there will be anger and fury.' And in his exhortations to the Galatians, Paul warns:

Don't delude yourself into thinking God can be cheated: where a man sows, there he reaps: if he sows in the field of self-indulgence he will get a harvest of corruption out of it; if he sows in the field of the Spirit he will get from it a harvest of eternal life. We must never tire of doing good because if we don't give up the struggle we shall get our harvest at the proper time.

These passages suggest that character and actions are the crucial variables, but again stress that purely motivated good works flow directly from a living faith. Earlier in the same chapter Paul states that what matters is 'faith that makes its power felt through love', and that the community should serve one another in works of love, in accordance with the greatest single commandment of love. The fruits of self-indulgence are to be shunned in favour of the fruits of the Spirit: 'Love, joy, peace, patience, kindness, goodness, trustfulness, gentleness and self-control'. Charity should be extended to everyone, leaving vengeance to God himself.

(c) A clarification of this issue can be found in the epistle of James, when he poses the question of whether someone's faith will save them even if they have not done a single good work. The answer is emphatically negative: 'Faith without good deeds is useless.' Faith and deeds are to work together, the faith being perfected through and reflected in the deeds. Put another way, one could argue that faith without good works is simply not genuine.

5. Despite developments in the details of Paul's eschatology, he remains convinced of the relative imminence of the *parousia* or second coming. In his early writings to the Thessalonians he envisages a period of tribulations dominated by the rebel, who will be annihilated at the coming of the Lord at the final judgement followed by the resurrection. In the second phase (I Corinthians) there is no reference to the rebel (antichrist) and judgement is according to works. Then in II Corinthians and Romans the timing of the resurrection is revised to immediately after death and Paul looks for a universal spreading of Christ's kingdom. Finally, Christ is regarded as the all-in-all, so that either all must be reconciled and summed up in him, or else the impenitent are destroyed.

It is generally agreed, however, that the kernel of Paul's ethics is not directly related to his eschatology, but consists rather in his mystical identification with and in Christ. Albert Schweitzer argues that his ethic is 'nothing else than the mysticism of the being-in-Christ ... a concept of redemption from which ethics directly results as a natural function of the redeemed state'. This mystical being-in-Christ, symbolized by the sacrament of baptism, is a participation in his death and resurrection which results in a freedom from sin and from the Law. In practical terms this means an alignment of the Christian's will with the will of God, so that ethical behaviour follows logically; there is no need for the restriction of the Law, which is necessary only for those still in an unredeemed state.

Schweitzer then grapples with some of the perplexing issues presented above. In attempting to recast the doctrine of the atonement in relation to freedom from the Law (since atonement is essential to the message, and observance of the Law is peripheral), Paul tries to claim that the only valid righteousness is to be derived from faith alone, not from works in observance of the law, and that 'work-righteousness is incompatible with faith-righteousness'. In pursing this logic Paul 'arrives at the idea of a faith which rejects not only the works of the Law, but works in general': ethics is not actually deducible from such a proposition. Paul is anxious to deny the value of law-works that he 'commits himself to the inherently irrational general assertion that faith has no need of and no desire for works'. It should now be clearer why Paul's ethics flow more essentially from his mysticism than from justification by faith. And yet, as Schweitzer indicates, it is this last doctrine which proved to be historically the most influential.

According to Paul, liberation from the Judaic Law places the Christian under the Law of Christ, the fulfilment of which is in love, in loving one's neighbour as oneself: 'he who loves his neighbour has fulfilled the Law.' The Law of Love is prized above every other principle and virtue, as enunciated in I Corinthians 13; it fulfils Christ's own commandment to his disciples that they love each other, so as to be recognized by the quality of their love. Love in action is selfless service of a purer motivation than straight duty, ritual observation, or works carried out with half an eye on a reward. In spite of the mystical basis of Paul's ethics, though, a crude version of the doctrine of justification by faith has led to some of the more outrageous claims to salvation by mere intellectual assent. Paul also warned his followers about the pride often accompanying esoteric knowledge, insisting that love was the key; he would probably therefore have been scathing about salvation through belief. But the very exclusiveness of his claims for Christ necessarily entailed a rejection of the quality of being of a pagan, however virtuous, as the criterion of spiritual worth and salvation. This has led to uneasy relationships with other religions, owing to the insistence of Christianity being the only path to salvation.

At the time of the Jewish revolts and crushing of Jerusalem in AD 70, the second coming might have seemed imminent in the light of such momentous events; but even by that stage expectation of Christ's immediate return was beginning to wane. The Church therefore had to adapt itself to continued life in the world and began to de-eschatologize its teaching. One of the most important consequences of this process is first expressed by the unknown author of Hebrews; Christ is no longer depicted as the eschatological judge, but is cast in the role of mediator, 'a great high priest who has passed through to the highest heaven'. His unique sacrifice transcends all past and future sacrifices by priests, and is absolutely sufficient for all time. The need for an intercessor became increasingly clear as Christians living on in the world were tempted and sinned; the Church was also extending its scope beyond the supremely dedicated elect, which led to repercussions which we shall touch on in the next section. The apocalyptical structure and philosophy of history has remained nevertheless, with many groups throughout the past 2000 years prophesying the impending demise of the world: history is seen as moving towards a consummation to be inaugurated in the second coming. More cautious people have maintained their expectation without ever setting a precise date.

The Role of Grace: Augustine versus Pelagius

A number of early theological controversies centred around the issue of whether the Church should be confined to the elect prepared to dedicate themselves unstintingly to living the spiritual life, even risking persecution and martyrdom. Becoming a Christian was no light matter: aspirants who had made a commitment to be baptised were called upon to undergo a preparation of three years which included fasting, vigils and training in prayer. Only after baptism could communion be taken. Many of the early heretical sects such as the Donatists and Montanists were simply not prepared to compromise with the growing worldliness and politicization of the Church after the reign of Constantine; it implied a watered-down version of Christianity which made less rigorous demands on its nominal adherents.

This issue gives us some of the necessary background to the Pelagian controversy, which had profound implications for Christian moral order. Its main focus was the relative importance and roles of grace and free will in the attainment of salvation. I shall begin by elaborating the doctrine of grace. Its central meaning has been defined as 'the mercy and forgiveness of God given freely to sinners along with the empowerment to meet the demands of the new life, and to resist temptation'. This definition breaks down into two parts: first, the mercy of God implied in the doctrine of justification by faith, that is 'being made righteous, by grace which is received and grasped by faith, not by moral effort'; and, second, the empowerment to lead the good life, which, according to this doctrine, cannot be achieved without the prior initiative of God. In other words the empowerment comes from outside the individual, not from an inward and autonomous act of will.

Before proceeding any further, we need to look at the background and temperaments of the two protagonists, since it is abundantly clear that these were contributory factors in this dispute. Augustine, bishop of Hippo, had a deep conviction of his own sinfulness and unworthiness, with an equally powerful experience of grace intervening in his life. In this respect his psychological profile resembles that of Paul. He did not feel that he could have achieved anything without the prior operation of the grace of God. Pelagius was a British teacher who arrived in Rome at the end of the fourth century, and was horrified to find what low standards of morality obtained in the city. He gained the impression that much of this was condoned or excused on the grounds that it was a weakness inherent in the human condition. Such reasoning failed to impress Pelagius, whose motto was 'If I ought, then I can', thus encouraging his contemporaries towards self-improvement through the exercise of free will.

We can now penetrate the heart of the matter. Joan O'Grady puts it succinctly: 'For Pelagius, the centre of Christianity was moral striving towards perfection; for Augustine, it was abandonment of God.' Not that the two aspects ought to be mutually exclusive, but the issue became polarized in the course of debate. Three main doctrines were the focus of attention: original sin, grace and redemption, and the status of free will. Pelagius rejected the idea of inheritance of original sin from Adam, insisting on the contrary that falls were individual, depending on a person's life and conduct rather than being an inherent taint. Augustine took up the opposite stance, stating that the Fall and permanently impaired human nature so that no salvation was attainable without the prior intervention of God. Pelagius did not reject grace, preferring the view that its function was educative and co-operative in allowing room for freedom and hence personal accountability. By the same token, he thought of Jesus as an example, not a saviour. Such a statement was anathema to Augustine, and indeed to the functioning of the Church as a whole. Denial of original sin means denial of the need for redemption or saving grace and the doctrine of atonement. Moreover, it was the Church which dispensed grace through the sacraments: no need for saving grace meant no need for sacraments, in which case exactly what role was left for the Church? The whole scheme rested on original sin and its reversal through death on the cross; sharing the benefits of redemption was only possible through the Church for those who had been granted the grace of perseverance. This closed shop was menaced by Pelagius; or, to change the metaphor, the Church was in danger of losing the power of its exclusive licence to dispense grace.

The third focus was the question of the sufficiency of free will, itself a gift of grace. Pelagius was more of a moralist than a theologian, while Augustine was more fundamentally a theologian. As we saw above, Pelagius was shocked by the loose conduct he observed around him in Rome, and convinced that standards could be raised through individual moral effort. A degree of circular reasoning can be found in Augustine's arguments about the necessity for grace; and, as we shall see, his reasoning led him to the obnoxious conclusion that God predestines some of his creatures to damnation. Grace, he maintained, came to those whom God had chosen; and it was precisely these people who had the capacity to persevere through the empowerment of grace. Thus anyone who managed to persevere at the same time as remaining loyal to the Church must by definition have received grace. That is, 'the very fact of striving towards God implies the reception of His grace.' Yet Pelagius himself was a prime example of someone striving towards God, even by Augustine's own account! But he repudiated the basis of the Church's teachings and his views were regarded as heretical. Hence he was damned.

Augustine found himself in a cleft stick similar to that of Paul when the latter was attempting to divorce the central message of Christianity from the sole performance of good works (good works alone could not lead to salvation): this was only attainable through the faith which would then *manifest* in good works. Augustine was arguing against the assertion that human beings could achieve eternal life without any outside help. If this were so, then faith in Christ and his death would be superfluous and the Church redundant. Because faith in Christ and his redemptive power is the distinguishing mark of Christianity (whereas anyone can perform good works for the best of motives), it is ultimately necessary to condemn the doctrine that human free will and moral effort are in themselves adequate to salvation. When pushed to its logical limit, this argument has to support the efficacy of faith over even selflessly motivated works by a non-believer; it thus risks becoming unethical, as Schweitzer pointed out (see above).

One further development of Augustine's position needs to be mentioned. It stems from the proposition that grace is bestowed on those chosen by God in their single life-chance. They were enabled to persevere in the faith and finally enjoy the blessings of heaven. It follows that those whom God has not chosen, for reasons best known to himself, have no chance of being saved; any effort on their part is of no avail. The situation is especially embarrassing when applied to unbaptized children. Baptism was considered an essential prerequisite to gaining salvation through grace, absolving the original sin which the child had been born with. Logically, then, unbaptized children were damned. Augustine admitted to St Jerome that he was at a loss as to how to answer this question! The fact remains that he laid the foundation of the doctrine of predestination, which was to be elaborated centuries later by Calvin. It makes God into an arbitrary tyrant and negates the justice of the moral order.

I have dwelled at some length on this controversy, since its echoes can be heard down to the present time. It is doubtful whether predestination or determinism can even be called moral orders if such order implies a certain degree of free will and autonomy. To overplay grace and dependency can sap moral initiative, as Pelagius upheld. The moral obligation of 'If I can, then I ought', while not implying 'If I ought, then I can', serves to encourage individuals to make an effort from within rather than rationalize their supposed incapacity by blaming it on their parents or social environment.

Purgatory, Penance and Indulgences

If the Church found itself obliged to adapt to the delay in the second coming and plan for a prolonged stay on Earth, development of its popular appeal necessitated a revision of the dualist metaphysical order of heaven and hell: most Christians were not ready for paradise without a prior process of purification. The doctrine of purgatory eventually came to fill this gap by postulating an intermediate space between Earth and heaven and an intermediate time between death and resurrection. It is defined by Jacques Le Goff in his classic work as 'an intermediary other world in which some of the dead were subjected to a trial that could be shortened by prayers, by the spiritual aid of the living'. He points out that the word *purgatorium* did not exist before the end of the twelfth century, although a number of earlier figures, in particular Augustine and Gregory the Great, contributed to the emergence of this new status in the metaphysical order.

The Catholic doctrine is based on a radical distinction between mortal sin which results in eternal loss of the soul in hell, and venial sin which can be expurgated in purgatory; it teaches that forgiveness of the sin does not entail remission of the penalty. Hence the need for punishment to be exacted before entry into heaven, whether it is meted out in this life as penance (or even appropriate earthly tribulation) or in the next as refining and purgative fire. The image used for these venial sins was wood, hay or straw, which could naturally be consumed in the fire. To complete the picture, the symbols of gold, silver and precious gems are associated with the righteous, while the worst sins are represented by iron, lead and bronze.

In the sixth century, Pope Gregory the Great furthered the development of the doctrine by his didactic use of anecdotal illustration. Le Goff observes that the astute pastor realized the need for 'authentic testimony delivered by witnesses worthy of belief and the need for details about the location of purgatorial punishments'. Gregory's keen sense of the political and ecclesiastical implications of the doctrine is apparent from the final book of his dialogues, in which he demonstrates 'the reality of postmortem punishment and the efficacy of masses and pious works on behalf of the dead'. These 'suffrages' link the dead to the living, and involve the Church in a pivotal role through the eucharistic sacrifice. One cautionary tale relates how a hermit, revived from death, had paid a visit to hell and had all but joined several eminent people he found there; he was spared by an angel and instructed to give careful consideration to his manner of living from then on! Needless to say, the hermit led an exemplary existence from that moment forwards. Carol Zaleski translated another of Gregory's influential narratives in full, observing at the end how it foreshadows various motifs which become familiar in medieval accounts of otherworld journeys: 'the river of hell, the flowery meadows of paradise, the while-clothed throngs in heaven, the test-bridge, and, above all the externalization of deeds'.

Towards the end of the twelfth century, according to Le Goff, 'purgatory found its place as man's social imagination expanded to embrace the other world as well as this one.' The belief that was central to the development of purgatory in the medieval imagination was the conviction that 'the dead could be helped by prayer, and more particularly by suffrages.' This participation satisfied the desire to help relatives and sustained the believers' own hopes of receiving similar benefits themselves. The Church's key intervention was in the eucharistic sacrifice in exchange for alms, and this 'helped to tighten its control over the living, who wished to avail themselves of its supposed power to intervene on behalf of the dead'. Le Goff notes that the enemies of the Church argued relentlessly against the doctrine of purgatory, maintaining that a person's fate depended only on their own merit and the will of God, and that there is no redemption between death and resurrection; hence purgatory and prayers for the dead are redundant. Consequently, also, opponents denied 'that the Church has any part in determining the fate of the soul after death, and opposed its attempts to extend its power over men by claiming such a role'.

Before we move on to consider the question of penance and indulgences, it is worth mentioning a moral revolution which was occurring about the same time, involving new concepts of sin and penance. It was Anselm who drew the key distinction between voluntary sin or vice and venial sin due to ignorance. Such a distinction brought the search for purity of intention into sharp focus, discriminating between acts externally similar but internally quite dissimilar. This represents a refinement of the moral order through an expansion and enrichment of personal responsibility, leading to an 'internalization and personalization' of moral life with an emphasis on confession and contrition. The faithful were all exhorted to examine their consciences, and verbal confession was made compulsory once a year. Penance would then be imposed; if the person should die after confession but before completing the penance, the venial (literally 'pardonable') sins would be 'dissolved in fire'. The connection between such venial sins and purgatory was thus reinforced.

The year 1300, declared a Jubilee of Pope Boniface VIII, marked a watershed in the development and provision of indulgences for venial sins and penance. Indulgence is defined by Canon Law as 'a remission in the sight of God of the temporal punishment due to sins of which the guild has already been forgiven'. Such remission is granted as absolution to the living and as intercession for the dead. It was underpinned by the theory of The Treasury of Grace, of which the Church was the sole guardian and cheque book holder. Although the sin may be forgiven, there is still a penance to be exacted in the form of works of reparation, prayer, psalms, fasts, mortification, vigils and alms. A system of Penitential Books was gradually established, enabling the priest to impose the correct type and duration of penance. The logic of indulgences, however, was mercy towards the sinner, who might have part of the penance commuted through the merit of grace transferred from the Church's account. Their treasury was in the happy position of being able to draw on limitless funds of grace, first through Christ himself, then through the superabundance added by the Virgin Mary and the saints. The development of this practice tended towards increasing concessions more easily obtained.

Plenary indulgence had hitherto been reserved for crusaders, but it was now extended to pilgrims who made their way to Rome. At a later stage this practice was extended to encourage pilgrimages. The Pope offered a free pardon for all sins committed since baptism to all those who entered the church at Assisi between the evenings of the first and second of August every year. Such was the popular enthusiasm for this bargain offer that more than 60,000 sometimes made the pilgrimage and a few were tragically crushed to death in the suffocating pressure at the church entrance. The normal transfer of merit from the living to the dead through good works was by-passed by the edict of the Pope. Even if subsequent incumbents did not avail themselves of the privilege during the fourteenth century, the initiative was nevertheless a decisive one. We shall return to the theme of purgatory and the abuse of indulgences when we reach the Reformation, but turn meanwhile to medieval developments in eschatology.

Death and Judgement in Medieval Europe

W. R. Alger asserts that the 'principal mental characteristic' of the medieval age, 'especially in regard to the subject of the future life, was fear ....living fear of men, fear of the State, fear of the Church, fear of God, fear of the devil, fear of hell, fear of death'. Keith Thomas makes a similar point when he reminds us how vulnerable and helpless people were in the face of disease like plague, fire, or other sudden misfortune. The superstitions which arose out of and thrived on fear and insecurity created a close alliance between religion on the one hand and magic or miracles which exerted some control over a capricious environment on the other: insecurity was allayed by miracles, which suggested that human beings were not all so helpless after all. As dispenser of grace and repository of supernatural power the Church occupied the position of mediator between people and God. Thomas indicates how the mass was associated with magical power, acquiring in the popular mind a 'mechanical efficacy' not so much due to the participation of the congregation as to the 'special power of the priest' through consecration of the host which accomplished the miracle of transubstantiation. The host itself acquired a distinctive reputation; some people retained it in their mouths and put it to use later on. One man even beating it into a powder which he then sprinkled over his garden as a charge against caterpillars! Although ecclesiastical authorities insisted that the Church's rites and prayers were primarily intercessional, that is they worked by supplication rather than control as in magic, the people themselves did not draw such a hard and fast demarcation.

From the twelfth century onwards we witness the appearance of sculptural depictions of the last judgement above the portals of many of the great Gothic cathedrals in Europe. It must have been an awe-inspiring spectacle to the pilgrim or worshipper, whose imagination was fired by this scene of the separation of the just from the damned. The initial phase was marked by a linking of the second coming to the last judgement, a connection which disappears by the thirteenth century, when representations portray a court of justice. As mentioned in Chapter 5, the weighing of souls, or *psychostasia*, was a prominent feature; but the measure of the scales is no longer seen as inexorably determining the fate of the soul. There are now intercessors – St John and the Virgin Mary – to plead the cause of the soul. If Christ is the supreme mediator with God, Mary and John assume this position *vis-à-vis* Christ as Judge (and pardoner); Ariès claims that the intercessors become just as important as the archangel who weighs the souls. This signifies merciful concessions to the impartial rule of law, and thus has implications for the moral order: strict justice may be overridden by the appeals of intercessors to the mercy of the judge; in other words the judge can be swayed by human considerations.

A legal atmosphere pervades the development of the concept of the book of life from that of a universal census to an individual register of account book in which are inscribed the sum total of a person's thoughts, words and deeds. It is a history or biography 'with two columns, one for the evil and the other for the good'. Towards the end of the Middle Ages, the book was thought to be retained by the devil as a means of laying claim to the soul, but by the end of the sixteenth century a person would have two books to be consulted at the hour of death.

The next important process, partly the result of an increasing acknowledgement of individuality, shifted the emphasis away from the last judgement as a general assize to the conviction that the fate of the soul was decided at the moment of physical death. Along with this went a stronger belief in purgatory as a waiting room for heaven, as opposed to the original notion of sleeping until the last trump of the second coming. The bedroom was transformed into the scene of judgement, and a last ordeal replaced the last judgement. The scales have disappeared, although the book of life is frequently grabbed prematurely by a demon. Ariès mentions two interpretations of this scene, in which God or Christ no longer appear as judges. The first is a straight struggle between good and evil, witnessed by the soul; the second, more plausible, involves the soul in an essential way: how will it react to the revelation of its life in the book? There are three temptations: pride, despair, and attachment to the world or to people. The first two temptations relate to the interpretation of one's life. The guardian angel does not parade the good works to balance the evil, but rather cites instances of divine mercy such as the penitent thief at the crucifixion in order to enable the soul 'to resist the morbid contemplation of his life and crimes'; the challenge is to prove one's faith by reliance on divine grace, not by parading one's good works. We can once more discern a moral order of dependence on grace and an implicit suspicion of what can be achieved by free will. The book has been transformed from 'a symbol of impartial justice into a reminder of the need for mercy and intercession'. Fourteenth-century mystery plays always depict the crucified Christ and the Virgin ready to intercede on behalf of the soul; Christ traditionally bares his five wounds and Mary her breast to provide six reasons why the request for mercy should be granted.

The third temptation, that of *avaritia*, attachment to the temporal, represents a great test of renunciation. The soul's attitude at this critical moment will either erase its sins or wipe out its good deeds at a stroke. It is not hard to see how this concentration on the moment of death as the supreme test led to the perverted belief that it was less important to live virtuously if a good death could redeem everything by cancelling out one's sins. A humorous tale gives this stratagem away, however. A man had heard that a good death consisted of remembering God at one's passing, and so he called each of his sons by a name of God, thinking that they would be present at his deathbed and therefore remind him of God. In due course the man came to die and called out to each of his sons to ascertain that they were present. When he reached the last son, he sat straight up in his bed and asked 'Well, who is minding the shop, then?', whereupon he promptly expired!

The motif of the encounter with deeds, a variant of which we discussed in the near-death experience life-review, is to be found in every version of judgement at death: its essence is an externalization of the character as manifest in actions. Nothing can be hidden; all is written in the book and weighed in the balance. In the deathbed ordeal, the soul is its own inner measure and judge; and yet its ultimate resources are supposed to be external in the form of grace, mercy and intercession; the doctrine of original sin would disqualify the soul from determining its fate on its own merits. In this version of the moral order we can see the re-emergence of the old dichotomy between faith and works, grace and free will. The trial is ultimately one of faith, as outlined above; works, or lack of them, can always be overridden by mercy and/or intercession. The soul is enjoined to rely on grace, and warned away from self-reliance by the looming spectre of spiritual pride. The underlying moral order thus remains one of dependence on mediation, faith and grace, thus rendering free will and works quite secondary.

Reformation Eschatology

The Protestant reformers were in many respects the elaborators of a bequest received from Augustine; they took up the tension inherent in his doctrine of grace and his doctrine of the Church. One commentator calls the Reformation the triumph of the former over the latter. His outline of Augustine's doctrine of grace is worth quoting in full:

> Sinful man depends, for his recovery to good and to God, entirely on the free grace of God; this grace is therefore indispensable, prevenient, irresistible, indefectible; and being thus the free grace of God, must have lain, in all the details of its conference and working, in the intention of God from all eternity.

We saw how Augustine defended this view against Pelagius, so that grace was declared indispensable to salvation; however, the Church did not go as far as pronouncing grace to be irresistible; a full-blooded Augustinianism did not develop without orthodoxy. His doctrine of the Church made it the vehicle and dispenser of grace, thus ensuring its role and power as a mediator between people and God. An irresistible grace flowing directly from God to the individual would render the Church's mediating function superfluous, and could not therefore be tolerated. Such a doctrine would also effectively destroy the freedom to choose and the moral consequence of wrong choice. It was left to Luther to take the critical step of attacking this monopolization of power.

Luther's psychology was similar to that of Paul and Augustine: he had an acute sense of his own sinful unworthiness, and, by his own account, was reduced to despair in his attempts to come to grips with Paul's doctrine of justification by faith. At first, according to Ninian Smart, he took faith in Christ as a 'further demand the punitive God made on men harassed by sin', but then realized that God's intention was merciful, making people justified through their faith, not works. Luther turned to Augustine's texts attacking the Pelagians and found his own interpretation bolstered. Moreover, he concluded that if works were not the means to his justification of God, then ascetic practices along with ceremonial works and rituals performed by the Church were similarly needless: grace was not mediated through the sacraments, but came directly from God; no necessity, therefore, for ecclesiastical mediation.

Luther was also incensed by the absurd lengths to which the sale of indulgences was being pressed. A system which had initially been firmly rooted in a system of penances reached its nadir in the practices of Tetzel. Alger catches the flavour in a classic piece:

> Ecclesiasticism devoured ethics. Allegiance to morality was lowered into devotion to a ritual. The sale of indulgences at length became too impudent and blasphemous to be any longer endured, when John Tetzel, a Dominican monk, travelled over Europe and, setting up his auction-block in the churches, offered for sale some famous indulgences of Leo X which promised, to everyone rich enough to pay the requisite price, remission of all sins, however enormous, and whether past, present or future! This brazen but authorized charlatan boasted that 'he had saved more souls from hell by the sale of indulgences than St Peter had converted to Christianity by his preaching'. He also said that 'even if any one had ravished the Mother of God he could sell him a pardon for it!'

This practice marks the demise of any credible moral order: money is able to purchase immunity for the most scandalous misdemeanours.

Escape from hell is no longer related to one's moral quality but rather to the size of one's bank balance. It is scarcely surprising that Luther reacted with indignation.

Before proceeding to a closer analysis of Luther and Calvin, it is as well to remind ourselves of the similarities of doctrine between Catholicism and the reformers. Both agreed that original sin led to death, and that heaven was barred to the human race sunk in depravity; that the incarnation, death and resurrection of Christ brought about the redemption of our lost estate; and that at the second coming there would be a general bodily resurrection and universal judgement which would assign people to heaven or hell. The essential differences between the two views lay in the nature and means of redemption. While the Catholics believed that the atonement had wiped away sin and enabled salvation to be attained by moral fidelity and with the help of the Church, the Lutherans maintained that Christ's death represented a pardoning of the sins of those who had faith; while Calvin argued that God foresaw the Fall and consequent damnation, but decreed that a few sinners should be saved nevertheless.

The 1530 Augsburg Confession sets out many of the essentials of Lutheranism. It insists on original sin, denying the Pelagian contention that 'man is made righteous by his own powers, thus disparaging the sufferings and merits of Christ'. It teaches justification by faith and forgiveness of sins by divine grace, for Christ's sake, through faith, not by 'our own merits, works or satisfactions'. It includes a long article on faith and works, which observes that the key to Christian life, namely faith, has been neglected, 'while nothing but works was preached everywhere'. In expounding the relationship between faith and works, the Confession refers to the authorities of Paul and Augustine:

> We begin by teaching that our works cannot reconcile us with God or obtain grace for us, for this happens only through faith, that is, when we believe that our sins are forgiven for Christ's sake, who alone is the mediator who reconciles us with the Father. Whoever imagines that he can accomplish this by works, or that he can merit grace, despises Christ and seeks his own way to God, contrary to the Gospel.

Reliance on works and personal merit is rejected for reasons reminiscent of the authorities appealed to. The only mediator allowed is Christ, thus displacing the Virgin Mary, the saints and the Church itself. Further on, the doctrine of justification by faith is referred to as 'most comforting and salutary' to weak and terrified consciences; it was, in addition, quite unreasonable to drive such weak consciences to rely on their own efforts, which brought no peace of mind comparable with that brought by the doctrine outlined above. The text is careful to insist that faith is not to be equated with mere knowledge of historical events, but is 'a confidence in God and in the fulfilment of his promises'. As in Paul, the good works are to spring out of the nature of the faith; indeed they are obligatory, even if not to be relied on to earn grace. It is surmised that without faith human nature is much too weak to perform good works, endure suffering, love one's neighbour and so forth. The English Thirty-nine Articles speak of justification by faith as 'a most wholesome Doctrine, and very full of comfort'; similar ideas can be found in Baptist and Methodist pronouncements.

The Augsburg Confession expects the return of Christ in judgement at the last day 'to give eternal life and everlasting joy to believers and the elect but to condemn ungodly men and the devil to hell and eternal punishment'. The Westminster Confession of 1646 speaks of a judgement according to thoughts, words and deeds, while the Second Helvetic Confession (1566) categorically states that the faithful go directly to Christ after death, whereas the unbelievers are cast headlong into hell. Implicit in this metaphysical order is a rejection of purgatory, tainted by its association with indulgences, so that prayers for the dead are quite irrelevant. Indeed, the doctrine of purgatory is argued to be contrary to faith's insistence on the forgiveness of sins through the atonement.

The Church of England's Thirty-nine Articles condemn, among other things the Romish doctrine concerning purgatory and the invocation of saints as 'a fond thing, vainly imagined, and grounded upon no warranty of Scripture, but rather repugnant to the Word of God'. We shall see in the next chapter how this reduction of the metaphysical order from three to two dimensions landed the reformers 'in the very difficulties that Purgatory had been invented to solve', the uncompromising harshness of definitive assignment to heaven or hell.

Calvin's temperament was quite different from that of the passionate and not altogether systematic Luther: he was a severe man with a powerful will and a brilliant legal mind. Publication of his famous *Institutes* is considered as epoch-making in its impact as Kant's *Kritik* or Newton's *Principia*, since in them for the first time the doctrines of the reformed churches were systematically laid out. The bedrock of Calvin's teaching is the absolute sovereignty of God, from which is logically derived his doctrine of predestination. Although the ancestry of this doctrine can be traced, as we have noted, through Augustine, there are significant differences and developments: Calvin repudiated the Church's claim to mediate between the soul and God, upholding 'the priesthood of all believers'. A more important distinction is that Augustine confined himself to speaking positively of pre-destination to life, while Calvin defends a double predestination – to salvation and to damnation. Nor is the doctrine as simple as many would think at first sight.

Calvin excludes the objection that such predestination is an arbitrary act on God's part, adding that he is acting on the grounds of 'good pleasure', which must imply wisdom, righteousness and love by definition, even if such qualities remain totally inscrutable and unidentifiable when applied to these circumstances. It must also be remembered that the whole human race is lost, so that it is a gain if anyone at all is saved. The real stumbling-block to this version of the metaphysical order is the purported motivation of love on the part of God in assigning some souls in advance to perdition: if these souls can be saved through divine omnipotence, then why not also out of divine love? James Orr comments in an understated fashion that this question can probably never be answered 'even with the admission of inscrutability'. Such arguments from inscrutability have cut less and less ice since Calvin's own day.

There is no doubt that the practical effect of the Reformation was a reaffirmation of the Christian moral order. Smart observes that a person individually confronted with divine grace 'felt an individual responsibility for self-reform'. The democratization resulting from the priesthood of all believers, however, carried within it the seeds of a crisis of authority, especially when authority is vested in scriptures open to a variety of relative and conflicting interpretations. The moral equivalent of such a process is the relativization of the moral order which reaches its logical conclusion in anarchic situation ethics where no principles extrinsic to the particular situation can be taken into account: the absolute drowns in the sea of the relative.

Fascinating insights into the purported fate of some of the leading reformers can be found in the writings of Swedenborg, who claimed to be able to converse with people in the spiritual world with a view to finding out whether they had changed their opinions since death. In our present context it is of particular interest to read his accounts of 'conversations' with Luther, Calvin and Melanchthon. It is very clear that he regards the doctrine of justification by faith alone as misguided and that of predestination as positively pernicious. He therefore attempts to persuade the reformers of their errors.

Luther is first pictured as holding forth to his followers from a kind of throne. Around him were seated those most favourable to his opinions, while the less enthusiastic kept their distance. At length Swedenborg reports Luther's admission that he had derived the dogma of justification by faith alone from his own intelligence and not from the Word; and after changing his mind, as if for dramatic effect, Swedenborg describes him laughing at his former views, but justifying his stance on the grounds that he had to break away from the Catholics: 'I do not wonder, therefore, that I erred; but I do wonder that the folly of one man should make so many others foolish, and that they did not see the contradictions of the Sacred Scripture, although these are so manifest.' All was not lost for Luther, though, since he admitted the pre-eminence of charity above faith. We see an interesting shift in the terms of reference with 'charity' substituted here for 'works'. It is Swedenborg's general view that charity arises from 'internal affection thus from the joy of well-doing', and thus claims no merit. In other words it is an inner impulse from the heart. He likens faith alone, separated from charity, to the cold light of winter when everything is inactive, while faith with charity is 'like the light of spring and summer in which all things flourish, and are productive'. The first is a light without love, the second a light infused with love and therefore warmth.

Melanchthon is portrayed at a writing-table scribbling for days on end about justification by faith, without so much as mentioning charity. By spiritual inner correspondence his clothes become shabbier and his surroundings dingier, even to the extent of his appearing in a fur coat 'because faith without charity is cold'. It is for Calvin that Swedenborg reserves most of his indignation, however: he abhors predestination as a 'detestable heresy', a cruel notion which depicts God as a tyrant instead of as a loving Father. He likens the monstrous idea to a wild beast devouring its own young. In encounters with Calvin he meets only a stone wall of solid conviction about an omnipotent God saving just the elect. In a graphic metaphor, Calvin is said to perceive arguments against his views as 'mere eructations of the stomach or the rumbling of the bowels', an appropriate turn of phrase for hot air!

Swedenborg's own metaphysical order admits a God who is Love and Wisdom embodied in Christ as the saviour of the world. He condemns no one to everlasting punishment; those in hell are in the state/place corresponding to what Swedenborg calls the ruling love, the inmost disposition of the heart and will. The vicarious atonement is rejected in so far as it is seen to provide an excuse for moral and spiritual indolence. Although he insists that all good comes from God, Swedenborg leaves a central role to freedom active through the will and understanding, which correspond to the divine Love and Wisdom. The degrees of heaven and hell in the metaphysical order are the expression of the internal state of the soul, the outcome of the 'encounter with deeds', a justice proportionate to the person's own development of the qualities of love and wisdom.

Grace and Free Will: The Abiding Dilemma

In our outlining of the tension between grace and free will, we have been considering issues arising in psychology and politics as well as in religion. We noticed that some of the early heresies appealed to the stronger brethren and took little account of the weak who did not feel that they could help themselves. Joan O'Grady puts it like this: 'Is this religion to be for those who are willing to strive for perfection and have already reached some degree of purity, or is it for everyone, however lax and apathetic?' Should there be two Christianities or just one Church? The doctrine of purgatory arose out of just such a concern, fuelled by people's belief in their own damnation and their wish to do something about it. Ariès maintains that the Church 'hesitated between the impossibility of changing the judgement of God and the desire to alleviate the fate of the damned'. Hence the intermediary purgative state and the intercessions and indulgences which eventually sprouted around it, as we have seen.

Nowhere is this issue more poignantly expressed than in Dostoevsky's *Legend of the Grand Inquisitor*. The scene is Spain, at the height of the Inquisition. Christ returns and is recognized by his 'gentle smile of infinite compassion'; he encounters the venerable Grand Inquisitor, who has him led away. A conversation follows, in which freedom is the central issue. The Grand Inquisitor, in his worldly wisdom, asserts that the burden of freedom is intolerable to individuals and society and that 'man is tormented by no greater anxiety than to find someone quickly to whom he can hand over the gift of freedom with which the ill-fated creature was born'. He accuses Christ of wantonly increasing man's dreaded freedom instead of taking possession of it. The Church, on the other hand, 'correcting the work' of the gospel, took pity on the weak creatures weighed down with freedom and assumed the responsibility in exchange for submission based on miracle, mystery and authority. By believing in the answers promulgated by the Church the individual is relieved of 'the great anxiety and terrible agony' of making a free decision. The mediating Church dispenses the grace and assumes the responsibility.

In the final analysis we are left with a series of polarities in the Christian moral order. There is an undercurrent of grace even where free will is most passionately espoused by the Pelagians. There is a hint of determinism rendered most explicit in the theology of Calvin. There is a tension between mercy and love on the one hand, and justice on the other. There is mediation of various kinds and assertion of an immediate relationship of the individual to God. Metaphysically, there is a loving God with the hierarchies of heaven and hell, with purgatory between for some; there is an urgency added to the moral dimension by the eschatological expectation of the second coming and last judgement. Although no entirely consistent picture can be drawn, the Christian tradition has exhibited all shades of opinion between irresistible grace and unfettered free will. It has always been hampered by the need to insist on its own exclusivity and therefore accord a higher value to the defining characteristic of faith as opposed to works, even if the works are regarded as an integral part of genuine faith. The reconciling key is surely the attribute by which Christ hoped that he would recognize his disciples: by the fact that they loved one another and loved God. This kernel must remain after all the passion of theological wranglings has been spent. We shall see in the next chapter how the ascendancy of metaphysical propositions over spiritual experience contributed to the uprooting of humanity from the context of metaphysical order on which the final sanction of the moral order rested. Belief in the afterlife has been eroded and the moral order has come to be seen as a simple expression of conformity to the social order.

CHAPTER EIGHT

THE ECLIPSE OF THE SPIRITUAL WORLD-VIEW

The answer to human life is not to be found within the limits of human life.

C. G. JUNG

Man is a useless passion.

JEAN-PAUL SARTRE

Background

The use of the world 'eclipse' in the chapter title is deliberate: although I deal with the emergence of the spiritual sun from behind the shadow in the concluding chapter, we need to bear in mind here that the trends of thought to be analyzed are showing signs of cracking up in the late twentieth century, in order to make way for a more complete view of reality and the human being. The two quotations above represent the poles of the debate about metaphysics and the meaning of life. It was Jung who said in an interview that he did not simply *believe* in the existence of God; he *knew* it deep within himself. Sartre, by contrast, was a militant atheist who regarded the idea of God as impossible, and was himself committed to an uneasy combination of existentialism and Marxism. The quotation is the closing sentence and conclusion of his vast *Being and Nothingness*, the ultimate victory being that of nothingness as it engulfs the consciousness at physical death: hence the futility of human strivings, in his view – a pessimistic nihilism akin to Bertrand Russell's 'firm foundations of unyielding despair'.

The scope and approach of this chapter require some explanation. The main aim is to outline the principal factors leading to a decline in the belief in a metaphysical order behind life and beyond death since the seventeenth century. It is a complex field about which many books have been written so that it may seem impudent to attempt a summary in a short space; moreover, the various factors which I shall isolate cannot in fact be treated separately and will invariably overlap and cross-refer. This strategy is necessary, however, in order to achieve a sufficient clarity about the issues involved. In this section we shall consider in a general way the relationship between the divine, metaphysical, physical and social orders. We shall then discuss the nature of world-views and explanations within them, moving on to the medieval and Hermetic backdrop to the development of modern science. The rest of the chapter will treat four main themes which run through the intellectual emergence of the modern scientific outlook: the question of the existence of God; the decline of organized religion; the loss of sense of purpose and meaning in life; and the decline in the belief in immortality or survival of consciousness after bodily death. Each of these themes will be subdivided and will, as implied above, complement each other as aspects of a complex process.

At the beginning of the Chapter 6 I defined various levels and dimensions of the context of the moral order: social, physical, metaphysical and divine. The eclipse of the title of this chapter will be seen to be that of the metaphysical and divine orders, so that the moral order is contained and defined within the social and physical orders. One might even go as far as saying that an awareness of the physical order has diminished, in so far as science and economics have ignored ecological factors in their pursuit of mastery over nature. The predominant context of the moral order, therefore, has become the social order of politics and economics, the optimum organization of material society. This signifies a profound shift of focus and values away from the medieval preoccupation with individual salvation towards a secular concern with social and economic welfare, a shift which was necessary to redress the balance but which has resulted in something of a spiritual vacuum. Spengler comments on the decline of metaphysics in a section of 'Buddhism, Stoicism, Socialism' in *The Decline of the West*. 'With the decline of metaphysics', he argues, 'ethics has outgrown its status as a subordinate element in abstract theory. Henceforth it is philosophy, the other divisions being absorbed into it and practical living becoming the centre of consideration ... Metaphysics, mistress yesterday, is handmaid now; all it is required to do is to provide a foundation for practical views.' The reversal of priorities has dethroned metaphysics and theology, so that ethics is no longer logically derived from a metaphysical framework.

MacIntyre makes a similar point when analysing the two greatest moral weaknesses of Christianity: 'the sheer extent of its metaphysical commitments', and 'the fact that it has to assert that the point and purpose of this life and this world is to be found in another world'. He goes on to say that Christian claims will be more appealing to people who find this life 'inherently unsatisfactory', but their interest will be weakened if the possibilities of earthly life are rendered more attractive by economic prosperity. Thus other-worldly considerations fade into the background and are even denigrated as 'morbid'; concomitantly, 'belief in a God of any specific kind becomes increasingly a formality – when not actually abandoned.' We shall see below how a nominal belief in God may disguise the psychological abandonment of a once living force through a half-hearted adherence to what is regarded as an outmoded idea.

World-views and the Nature of Explanations

World-views, or *Weltanschauungen*, consist of the largely unconscious presuppositions which underlie the thinking of any age. Among thinkers who have contributed to our understanding of the nature of world-views are Albert Schweitzer, A. N. Whitehead, C. G. Jung, W. T. Stace and Ninian Smart. We can begin with the psychological observations of Jung, who defined a world-view as 'an attitude that has been formulated into concepts'; an attitude is defined in turn as 'a psychological term designating a particular arrangement of psychic contents oriented towards a goal or directed by some kind of ruling principle', a psychic attitude being 'a general guided idea which is reinforced by a wide assortment of experiences, principles, affects of all kinds etc.'. In distinguishing between attitudes and world-views, Jung reserves the latter term for people who have actually made a conscious effort to formulate a personal philosophy through which one creates a picture of the world and of one's place in it.

Jung warns that the basic error of every world-view is 'its remarkable tendency to pretend to be the truth of things themselves, whereas actually it is only a name which we give to things'. Ideas regarded as 'common sense' may well conceal unjustifiable hidden assumptions taken for granted by the majority and therefore left unquestioned. Jung considers in some details the conceptual reversal from the priority of spirit in medieval philosophy to the primacy of matter in the modern outlook, remarking that ideas are postulated or denied 'according to the temperament of the individual or as the spirit of the age dictates': 'otherworldliness is converted into matter-of-factness.' We shall examine the mind/matter issue in more detail in the section on immortality, but it is worth remarking at this stage that our predominant scientific materialism concludes that mind is a by-product of matter and the soul a bygone illusion. Conventional scientific and medical training inculcates and reinforces this conclusion as the received wisdom. It brings to bear powerful considerations in its favour, ignoring those areas of human experience which might suggest a contrary hypothesis. The important historical realization will be that the current penchant for 'horizontal', physical explanations was in fact a reaction against the medieval predilection for 'vertical', metaphysical categories. A post-modern synthesis will recognize both factors and attempt to discriminate which level of explanation is adequate or appropriate, without reducing one to the other.

Smart has usefully defined world-views, a category missing in English, as covering 'both traditionally religious systems of belief and practice and secular systems of a similar nature'. Elsewhere, in the context of a discussion on the nature of ideologies and religions, which both confer a sense of identity and place in the world, he proposes that world-views can be seen as a triangle: in one corner is the individual, in another fellow human-beings, and in a third the cosmos. Thus 'the fully satisfying myth or doctrine tells a person where he is in relation to society and the universe, and what the true constitution of his self is'. If we reformulate this in terms of our four orders, the individual is placed and defined in the social and physical orders, depending on whether or not the world-view is secular or spiritual, profane or sacred. The nature of the individual's identity and purpose is also defined in terms of these orders: social and physical identity in family, economics, politics, geography and ecology; the metaphysical and divine identity of the individual soul and universal spirit. A denial of these last two orders leads to a shrinking of identity and contraction of purpose, or even dehumanization through repudiation and denial of non-physical explanatory categories.

It is important to realize that explanations are embedded in the assumptions of world-views, that facts cannot be entirely separated from interpretation, even in perception. This line of thought is clarified by Whitehead in his distinction between the 'observational' and 'conceptual' orders. The former is constituted by 'the direct, immediate discriminations of particular observations'; and the latter by 'our general way of conceiving the Universe'. He argues that 'the observational order is invariably interpreted in terms of the concepts supplied by the conceptual order', in terms of both language and ideas. He then stresses that observational discrimination is selective, as hinted in his careful definition above: certain facts are highlighted, others ignored, and the whole rearranged and presented 'in a subjective order of prominence'. Whitehead illustrates his point by the simple analogy of sunlight which illuminates the world but conceals the stars. A daytime or night-time explanation of the sky would be 'delusively complete' if it rejected the other viewpoint; the same goes for the reduction of spirit to matter or matter to spirit.

The categories of the conceptual order enable certain connections and classifications to be established, which in turn render the world intelligible. Such classificatory ideas are, however, 'incomplete tools' which put the world together again after it has been analyzed into component parts; they both represent and misrepresent the world in thought by referring it to a context of ideas. We feel that we have 'explained' something when we are able to classify it in a familiar pigeon-hole. We now need to ask about the nature of explanation. Why is it that certain explanations are felt to be satisfactory and others doubtful or problematic?

Basil Willey tackles this issue by defining an explanation as 'a restatement of something – event, theory, doctrine, etc. – in terms of the current interests and assumptions'. It is crucial that such assumptions should seem ultimate and incapable of further analysis, according to Willey, since an explanation of the explanation leads one immediately into the metaphysical or psychological arena, which most thinkers shun. Ignorant as they are of the presuppositions of their thinking, in turn derived from their training, unconscious thinkers fall straight into the basic error identified by Jung and quoted at the outset of our discussion. Willey's central assertion is that explanation cannot be defined absolutely, but only in terms of the demands of a particular time or place.

At certain epochs, he explains, there arises the demand for a reformulation of explanatory principles resulting from 'a disharmony between traditional explanations and current needs', which need not necessarily imply the falsehood of the older statement but rather a change of categories. In practice, though, one or other of the categories is accorded the status of truth, while the other is treated as false, superstitious or mythical: thus 'scientific' explanations supplanted theological ones as the focus shifted 'from metaphysics to physics, from the contemplation of Being to the observation of Becoming'. The criterion of truth becomes consistency with the prevalent world-view. This procedure has encouraged an either/or approach to knowledge, corresponding to the simple assertion of true/false. Such at least was the case until the advent of systems theory, which proposed that complementary explanations could coexist at different levels of analysis. It would be legitimate, for instance, to describe the efficient cause (the 'how') of a disease as a virus and its purpose, or final cause (the 'why'), to bring about a change in the person's lifestyle.

I shall argue in the last chapter that we are now living through another epoch, one in which we are being subjected to a demand for a reformulation of explanatory principles. Meanwhile we can conclude that it would be unwise to ignore the existence of world-views underlying our thinking processes and explanations: the assumptions of a particular culture or way of thinking lie behind their conceptions of the relationship between social and physical orders, and determine whether or not the metaphysical and divine orders are even acknowledged.

The Medieval and Renaissance World-views

Both the medieval and Renaissance world-views were firmly based on the existence of God and an afterlife; that is, the context of the physical and social orders lay within the metaphysical and divine. The images of concentric circles encompassing the flat Earth, with heaven above and hell below, provide a diagrammatic picture whereby the world is literally contained within the planetary orbits and heavenly spheres. The Earth is at the centre, with the heavenly bodies encircling it. Only the earthly realm is subject to change and decay, while the heavens remain changeless and incorruptible. Such a scheme was backed by the authority of Christian doctrine.

In a more general sense, human life was set within the metaphysical certainty of the existence of God. Jung puts it like this: 'The medieval man we have talked of had a beautiful relationship with God. He lived in a safe world, or one that he believed to be safe. God looked out for everyone in it; he rewarded the good and punished the bad. There was the Church where the man could always get forgiveness and grace ... his prayers were heard. He was spiritually taken care of.' Although Jung may be correct in his use of the word 'safe' in a psychological sense, the medieval world was scarcely a comfortable place to be. The safety lay in the prevailing theodicy which explained all events in terms of the providence of God, which itself was increasingly called into question, as we shall see; but fear and insecurity lurked round every corner, if not in the form of disease and disaster, then in the post-mortem threat of hell-fire.

W.T. Stace accounts for the coherence and stability of the medieval world-view through the presence of three key factors in people's mental outlook: the idea of God, that of world-purpose and what he calls the moral order of the world. The effect of this scheme is to make sense of human life and the physical order within the metaphysical and divine orders. The medieval God was personal and intimately concerned with the world and its inhabitants. Natural phenomena were explained with reference to their purpose, not merely their physical and mechanical causes. This distinction between teleological and mechanical explanations will be pursued below: 'mechanical' came to mean 'purposeless', thus actually excluding the notion of purpose rather than simply pushing it into the background. The assertion that the world is a moral order is common to all spiritual world-views. By this Stace means that moral values are objective, guaranteed by God, and not just the projections of the relative workings of the human mind or emotions. One important implication of seeing the world as a moral order is that apparent injustices will be remedied in the afterlife; this theme will be treated more fully in our discussion of changes in views of God and the problem of evil.

The Hermetic world-view of the Renaissance is frequently ignored or minimized in the history of science. It arose from a combination of four sources, namely the writings attributed to Hermes Trismegistus, the renewed interest in Platonism, the study of the Jewish mystical tradition of the Cabala, and alchemy. Cosmology retained the Earth at the centre of the universe, but wove an elaborate astrological scheme of cosmic harmonies, affinities and correspondences which related the part to the whole and the microcosm to the macrocosm. Such connections impregnated life with meaning and significance; Nature was explained as animated, alive, having not yet succumbed to the deadening influence of mechanical philosophy.

Sympathetic connections between mankind and the world lay behind the development of the Renaissance idea of the magus's capacity to dominate and control nature, a legacy which persisted well beyond the cultural demise of the magus himself. As a pivotal part of the great chain of being between matter and spirit, the magus reached into the supernal realms of spirit as well as descending into matter with the golden keys of number and geometry. Investigations of the natural world were guided by a reverential spirit of enquiry, which was reflected in the pioneering scientists of the seventeenth-century revolution. Thus Frances Yates can say that 'The Renaissance magus is the immediate ancestor of the seventeenth-century religious scientist.'

Yates puts magic at the centre of what she calls the Rosicrucian outlook, but emphasizes that it works as 'a mathematics/mechanics in the lower world, as celestial mathematics in the celestial world, and as angelic conjuration in the supercelestial world'. The link between mathematics and mysticism, dating back to Pythagoras, is a strong element at this stage and remains until as late as Kepler. But in the course of the seventeenth century there was a definitive shift from the philosophy of magic to that of mechanism, from a perception of the connections within the whole to a concentration on the working of the separate parts. Yates comments on the profound irony of the emergence of mechanical science from the Renaissance magical tradition: 'Mechanism divested of magic became the philosophy which was to oust renaissance animism and to replace the "conjuror" by the mechanical philosopher.'

Before leaving this theme, it is interesting to note the ideological and political tensions surrounding the formation of the Royal Society in England. The Rosicrucian Hermeticists envisaged a thoroughgoing reform of society, education and religion, and therefore posed a radical threat to existing institutions if they became too influential. Evelyn Fox Keller explains how interest in the alchemical philosophy of Paracelsus reached a high point during the puritan revolution of the 1640s and 1650s, dividing the 'new science' into the Hermetic and mechanical camps. During the 1650s a number of leading intellectuals such as Robert Boyle and Henry More shifted their allegiance to the mechanists and paved the way for the establishment of the Royal Society along mechanical and experimental lines in 1662. A moment's reflection on the political and religious upheavals of the previous twenty years suffices to account for the conservatism of the Royal Society founders. A cautious policy was adopted: the Society stuck to discussions on experimental science, avoiding in the interests of its own self-preservation such inflammatory topics as utopian social reform, witch-scares and religious pronouncements on private illuminations, which might be offensive to the Church.

In his article on a Festschrift for the physicist David Bohm, the biologist Brian Goodwin outlines an approach to what he calls 'A Science of Qualities', in which he envisages the re-emergence of the connective patterns reflected in the Hermetic world-view. It is a vision in which 'subject and object, the known and the unknown, can relate and participate in an appropriate unity, made possible by the fact that reality is a single co-ordinated domain'. We may well find that Renaissance Hermeticism and Platonism will underpin the metaphysic of the emerging new science, albeit with the accent on dynamic and evolutionary processes rather than static correspondences.

God

The trend away from living religion has taken many thinkers from personal theism through impersonal deism towards a position of explicit agnosticism or implicit atheism. In these last two cases the divine and metaphysical orders are eliminated, all phenomena being accounted for by natural physical causes. We shall explore four avenues of thought which have proved persuasive in the decline of religious faith: developments in astronomy and physics, which have altered the cosmological scheme within which God might be seen to operate; the controversy over proofs of the existence of God; the nature of God in relation to issues of theodicy, including the problems of free will and evil; and finally the question of providential interference in the everyday physical world.

197

Cosmology

It is well known that the scientific revolution in astronomy and mechanics destroyed the medieval world-view outlined above. The metaphor of the organism was succeeded by that of the clock, a mechanical analogy which held within it the seeds of implications which would only germinate at a later stage. The clock consists of mechanical parts which are co-ordinated but which can be dismantled and reassembled without integrally damaging the structure. Knowledge of the workings of the clock can best be obtained by taking it apart. The clock needs to be wound up periodically; applied to the universe, which is only once set in motion, the idea corresponds to the second law of thermodynamics whereby the universe is running down to an inevitable heat death.

Two cosmological themes stand out: the displacement of the Earth from the centre of the universe and the subsequent growing realization of the sheer scale of space and time; and the gradual perception of the autonomy and independence of physical processes. We shall take these in turn.

The displacement of the Earth from the centre of the universe was paralleled by the psychologically more important doubt cast on the place of mankind in the overall scheme of things. Could the universe really have been made especially for human beings? Such a supposition became less and less plausible as instruments demonstrated the vast extent of space and the relative insignificance of our galaxy, let alone of the solar system. We shall see how the question of scale also affected perception of purpose and the role of providence. For the time being, however, our attention is focused on its effect on the idea of the existence of God. Stace rightly points out that the principal scientific discoveries do not in themselves invalidate or disprove God, but they do exert an effect through association, which non-logical sequence he calls a 'psychological transition'. He isolates two key factors: the growing feeling of the remoteness of God in the astronomer's universe; and the pushing back of the role of God in time to creation, that is setting the divine clockwork in motion, and subsequently only tinkering with the irregular motion of the planets God becomes the First Mechanical Cause, becoming more or less redundant once the workings of the laws of motion have begun. Stace concludes that an imaginative picture of a 'God far away and long ago is death to a living religion'. God then becomes an abstract intellectual belief devoid of psychological reality, a proposition to be argued for or against.

The argument for the independence and autonomy of natural processes runs on from Newton's 'First Cause of Clockwork Designer' picture. Galileo's idea of God was that of a huge 'Mechanical Inventor', who was required to create the universe and set it in motion, but subsequently left causal power in matter itself. As mentioned above, Newton left room for God to correct irregularities in the planetary motion. Laplace then discovered that it was not necessary to introduce God, as the effects were in fact self-correcting. Hence his famous retort to Napoleon that he had no need of the hypothesis of God to explain the workings of the universe. He argued that the processes could be understood as a self-contained system. This logic is also implicit in Big Bang cosmology, in which there is no need to assume either a creator or a designer of the universe. We are left with chance and necessity as explanatory principles in both physics and biology.

Proofs of the Existence of God

The primary impact of discussions about the proofs of the existence of God has been restricted to the philosophy tradition, although its effects have permeated through to informed public opinion. The various proofs set out by Anselm and Aquinas were subjected to systematic criticism by Kant, who then proposed his own moral argument for God, freedom and immortality on the grounds that they were practically necessary for a coherent moral order. In other words, justice must surely be achieved in a redress in the next world if not in this. Few people have found this *a priori* argument very convincing; it will be further discussed when we consider moral arguments for immortality below.

We saw above how Newton held to a version of the 'first cause' argument, rendered scientifically unnecessary by Laplace, and a form of the argument from design: that the clock implied a clock-maker. This theory was further elaborated by Paley at the beginning of the nineteenth century, but met its match in Darwin's theory of natural selection, which explained adaptations without invoking purpose or design. We shall examine this in greater detail below, but it is worth mentioning at this stage that the latest incarnation of the argument from design has appeared under the guise of the anthropic cosmological principle, which maintains that the improbability of the physical constants being exactly right for the emergence of conscious life indicates a form of cosmic intelligence. Detractors point to the circular nature of such an *a posteriori* argument which explains the present in retrospect, already knowing that life as we know it has actually developed. At any rate, the appeal of such a position is partly intuitive, and it can be argued both ways.

Another type of argument is psychological rather than philosophical, stemming as it does from the proposition that man made God in his own image. Traces of this can be found in Voltaire, who maintained that if God did not exist he would have to be invented, and then in Feuerbach, who regarded God and religion as human projections. The theme reaches full development in the writings of Sigmund Freud, where helpless humanity projects the need of a protective father and creates a wish-fulfilling illusion. With this flourish Freud thinks that he has explained the matter, and that the question of the truth-claims of wish-fulfilments need not be addressed. But, as John Gaskin indicates, he ignores the distinction between reasons and causes: once he has explained the causes of belief in God, he regards all possible reasoning as specious, neglecting the possibility that human beings may have deep-seated dispositions to believe in something for which there is also good evidence. We shall return to this consideration when discussing wish-fulfilment arguments against immortality and survival.

Theodicy and the Nature of God

Many of the most intractable theological problems arise from attempts to reconcile apparently conflicting attributes of God. The issues that will preoccupy us in this section are among such problems: the question of evil, classically expressed by Augustine in the proposition 'Either God cannot abolish evil or he will not; if he cannot, he is not all-powerful; if he will not, he is not all-good'; the question of hell and eternal punishment under which the implied vindictive lack of forgiveness was seen as inconsistent with a God of love; and the question of predestination and free will, by which the foreknowledge of God ordains some for heaven and others for hell, thus making a mockery of the freedom required for moral conduct.

We begin with the problem of evil. It is customary to draw a distinction between moral evil as unnecessary suffering caused by the free action of other human beings, and physical or natural evil as suffering imposed on creatures, including humans, by natural processes independent of human agency. The evil of Auschwitz typifies the first kind, while one of the most famous of the second kind was the Lisbon earthquake of 1755. In fact the atrocities of concentration camps do not fit exactly with the above definition in view of the word 'free'. The torturers were free in one sense but locked into a system by fear and obedience; in some instances they might have lost their own lives if they had ceased to co-operate with the war machine. Some did just that, and their moving testimonies are recorded in *Dying We Live*: examples of supreme moral and physical courage. The Christian answer to moral evil is the doctrine of original sin, the basic concept of which is still persuasive even if detached from its biblical moorings.

Natural disasters and epidemics are not attributable to human error. The traditional explanation in terms of providence was that all misfortune was deserved by definition (we shall return to this in our discussion of providence): if the person struck was not overtly sinful, then they must have had some hidden vice for which they were being chastised. While this may have an air of plausibility when applied to individual cases, the argument wears thin when applied to 20,000 individuals killed in an earthquake. It was nevertheless the conventional approach at the time of the London fire and plague, as recorded by Defoe. It is also the position originally taken by the priest of Albert Camus's novel *The Plague*, but Camus forces Paneloux out of this harsh verdict by confronting him with the unmerited suffering of a child. A similar illustration occurs in Dostoevsky's *Brothers Karamazov* in a conversation between Ivan and Alyosha. Ivan tells the story of a child's excruciating suffering at the hands of cruel parents and demands poignantly: if all must suffer to pay for the eternal harmony, what have children got to do with it?' A full discussion of this question would require a chapter in itself, but the following observations are in order: the Christian response is usually to invoke the mystery and inscrutability of God without questioning his/her basic goodness; the agnostic, like Sir Leslie Stephen, will conclude that something is wrong with the usual image of God; and the atheist, such as Camus, used physical evil as one of his main arguments for disbelief in God. The Indian would explain such events through karma, thus referring the responsibility for the disaster back to the sin of a previously earthly existence.

Other arguments and stratagems have been discussed in detail by Gaskin. What is at stake here is the 'plausibility structure' (a phrase coined by Peter Berger) of the religious explanation of suffering and evil. Such explanations are meant to furnish a plausible account of suffering, evil and death, thus integrating these anomalous events into an overall scheme and giving them a meaning and significance. The wider context of such questions is referred to by Max Weber as the 'theodicy of disprivilege' in which one of the principal requirements is just compensation for trials and tribulations undergone. In other-worldly salvation religions promising compensation in another life, the revolutionary spirit of the desire to change existing social conditions is conspicuous by its absence. Weber then argues that 'the need for an ethical interpretation of the "meaning" of the distribution of fortunes among men increased with the growing rationality of conceptions of the world.' He goes on to list possible justifications for suffering and injustice: reference to deeds committed in a former life; the transferred guilt of ancestors; or original sin and the wickedness of all. As compensatory promises he lists a good rebirth, a messianic hope for a better life on Earth, or a better life in the hereafter. One should note that this compensation may be independent of the moral person's moral deserts. There are also three closed-system answers in karma, Zoroastrian dualism of good and evil, and predestination. The twentieth-century materialist humanist would tend to reject all these metaphysical considerations, and, if an ardent socialist, would regard them as comforting intellectual illusions.

One further pragmatic point: Leszek Kolakowski remarks, and Viktor Frankl bears out, that trust in God and a strong belief in a purposeful moral order helps people cope with vicissitudes as distressing as incarceration in concentration camps. That is to say, the belief has survival and psychological value quite independent of its truth or falsity; indeed one woman cited by Frankl goes as far as admitting that she is glad that life hit her so hard, as she would otherwise never have appreciated its deeper significance. The power of such confessions *in extremis* needs to be weighed against the more superficial pronouncements of normally comfortable individuals.

We pass now to the question of the existence of hell in relation to the attributes of God, an issue to which we shall return when we consider the arguments around immortality. Hell-fire preaching inculcated a fear of hell into the faithful and thus increased the clergy's control over their flocks. Such preaching was backed up by selected passages on eternal punishment from the New Testament but was being challenged as early as the seventeenth century. By the nineteenth century the issue had moved to the forefront. It jarred with both the emerging humanitarian sensibility and a revised philosophy of punishment advanced by Jeremy Bethak; this put the accent more on reform than on retribution, thus calling into question the logic of hell as a deterrent to wicked behaviour. (The same structure of argument continues to this day, applied to capital punishment.) The really uneasy tension was between the teaching of eternal punishment and the assertion of the love and forgiveness of God, who could surely not impose eternal punishment for sins committed in the course of one short earthly life: the retribution would be quite dis-proportionate.

On the other hand, Christianity insists on 'the reality of "abiding consequences" of every act of moral choice', while Nicolas Berdyaev goes as far as contending that 'hell is the moral postulate of man's spiritual freedom.' This harsh imperative can still be mitigated by some form of ultimate salvation for all; the possibility of post-mortem reform concedes that one's fate is not irreversibly decreed at death. For Pusey in the nineteenth century, the moral poles were the fear of hell and the love of God, the first perhaps useful in initiating conversion, while the second perfected the intention beyond an expedient calculation of spiritual self-interest. Even today, though, some 53 per cent of Americans believe in eternal damnation for unrepentant wrongdoers, a reflection of fundamentalist influence; on the other hand, some 71 per cent believe in heaven, and of those 20 per cent reckon they have an excellent chance of going there, 44 per cent a good chance, 29 per cent a fair chance, and only 7 per cent admitted to a poor chance or abstained from comment. In summary it can be said that secularization has brought about a decline in the belief in hell as a deterrent; the believer, if not fanatically fundamentalist, is less willing to countenance an eternal hell in view of a conviction of the underlying goodness of God. The full impact of the denial not only of hell, but also of an afterlife, will be considered below.

I referred to the predestination theodicy as one of Weber's solutions to the problem of evil and suffering: it arises from the attributes of omnipotence and omniscience, which combine to rule out the potential for genuine free moral choice and action by human beings. Its ancestry has been discussed in Chapter 7. The controversy reached a peak in the seventeenth century during the lifetime of Blaise Pascal. The idea of predestination to hell was considered particularly odious, the product at best of an inscrutable God and at worst of a monster. Such assertions are hardly guaranteed to persuade the unbeliever of the existence of a benevolent God. The harsh picture contributed towards disillusionment with that image. It is an interesting reflection that theological predestination has been translated in its implications into materialist determinism, but without its metaphysical trappings. It is no longer God who determines, but the material or psychological forces of mechanical philosophy.

Providence

'The doctrine of providence,' asserts Keith Thomas, 'was a conscientious attempt to impose order on the apparent randomness of human fortunes by proving that, in the long run, virtue was rewarded and vice did not go unpunished.' Moral chaos was unacceptable, so God's providential sovereignty was posited instead, added to which was full compensation for residual injustices in the next world. The strength of the doctrine, while it lasted, was its self-confirming or circular nature, by means of which religion was actually strengthened by the hardships encountered in life. The logic, as stated in the discussion above on the problem of evil, was that all misfortune (and by implication good fortune) was deserved, including disease. The next step was to insist that religious conformity might provide immunity against disease, with the caveat that hidden sins might still beat the immunization. Such injunctions were reinforced by cautionary tales illustrating mishaps which revealed an appropriate connection between physical events and moral disposition. Tawney cites the case of a usurer being crushed by a falling statute of another usurer on entering a church to be married!

Another focus of the providence issue of intervention in the physical world is miracles, eloquently denounced by David Hume in his famous essay on the grounds that natural laws could not occasionally be suspended. The classic Augustinian riposte to this statement is that (assuming that the witnesses were truthful) we do not yet know enough about the workings of the law in question. Obviously, different kinds of miracle need to be treated on their merits, and an adequate definition of miracle formulated. All these considerations aside, the basic scientific objection to the doctrine of providence is that it has been rendered redundant by advances in scientific knowledge: there are no more gaps into which God might squeeze; besides, the scale of the universe, as we have seen, seems to militate against divine intervention in the affairs of humanity. The astronomer Hanbury Brown condemns the idea of supernatural intervention in the physical world as belonging to an obsolete world-view and as hopelessly at odds with the world-view of modern science. In a sense, Brown's argument is a restatement of the remoteness of God shading into non-existence. As a postscript it is worth pointing out that the parameters of the debate have remained the personal intervention of God or the total absence of such intervention; rarely does one see arguments for intermediary forms of discarnate influence as it were on behalf of God. Such a possibility renders the alternatives less stark, but the notion naturally remains unintelligible to those who disbelieve in any kind of post-mortem or extra-terrestrial consciousness.

The Decline of Organized Religion

In so far as organized religion has upheld the metaphysical and divine orders, its decline is mirrored in a parallel evaporation of the significance of these orders in the lives of those who have not turned elsewhere for spiritual guidance. Part of the trend may be accounted for by an insufficiently clear demarcation of the respective domains of science and religion. Whitehead, for instance, contends that 'Science is concerned with the general conditions which are observed to regulate physical phenomena; whereas religion is wholly wrapped up in the contemplation of moral and aesthetic values.' No doubt the distinction is altogether too sharp, ignoring as it does philosophical questions under dispute between the two, but it springs from Whitehead's genuine religious concern and dismay that religion is tending to degenerate into 'a decent formula wherewith to embellish a comfortable life', what Weber would call the 'psychological reassurance of legitimacy' required of religion by the privileged classes. For nearly three centuries religion has been on the retreat in the face of the intellectual advance of science, and can be hampered by its difficulty in adapting to changing circumstances from more or less fixed positions.

In this section we shall examine four factors which have reflected the decline of organized Christianity in the West: fanatical intolerance, as manifest in the seventeenth-century wars of religion; the dogmatic rigidity and bigotry associated with fixed tenets of belief; the impact of the moral arguments of humanism; and issues relating to the relative authority of religion and science.

Fanatical Intolerance

A cursory glance at history will confirm the spectacle of human beings ready to die for and kill in the name of ideologies and religions. Fanatical espousal of an idea and its absolute rightness drives out any vestiges of humanitarian feeling and enables blood-curdling atrocities to be perpetrated in the name of justice and in pursuit of the realization of some ideal. The history of the Inquisition and that of contemporary sectarian warfare shows that this capacity has persisted through the centuries and is unfortunately alive and well in the world of today. The fanatic achieves a sense of identity and purpose of aligning with the idea, and is prepared to pursue its realization with remorseless zeal.

In the seventeenth century the wars of religion sent a shock-wave through the sensibilities of Europe. Arnold Toynbee describes the moral revulsion at the exhibition of malice, uncharitableness, fanaticism and also hypocrisy:

The theological controversialists on both sides have been fanatical in so far as they had been sincere; the politicians had been hypocritical in exploiting sincere religious fanaticism for furthering the interests of their respective states; the combatants, whatever their motives and aims, had been guilty of committing appalling atrocities.

Fanaticism, said Jung, is overcompensated doubt. The Church traditionally insisted that no salvation was possible outside its confines, and attempted to impose its views by force when persuasion proved ineffective. After all, the salvation of the soul was at stake, even if the body had to be mutilated as a means to that end. The exclusiveness and correctness of one's doctrinal stance became more important than ethical qualities, which necessarily came second to the primary requirement for orthodoxy. The issue is delicate even today: what is the irreducible minimum for identifying oneself as orthodox in a particular tradition? And what attitude should be adopted towards manifestly ethical 'non-believers'? We can only hope that religious maturity will bring with it not simply tolerance but acceptance and empathetic understanding of other views.

Dogmatism

It is not easy to separate out the influence and effects of fanaticism and dogmatism, which tend to go together. In the eighteenth century Voltaire's message was 'Ecrasez l'infâme' (crush the infamous), his disgust being directed not only at fanatical intolerance but also at the metaphysical meanderings which were frequently used to justify cruelty and barbarism.

In the twentieth century, scientific and anti-dogmatic views can be typified by Bertrand Russell, who defined faith as a conviction which cannot be shaken by contrary evidence. Leaving aside the fact that this is a better definition of belief than of faith, he represents the shift of focus from the deductive approach of scripture towards the inductive method of observation and experiment, a theme which I will take up in relation to authority below. More generally, it is the whole Christian scheme of creation, the fall, the incarnation and virgin birth, the redemption, the resurrection, the judgement and the second coming which has been under attack, even from within theology itself. Traditionalists have had to maintain their position by means of a variety of theological arguments and distinctions against those who think that doctrine should move with the times; it is probably a matter of temperament as much as anything else. The neglected factor is perhaps the inner dimension of spiritual and mystical experience, a kind of inner empiricism (long familiar in the Indian Yogic traditions) which confirms certain universal patterns of spiritual development and shuns dogmatic pronouncements on subtle aspects of the inner life. In the event, there is no doubt that the arrogant certainties of dogma have alienated many more than they have attracted.

Humanist Morality

The humanist movement began by reacting against the fanaticism and dogmatism described in the previous two sections. It stands for humane toleration taking priority over theological rectitude. It rejects many religious beliefs as outdated superstitions or comforting illusions. It also focuses its concern exclusively on this world and its problems, regarding another life as both improbable and irrelevant. In other words it is philosophically materialist and socially aware, critical of conservative or compensatory doctrines advanced by the Churches as stabilizing or palliative proposals which do nothing to empower people to demand social change.

The basis of humanist ethics is social, since obedience to the will of God or individual conscience means nothing within their categories. As early as 1699, Shaftesbury was debating the metaphysical basis of morality and arguing that the scheme of heaven and hell inspired selfish hopes and fears, corrupting morality which ought to be based on the beauty of virtue itself. The opposite view, that the metaphysical order is a necessary basis for morality, will be discussed in a later section. Bertrand Russell also criticizes the individualism of the Christian scheme of salvation, saying that welfare has to be conceived in the light of the state of the whole community. These views are, however, by no means irreconcilable, for instance in the approach of Albert Schweitzer through ethical mysticism, whereby individual enlightenment is intimately bound up with the love of and service to creation. Besides, the change of lack of Christian social concern has been widely responded to in our time with a proliferation of humanitarian agencies sponsored by official religions.

In a penetrating study of psychoanalysis and religion, Erich Fromm makes it clear that it is a caricature to regard Freud as totally anti-religious. He argues that the dangers which Freud saw in religion threatened his own ideals and values, namely knowledge, (reason, truth, logos), brotherly love, reduction of suffering, independence and responsibility. Speaking in the name of the ethical core of religion, Freud 'criticizes the theistic-supernatural aspects of religion for preventing the full realization of these ethical aims'. Superstitious belief will be used to suppress critical thinking and infantile projection will prevent the development of mature moral responsibility. It is open to question though, whether Freud did not ditch the baby with the bathwater by over-reacting to the religious world-view; he certainly threw out the metaphysical dimension, which need not be approached only through the avenue of superstition. His analysis is more valid for pathological and immature forms of religious belief.

A similar pattern can be discerned in Russell, who remained implacably hostile to organized religion throughout his long life. He maintained that the great religions of the world were both untrue and harmful, and yet showed in his autobiography a sensitivity to the profound mysteries of existence and what he calls 'unbearable pity for the sufferings of mankind'; this he translated into vigorous social campaigns, twice going to prison for his beliefs. The unbearable pity forms one part of a triad of passions which governed his life, the other two being the longing for love and the search for knowledge. He defines the good life as one 'inspired by love and guided by knowledge'. Elsewhere he mentions that the important virtues are kindness and intelligence, adding that intelligence is impeded by any creed and kindness inhibited by the belief in sin and punishment.

In a television debate a few years ago between the atheist philosopher Sir Alfred Ayer and the Christian politician Lord Hailsham, it was striking that ethical differences were so minimal when compared with their religious views. From the foregoing it can be seen that the humanist protest stems at least in part from a Christian failure to live up to their own precepts. The ideals of Russell and Freud could be espoused by most Christians, even if such ideals could never exert the degree of moral obligation inherent in a morality grounded in the metaphysical and divine orders.

Authority

In an aphoristic remark in one of his letters, C. G. Jung attributes the loss of the Churches' spiritual authority to their inability to come to terms adequately with the scientific spirit: 'Science seeks the truth because it feels it but does not possess it. The Church possesses the truth and therefore does not seek it.' Despite the invariable oversimplification of such generalizations there is more than a grain of historical validity in the remark: the source of the Church's truth was its tradition and scriptures which were meant to present an adequate account of the world and human life. Answers were to be deduced from what had already been laid down. As against this, as we have seen, the seventeenth-century scientific revolution followed the canons of experiment and observation, establishing a different approach to and definition of truth with a corresponding world-view. That the question of authority and tradition is not so clear-cut as the historical accounts suggest has been made apparent by Alexander Thomson's work on tradition and authority in science and theology. Science itself has a tradition and authority structure resting on particular epistemological and philosophical assumptions and methods such that the personal factors are artificially excluded from consideration; and science too has an establishment, orthodoxies within various disciplines, and even a 'central dogma' in biology, which is now under attack. But it has certainly been influential in the decline of the Church, despite its own vulnerability.

The Catholic theologian Hans Küng observes that 'the Church's power over human soul ... seemed to be secured better by the fear of eternal damnation than by anything else.' He adds that the result was that 'intimidated, browbeaten Christians, suffered from fear and created fear'; terrorized themselves, they put the fear of God and man into others in their turn. Many anthropologists have indicated how fear lies at the root of primitive religion. In a chapter of the omnipresence of demons, Sir J. G. Frazer comments that at a certain stage of moral and spiritual development 'men are undoubtedly influenced far more by what they fear than by what they love.' Russell argued that fear of nature gave rise to religion, which attempts to placate spirits and gods through all manner of sacrifices. He also saw fear of death and the unknown at the root of dogma, quite apart from the political overtones referred to by Küng above. Indeed even Adam and Eve in the garden were afraid after they had eaten the apple and disobeyed the commandment of the Lord God. Erich Fromm speaks of the authoritarian and humanistic consciences, explaining that the authoritarian religious structure requires conservative obedience from its perpetuation, but commenting that most social innovations depend on a disobedient attitude towards current norms. Religious fear in the Middle Ages thrived on superstitions which have since been shown to be groundless by advances in science and technology. Thunderbolts were interpreted as an expression of the wrath of God, and should not therefore be diverted by the wicked invention of lightning conductors, as we noted above. We may still retain a fear of thunder, but no longer compound it with the conviction that divine anger is being directed at us. Cautionary tales of the kind discussed in the section on providence do not impress the modern mind.

In the Protestant denominations the authority of the Church was partly passed on to the Bible, as the infallible world of God. The advent of biblical criticism in nineteenth-century Germany initiated the process of undermining the authority of the Bible as the absolute literal truth and word of God. It could no longer be regarded as the guarantee of the authenticity of every story it contained. Scholarship analyzed the historical elements and was able to locate passages which might have been tampered with and interpolated, not to mention actual inconsistencies within the texts themselves. In spite of 150 years of work in this field, fundamentalist evangelicals still close their eyes to the issues raised and continue to treat the Bible as the oracle of God; moreover, if you do not agree with their approach, you are seriously misguided or even doomed. Such a dogmatic and uncritical outlook can only be treated as an anachronism likely to deter many seekers from taking religion seriously. The concentration on the letter at the expense of the spirit was not consonant with the attitude of the early Christians themselves.

Prior to the rise of critical thinking in theology came the advent of individualism in philosophy and democracy in politics. The turning-point of modern philosophy in Descartes began with the subject's analysis of his own experience: *Cogito ergo sum* (I think, therefore I am). As well as asserting the primacy of the subject in establishing certain and clear knowledge, Descartes formalized the principle of doubt, the antithesis of faith. Instead of believing in order to understand, we have disbelief and scepticism applied to all investigations with the sole exception of the original doubt itself: sceptics are rarely sceptical about their scepticism. In ethics the trend moved away from the absolute values of the objective moral order towards a subjectivism and relativism which made it increasingly difficult to discriminate between good and evil. In the atheistic existentialism of Sartre there is no set human nature and purpose; these are created by the choices of the individual. The situation is far from satisfactory: the individual looks for a certain amount of spiritual and ethical guidance, but if everything is relative (a term used extraordinarily sloppily) where is the guarantee they hope for? A return to medieval dogmatism, though, will not do either.

Survival and Immortality

Within the framework of our discussion we now come to a consideration of the decline in belief in the metaphysical order of life after death, judgement, purgatory, heaven and hell. Since I have already written extensively on this topic, I will here confine discussion to the essentials required to understand the changing picture. Ariès sets out in his monumental (no pun intended) study *The Hour of Our Death*, we have become less and less familiar with death in the last hundred years, over which period the subject has become taboo, the shadow side of rapid technological progress which has in fact done little to enhance the life expectancy of those over twenty. Decreasing familiarity has brought with it increased fear, reinforced by the nihilism of the prevailing materialist philosophy. We shall look at this philosophy first of all, and then move on to the more specific influence of Darwinism, Freud and Marxism in the criticism of the idea of the immortality or survival of the soul.

Materialism

Since the seventeenth century the whole trend of natural scientific explanations has been towards explaining all phenomena, including mind, as by-products of matter and physical forces. We examined the basis of this world-view at the beginning of the chapter. The method has focused on looking at things objectively from the outside and with ever-more sophisticated instruments, looking for necessary laws to explain the workings of the experiment in hand. This external, objective angle of vision has naturally sought to explain the inner in terms of the outer, the subjective in terms of the objective: thus mind in terms of matter. Materialism has constituted the research programme of both philosophy and neuroscience, so that one can count on one hand the number of distinguished philosophers and neuroscientists who do not subscribe to the monist reductionist view of mind.

Recapitulating the thesis of my earlier book, theories of consciousness can be divided into various categories: the orthodox 'productive' theory, which assumes that consciousness is produced by the brain; and the 'transmissive' or 'permissive' theories which postulate with a certain type of consciousness is transmitted through or permitted by the brain, but that consciousness itself need not be entirely dependent on neural wiring. The first theory predicts extinction of consciousness at brain death, while the second allows the escape or expansion of consciousness into another dimension. I argued that normal conscious experience could be explained by either theory, but that the materialist productive theory failed to give adequate account of certain types of psychic and near-death experience. Such data are quite simply ignored by the vast majority of philosophers and scientists, since it poses a fundamental challenge to their world-view.

The decline of the belief in an afterlife cannot of course be divorced from the factors of belief in God and the strength of organized religion already discussed. We are talking about a change in mental climate which cuts across the disciplines and imprints them with the mark of a new world-view. One other argument for immortality deserves mention here, namely the moral argument advanced by Kant, related to which is the argument that God would not allow creatures like ourselves to perish after a lifetime of striving. Needless to say, such proposals have cut little ice with materialist philosophers, who simply regard them as incidental and irrelevant. The argument amounts to saying that this life would be morally incomplete without a larger context, a demand for moral order to be extended into the metaphysical order. As an *a priori* proposal it can only appeal to the intuition and not to any direct evidence; acceptance or rejection will depend on one's previous philosophical commitments.

Such has been the power and influence of philosophical materialism that it has actually entered the ranks of Christian theologians in their deliberations on the meaning of resurrection, immortality and eternal life. Paul Badham quotes two of them as saying that there is no reason to suppose that life continues beyond the grave and that subjective existence after death is not an article of Christian belief. Such assertions would have astonished their forebears. No less amazing is the interpretation of resurrection as unreserved assent to life or the present life experienced from the standpoint of God. Eternal life is sharply differentiated from life after death, but, as Badham points out, the ability to enter into an eternal relationship with God in the present actually presupposes a continued existence after death. Having said all this, part of the present disarray in Christian Eschatology arises from the tension inherent in the two traditions of the resurrection of the flesh and the immortality of the soul, Hebrew and Green respectively, and from the reluctance to look at any of the empirical material such as near-death experiences which might throw light on the nature of consciousness. Fundamentalists who believe that the soul sleeps until bodily resurrection are ironically aligned with materialists in rejecting the survival of consciousness independently of the body after physical death.

Evolution

We have already touched on the effect of the theory of evolution on the argument from design, and will return once more to it in looking at the disappearance of a sense of purpose and meaning in life. We will consider here the effect which the theory had on the plausibility of the metaphysical order.

The story begins with Descartes, who thought that animals had no souls, and were to all intents and purposes automata. Descartes maintained a distinction between humans and animals by endowing humans with a soul. Then along came Darwin to undermine the classification by positing a continuity between animals and humans. There were two possible developments: one could endow animals with souls as well, but where does one draw the line, and why? Do cockroaches have souls?, asks biologist Richard Dawkins. Or one could argue that neither humans nor any other life-form have souls capable of surviving bodily death. Since the general trend of thought was in line with the second avenue and the first seemed to present insuperable difficulties, most biologists dropped the idea; besides, it was associated with the unorthodox school of vitalism, while mainstream biology was and is mechanistic. In support of the first line of enquiry one would need to posit some kind of panpsychism, whereby mind is inherent in all matter, but only becomes organized and increasingly conscious as matter becomes more complex; then at a certain level of organization (hard to pinpoint, admittedly) the mind becomes capable of an existence independent of the physical body. Another approach would draw more heavily on the Indian Advaita metaphysic which treats mind as the basic stuff of the universe and matter as a condensation of mind. The mind would then predate the form, just as the soul would exist prior to the creation of a new bodily vehicle. Such a formulation would be profoundly distasteful to most modern scientists, who have a metaphysical horror of any kind of dualism of soul and body and can only recognise monism when it means mind arising from matter, not vice versa.

One nineteenth-century response to Darwinism was to concede that the soul was not naturally immortal, but was conditionally so, depending on the good grace of God. The reaction was not a direct one, but extricated theologians from an awkward dilemma if they were to accept the consequences of the loss of the natural immortality which had previously been accorded to humans but not to animals. Richard Swinburne, among others, argues that although we each have a soul, it can be kept in being after physical death only if God chooses; it (or we) is not (or are not) naturally immortal. The exact mechanism of the choice of who survives is not clear, nor at what point in evolution this process is meant to have begun. In summary, evolution as it is currently formulated contributes to the arsenal of materialist arguments, but once again, as with the theologians, only a handful of biologists such as Sir Alister Hardy and Rupert Sheldrake have any acquaintance with the literature of psychical research into communication with the departed and out-of-the-body experiences.

Freud

The Freudian wish-fulfilment criticism of the afterlife, sometimes combined with rhetorical calls for Stoic courage in the face of inevitable extinction, has proved influential among a certain class of sophisticated intellectuals who think that they have outgrown infantile religion but have not taken the trouble to delve into the depths of spiritual traditions. The most serious omission from their scheme is that they look only upon the positive side, neglecting the prospect of hell in the afterlife, a much less comforting illusion. Straightforward wish-fulfilment makes no demands on the will or moral energy, while the possibility of having to account for our actions in a post-mortem assessment puts one ethically on the spot. From this angle, it is the wish-fulfilment theory itself which is escapist!

Marxism

The basis of Marxist philosophy is materialist, with the central premise that consciousness is the product of the brain; correspondingly, human beings are products of society. Marx was also an atheist, following in the footsteps of Feuerbach, considering religion a social creation rather than a divine dispensation. At the same time Marx realized that the distress alleviated by religion was genuine:

> Religious distress is at the same time the expression of real distress and the protest against real distress. Religion is the sigh of the oppressed creature, the heart of a heartless world, just as it is the spirit of a spiritless situation. It is the opium of the people.

> The abolition of religion as the illusory happiness of the people is required for their real happiness. The demand to give up the illusions about its condition is the demand to give up a condition which needs illusions. The criticism of religion is therefore in embryo the criticism of the value of woe, the halo of which is religion.

With these words Marx launches into an attack on the metaphysical and divine orders, while acknowledging the psychological value of religion as a compensation for physical tribulations. His fundamental point is that religions have prevented the formation of the kind of social consciousness which insists on transformation of the world, and no longer pins its hopes on what, from a materialist angle, must seem the illusory hope of afterlife rewards. In fact the Christian theodicy was already in trouble by the time that Marx was writing, and the age of revolution arose out of its collapse as a viable plausibility structure for explaining the injustices of life.

Lenin was even more vituperative in his diatribes against religion. 'Marxism is materialism,' he declared. 'As such, it is relentlessly hostile to religion', which must be combated with all available weapons. The chief task of Marxism is the dissemination of atheist views and the extirpation of the deepest root of religion, 'the socially oppressed condition of the working masses'. The pervasive influence of Marxist doctrine has strengthened the already powerful wave of materialist thinking, but there are now signs, expressed by authors like Solzhenitsyn, that the spiritual aspirations of humanity cannot be satisfied by such a creed which turns its back on the deepest realities of spiritual life, entirely reducing the divine and metaphysical orders to the social and physical orders. The next phase of culture may include the transmutation of the Marxist impulse into an eco-spiritual as well as social order; liberation theology may also have a role to play here.

The Loss of a Sense of Purpose and Meaning

One of the seminal works of twentieth-century psychology is Viktor Frankl's *Man's Search for Meaning*, an autobiographical account of the origins of what he calls logotherapy, a response to the consequences of the 'existential vacuum' of human beings adrift in an alien universe. It represents the spiritual bankruptcy of the scientific-materialist world-view. Even proponents of 'positivistic naturalism' like John Gaskin concede that it 'stifles and renders illegitimate any sense of hope or purpose evoked by contemplation of the universe or of any place in it'. He states that the universe is exactly as it appears to be, with 'nothing to hope, nothing to seek for, no quest to be undertaken, no final purpose to be achieved'. The biologist Jacques Monod, like Russell before him, expresses a similar sentiment: 'Man must at last wake out of his millenary dream and discover his total solitude, his fundamental isolation. He must realize that, like a gypsy, he lives on the boundary of an alien world; a world that is deaf to his music, and as indifferent to his hopes as it is to his suffering or his crimes.' If this bleak picture were really the whole story, there would be nothing for it but to brace oneself against the worst, or, like Monod himself, nobly to gather one's ideas together for the creation of a socialist ideal, a pocket of caring in 'the unfeeling immensity of the universe'. Peter Atkins makes it clear, though, in part of a talk entitled 'The Ethics of Purposeless Decay', that there are simply no ethical implications to be derived from such a world-view; 'pragmatically advantageous values', may emerge in the interests of survival, but these are inventions quite devoid of any metaphysical foundation. Logically, as Dostoevsky pointed out, everything is permitted, although no society could last long without an ethical framework of some kind.

If we examine more closely the scientific lens through which such conclusions are seen, we can ascertain that it is a case of 'garbage in, garbage out'. This exploration will take us into the heart of scientific epistemology. Sir Arthur Eddington developed a philosophy, which he called 'selective subjectivism', with the help of a fishing analogy. He imagined an ichthyologist casting for fish in the ocean with a net having two-inch holes. The employment of such a device might lead him to the general conclusions that no sea creatures are less than two inches long, and that they all have gills. Eddington's main point is that the nature of the observer and instruments limit and condition the kind of knowledge which can be acquired. The exclusion of certain ideas and categories automatically limits the range and nature of the explanation which can be given within a particular world-view. We shall now sketch out some of the essential epistemological presuppositions of the view typified by Monod above.

Value-neutrality

Huston Smith suggests that four realms lie beyond scientific method characterized by number, objectivity, prediction and control: ultimate values, purposes, life-meanings and quality. If this is the case, it is hardly surprising that science as it is discovers none of these four themes in its investigations, since they are by definition excluded from consideration. Monod's statement begins to look circular. Value-neutrality itself is an illusion, since it simply means accepting whatever values are prevalent in society at the time, along with their political implications in, for instance, the structure of research funding. Value-neutrality is the equivalent of metaphysics-neutrality and is invalid for the same reason: to state that science is value-neutral is itself a value-judgement. Evelyn Fox Keller has shown how masculine assumptions are built into the very structure of scientific method; and Nicholas Maxwell goes as far as equating value-neutrality with value-blindness. Values are not perceived simply because they are screened out by the lens.

Purposelessness

Galileo was the most influential figure in the shift of attention away from purpose or final causality to cause or efficient causality: the 'why' was now neglected to make way for the 'how'. The rise of mechanical philosophy outlawed final causes, castigating them as 'unscientific'. Teleology became an illegitimate category shunned even by biologists investigating apparently purposeful behaviour! The two categories are not in fact mutually exclusive, but an excessive reaction against the extravagances of medieval metaphysicians frightened scientists off the idea of purpose. It would in fact have been 'unscientific' for Monod to have reached a purposeful conclusion.

Distinction between Primary and Secondary Qualities

This was first coherently formulated by Galileo, and had far-reaching consequences. Primary qualities were seen as inherent in the object and included shape, position, motion and number, they are real and objectively measurable, thus constituting genuine knowledge. Secondary qualities such as taste or feel are subjective and based upon opinion. The Platonic distinction between knowledge and opinion reappears in a new guise to legitimate the measurable and external aspects of reality, relegating consciousness and the inner world to secondary, derivative status. And since meaning is to be found in consciousness, the exclusion of consciousness from the methodological picture also eliminates meaning.

Mechanical Determinism

The study of mechanics by Galileo eventually provided an analogy – the clock – which was extended to the rest of nature. Inanimate objects necessarily followed certain inexorable mathematical laws summarized by Newton. No deviations were possible, since causal laws were held to determine all events that could, given the requisite knowledge, be predicted in advance. At the turn of the century the mind was compared with a machine. Now it is likened to a computer and debates about artificial intelligence are formulated in ways which minimize the differences between the machines and their creators. The irony of such analogies is that human beings explain themselves in terms of their own inventions. Although determinism is now under pressure from quantum mechanics and new approaches to physics in general and biology, the underlying thrust of the search for external determinants continues.

Materialist Reductionism

The power of Occam's razor, or Occam's hatchet (for lopping of inconvenient data) goes back at least as far as Newton, whose first 'Rule of Reasoning in Philosophy' was: 'We are to admit no more causes of natural things as are both true and sufficient to explain their appearances.' The principle of parsimony is implicitly favourable to materialist reductionism, which probably explains its popularity. It is frequently invoked in the philosophy of mind in order to justify a purely physical explanation of consciousness along the lines of the productive theory discussed above, whereby mind is a by-product of brain activity. If one is looking only for physical causes, one will not find any other kind.

Impersonal Objectivity

Similar in a way to value-neutrality, the impersonal objective approach emphasizes accurate and impartial measurements which can be reproduced by others in the scientific community, but it is only one step away from the statement that only what is measurable is real. Moreover, measurement has to be from the outside, thus explaining the 'inner' in terms of the 'outer', the 'secondary' in terms of the 'primary' along the lines of the reductionism just discussed. The most serious limitation of this approach is when it is applied to unique or qualitative events which do not prove amenable to laboratory experimentation.

The foregoing considerations should make it clearer why the methodology of scientific materialism leads to a picture of the universe devoid of purpose, value and meaning. They also complete our survey of the major forces responsible for the decline of the spiritual world-view since the seventeenth century. The final chapter will bring us back to what Arnold Toynbee called the post-rationalist vista, where the enquirer 'faithfully follows experience, wherever this may lead, as his predecessors followed, respectively, revelation and reason'.

CHAPTER NINE

ETHICS, INTERCONNECTEDNESS AND RESPONSIBILITY

———⟫●⟪———

Three kinds of progress are significant for culture: progress in knowledge and technology; progress in the socialization of man; progress in spirituality. The last is the most important.

ALBERT SCHWEITZER

A man to be greatly good must imagine intensely and comprehensively; he must put himself in the place of another and of many others; the pains and pleasures of his species must become his own. The great instrument of moral good is the imagination.

SHELLEY

The first day or so we all pointed to our countries. The third or fourth day we were pointing to our continents. By the fifth day we were aware of only one Earth.

SULTAN BIN SULMAN AL-SAUD, ASTRONAUT

The Apocalyptic Prospect

The Western world is teeming with apocalyptic prophecies foreshadowing the end of the world, or at any rate widespread destruction signaling the demise of the old order and the imminent arrival of a new age. Nostradamus announced an Earth-shattering world war for 1999, while lesser pundits predict ecological cataclysm, population explosion, nuclear devastation and social disintegration. Fundamentalist Christians are convinced that they are the elect who will be saved to found a new civilization, while other sects similarly define themselves as the elite, the creative minority who will somehow survive the full-scale purge and preside over the new order. All this lends a certain urgency to our time, even if days set for the dreaded apocalypse come and go, requiring periodic adjustment. If a man knows he is to be hanged in a fortnight, said Johnson, it concentrates his mind wonderfully. The generalized fear evoked by such a prospect of global collapse is allied to an equally widespread apathy and helplessness, as if the problem is so large and intractable that nothing can be achieved by individual effort; such a feeling of helpless passivity is self-fulfilling, pre-empting effective action and concerted responsibility.

In Kenneth Ring's and Margo Grey's near-death studies, it emerges that some people not only had flash-forwards of future events in their own lives, but caught glimpses of a larger planetary vision. This was experienced during a wider state of consciousness; remarkably, the accounts seem to converge around a general picture, although the overall explanation may well be psychological, archetypal, or a projection of their own NDE on to a global scale. It was also stressed that the patterns were simply probabilities, and that they were by no means inevitable if humanity changed course in the interim. The main features accord with the apocalyptic prospect: earthquakes, volcanic eruptions, geographical and land-mass upheavals, meteorological disruption, food shortages as a result of droughts, economic breakdown, social unrest, the prevalence of new incurable diseases, possible nuclear war and overall natural holocaust. There is some independent support for such predictions, at least in the medium term: increased sunspot activity over the next few years leading to seismic and volcanic disruption; the possible recurrence of drought conditions in the American grain-belt; the raising of global temperature leading to a melting of the ice-caps and a rise in sea-level with consequent flooding in coastal cities; the breakdown of the social order in South America owing to drug-trafficking; the fragility of the world economic system and the problem of third-world indebtedness; and diseases like AIDS which are challenging the capabilities of orthodox medicine.

The context of such breakdown scenarios emerging from the NDE is by no means gloomy, however, with breakthrough occurring in the rubble of the old order. The message is ultimately one of hope, of metanoia replacing paranoia. At a recent seminar, the participants were asked to suggest words which expressed their feelings about world prospects over the next fifteen years. All suggestions fell into the two categories of disintegration or renewal, death or rebirth, breakdown or breakthrough. It is almost as if this archetype is deeply embedded in our collective unconscious, a prior explanation of events to come. Another way of looking at things is suggested by Peter Russell in his *Awakening Earth.* He suggests that humanity is facing an evolutionary test of consciousness in order to determine whether or not we are fit to continue living on the planet. Our ecological and social problems are, for the most part, man-made (the use of the word 'man' is deliberate here) and represent evolutionary selection pressures which we are imposing on ourselves. We actually create the situation from which we will necessarily learn something. Having made the bed, we have no option but to lie in it. The NDE visions introduce a moral and spiritual angle to the process by stressing that humanity has not been living in harmony with natural and spiritual laws, as witnessed by the moral degeneration and social disintegration brought about by materialistic values. The purgation is meant to allow the rise of a new consciousness and values.

Whatever one's feelings about the likelihood of a generalized apocalyptic debacle, one thing is certain: that our bodies will one day die, and that our philosophy of life is intimately related to our philosophy and expectations of death. The Tibetan Buddhist tradition actually makes a practice of meditations on death and impermanence as a spur to spiritual application. The three roots are the inevitability of death, the indefinite nature of the time of death, and the fact that at the time of death nothing but spiritual practice is of any value. The roots are elaborated along with training for a conscious passing through death and the ethico-spiritual aspiration towards the ideal embodied in the Bodhisattva spirit of love, compassion and the wish for enlightenment as a means of benefiting the world.

Thinkers such as Albert Schweitzer, Sir Sarvepalli Radhakrishnan, Arnold Toynbee and C. G. Jung have concurred that nothing short of a worldwide spiritual revolution will suffice to bring about a renewal of civilization. They are equally convinced that the revolution begins and ends with the individual. The challenge is to overcome what Toynbee has called the 'morality gap' between moral pygmies and technological giants, or, as Jung puts it, to realize the dangers of power in the hands of the modern 'technicalized savage'. In his Nobel Prize acceptance speech, Schweitzer expressed similar concern about the discrepancy between knowledge and wisdom. The individual may only be a small part, but part nevertheless of a large whole or system with which there is a constant interaction. Negligible as our individual contributions may seem, they do contribute to the final outcome and constitute a share in the responsibility for our collective future.

Levels of Interconnectedness

The purpose of this section is to sketch out the various different levels of human interconnectedness which constitute the basis of a systems ethic in which the parts are intrinsically and dynamically related to the whole and to each other. After looking at systems theory in general, we shall move on to consider physics, biology, ecology, psychology and finally the spiritual dimension. The same structure will be apparent at each level, perhaps best characterized by Arthur Koestler's notion of the holon, which is at once a whole and a part. One can begin at the molecular level, for instance, and show how individual molecules exist in their own right but equally as part of a cell; then the cell as part of an organ; the organ as part of the body; the body as part of nature and the person part of society; local communities as part of nations, and nations as parts of the world; the Earth as a whole but part of the solar system; the solar system as a whole but part of the galaxy, and so on. Each holon, according to Koestler, lives in dynamic equilibrium with the whole and has two polar tendencies: self-assertion as the dynamic expression of its wholeness, and integration as a manifestation of its partness. Exaggerated self-assertion might be characterized as aggressive or anarchic, while the opposite tendency would culminate in submission and obedience. The ideal is harmony between the two, adapted to circumstances. The basic conception is organic rather than mechanical in nature, assuming the possibility of creative human action beyond simple stimulus/response.

General Living Systems Theory

Much of the early theoretical work in this field was done by Ludwig von Bertalanffy, reaching a classic statement in a book by J. G. Miller. The first distinction to draw is between an open and a closed system, the former interacting and exchanging with its environment, while the latter is self-contained. As human beings we are open systems as regards our bodies, but also in social, cultural, artistic, intellectual, emotional and other terms, since we interact, influence and are influenced by the various milieux in which we operate. Examples would include food, air, conversation, art, books and so on. Systems are integrated wholes with properties that cannot simply be reduced to those of the parts, as expressed in the adage that the whole is greater than the sum of its parts. They are also dynamic, and can only be fully understood through the processes which go on within and outside; in other words a knowledge of the structure would not be an adequate guide to these inner and outer processes. Within and between systems there exists an order based on the organization of the dynamic processes, which tend to be self-regulating, thus exhibiting the balance of homeostasis. As a result of the foregoing properties of systems, the emphasis lies on the nature of the interconnections and interdependence of all phenomena within a given system, the parts affecting each other through their involvement and mutual feedback in the context of the whole.

Physics

> The universe does not exist 'out there', independent of us. We are inescapably involved in bringing about that which appears to be happening. We are not only observers. We are participators. In some strange sense this is a participatory universe.

> JOHN ARCHIBALD WHEELER

The inseparability of the observer from the observation has been accepted since the 1930s as a result of advances in quantum physics. Fritjof Capra suggests that the world of modern physics has to be pictured as 'one indivisible, dynamic whole whose parts are essentially interrelated and can be understood only as patterns of a cosmic process'. He quotes Heisenberg as describing the world as 'a complicated tissue of events, in which connections of different kinds alternate or overlap or combine and thereby determine the texture of the whole'. Geoffrey Chew's bootstrap approach to the subject stresses the self-consistency of the overall pattern, including consciousness as a necessary part of the whole. He rejects the idea of the fundamental building of the correspondence theory of truth, preferring the internal consistency of the coherence theory. His vision of future science is that of 'an interconnected network of mutually consistent models, each of them being limited and approximate and one of them being based on firm foundations'. This is systems theory applied both within and between scientific disciplines.

Probably the most penetrating current insights into the philosophy of physics are coming from David Bohm, whose categories of implicate and explicate order may eventually become as commonly known as Jung's extraversion and introversion. Bohm is acutely aware of the importance of world-views in shaping our ideas of reality, and diagnoses a current widespread fragmentation of approach which leads to a sense of separateness, alienation and meaninglessness. He even goes as far as equating meaning and being, so that a change of meaning becomes a change of being. If being and knowledge are inseparable, the mode of being or state of consciousness will determine the mode of knowing, which in turn makes up the content of consciousness. Thus the quality and content of consciousness actually constitute the meaning of a person's life or outlook. A world-view which fragments reality necessarily disconnects people from their context and leads directly to a lack of meaning. Conversely, a world-view which connects life, matter and consciousness to an underlying process reinstates the sense of meaning and over-comes fragmentation.

For Bohm the new insight or theory (or way of looking at things) is characterized as 'Undivided Wholeness in Flowing Movement'. The parts are abstracted from and manifest out of this prior wholeness or flux. In the non-manifest reality of the implicate (literally 'enfolded') order, all is interpenetrating and interconnected, while the function of the explicate ('unfolded') order is to display phenomena separately and unconnected. If one did not know better, it would be easy to take the separateness as ultimate, thus falling into the *avidya* or *maya* in the Hindu tradition. Fragmented mechanical perception concentrates on the isolated parts at the expense of their context, while Bohm regards parts are relatively autonomous subtotalities within the whole. This language has much in common with Koestler's holons, stressing autonomy and its limitations. Matter, life and consciousness arise in the implicate order precisely as such relatively autonomous subtotalities, like waves on the ocean. They have individual form but are embedded in the whole. And if matter is a condensation in the physical field, self-consciousness can be seen as a condensation/limitation/form in the field of Being or cosmic consciousness. We shall return to this theme when we discuss the spiritual dimension.

Biology

Orthodox biologists, subscribers to the 'central dogma' of neo-Darwinism, usually describe themselves as mechanists, and imagine that their ancient enemies the vitalists (those who believe in some kind of animating life-force) have been eliminated. Yet a dissident school of biology is alive and well, one which takes a dim view of the inherent limitations of a mechanistic approach to living organisms. Among its most influential figures are Gregory Bateson and Rupert Sheldrake. Bateson, according to Capra, was always searching for 'patterns behind patterns and processes beneath structures', a shift of focus from objects to relationships. He saw the structure of mind and nature as reflections of each other – a 'necessary unity', with mind as a systems phenomenon characteristic of life, 'the essence of being alive', the principle of self-organization.

In discussing the philosophy of organism, Sheldrake notes that the very organizing principles must themselves have evolved, while taking as read the hierarchical nature of living systems. The basis of his idea of morphic resonance implies a dynamic feedback and interaction between individual members of a species or particular types of behaviour over time. Without the underlying connection of form, morphic resonance (the influence of like upon like, of one pattern of behaviour or order on another across time and space) simply could not operate. Individual forms arise in and affect the morphogenetic field, itself stabilized through the cumulative contributions of past organisms.

Two more points deserve mention before we leave the biological realm: the role of symbiosis in nature, and the philosophy of healing. Symbiotic relationships represent a co-operation between two organisms for mutual benefit, a creative interdependence in contrast with the destructive interconnectedness of dysbiosis or mutual antagonism. Another related notion is that of synergy, whereby individual elements in a system spontaneously work together for the harmony and good of the whole. This natural homeostatic tendency of the physical body could also be extended by analogy (even if not always in practice) to the body politic. Without an energetic connection between healer and healee, no healing could occur; and healing only makes sense within a holistic framework of interconnectedness with an inherent and dynamic tendency to re-establish order within a system. The healing power is said to flow through the system of the healer in order to encourage the self-healing capacity in the healee. Dora Kunz refers to illness as a disharmony in the organizing patterns of the body, while the healing energy has the features of order, wholeness and compassion and thus brings about a new dynamic harmony within the system. Healer and healee are simply channels of the energy which heals and makes the wholeness.

Ecology

The 'Gaia hypothesis', a term coined by Jim Lovelock (with the help of novelist William Golding) in the late 1970s, treats the entire range of living matter on the Earth as a 'single living entity, capable of manipulating the Earth's atmosphere to suit its overall needs and endowed with faculties and powers far beyond those of its constituent parts'. A more precise definition of Gaia is as a complex entity 'involving the Earth's biosphere, oceans and soil'. The totality constitutes 'a feedback or cybernetic system which seeks an optimal physical and chemical environment for life on this planet'. A further implication of the basis hypothesis emerges from Lovelock's latest study, namely the impossibility of completely separating organism from environment: 'the evolution of the species and the evolution of their environment are tightly coupled together as a single and inseparable process'.

The hypothesis is an application of systems theory analysis and more especially of cybernetics, which is concerned with 'self-regulating systems of communication and control in living organisms and machines'. The number of variables in the Gaia system is beyond computation, but each participates inter-dependently in the whole. This interdependence has become all the clearer since the effects of acid rain have been felt, and nuclear pollution from Chernobyl has been detected so far from its source; these examples demonstrate the impact of the human species on the environment, effects which deeply concern Lovelock.

The systems approach has also been applied to new thinking in economics, one of the premises of which is the recognition that the economic system is embedded in the ecological, and that long-term environmental effects must be accounted for. The economic and financial system is made up of interacting human beings and organizations: repercussions in one area or city are transmitted round the world with lightening speed, and stock markets are now so closely tied that a jitter in one centre ripples right round the world and feeds back into its originator. Likewise, the massive destructive power of nuclear weapons, not to mention the environmental consequences of nuclear holocaust, has fostered a sense of an interdependent world. A recent book compiled jointly by Soviet and American scholars and aptly titled *Breakthrough* makes interdependence a central theme. Anatoly Gromyko, for instance, asserts that genuine security in the nuclear age can only be universal international security: 'In a world of nuclear overkill and growing interdependence, it is impossible to secure a unilateral advantage for oneself to the detriment of the other side without ultimately impairing one's own interests.' Finally, in the philosophical field, we are seeing the birth of eco-philosophy as a comprehensive global approach which is environmentally sensitive.

Psychology

The work of C. G. Jung has given us the concept of the collective unconscious, distinguished from the personal unconscious by the fact that its contents have not been acquired through personal experience. It is 'of a collective, universal and impersonal nature which is identical in all individuals'. Archetypes are definite forms in the psyche which are omnipresent and which mediate the mythological motifs and 'categories of the imagination'; thus similar myths and legends arise spontaneously in different parts of the world without ever having been incorporated in the personal unconscious. It is as if there is a deep shared level of consciousness from which archetypes arise, or of which archetypes are the outer expression. Our waking consciousness floats on an ocean of consciousness which connects us.

Jung also contributed to the correction of an overemphasis on masculine values and modes of perception by drawing attention to the feminine within each human being and through his study and popularization of Chinese thought such as the 'I Ching'. Some of his followers such as Edward Whitmont have continued and extended this work into an analysis of the goddess principle, while writers such as Capra have diagnosed an excess of Yang in our culture and pointed out links between feminism, ecology and spirituality. For our purposes the key insight is the importance of receptivity and relatedness for a culture which has uprooted itself from nature and divorced itself from the feminine principle. This rootless loss of relatedness, as I pointed out in discussing David Bohm above, has led to a sense of alienation and isolation, where the part is abstracted from its participation in the whole system. The degree to which our Western science is underpinned by masculine values and attitudes is only now becoming apparent as scholars reassess the scientific method.

The Spiritual Dimension

It has become fashionable to draw comparisons between science and mysticism, some of which are facile and do justice to neither. Ken Wilber has indicated that it is worth discriminating between what he calls subscendence and transcendence. The former term is used with respect to the underlying unity of the world of physics, while he uses the latter to refer to the unity perceived by the mystics and which is of a different order. It is, however, valid to compare scientific and mystical themes from a systems angle, as Capra does when he asserts that the study of living and non-living matter points to insights repeatedly emphasized by mystics: 'the universal interconnectedness and interdependence of all phenomena, and the intrinsically dynamic nature of reality'.

David Bohm argues that the difference between ordinary and mystical experience is one of degree rather than kind: mystical experience enters more deeply into the interconnected and dynamic unity of the implicate order. He sees mystical experience as a 'heightening, and intensification, a deepening of something they participate in'. If this represents a deeper level of reality, it is possible to say that it is actually obscured by our normal waking consciousness. As suggested by Blake, a cleansing of the senses would reveal phenomena in their infinite dimension, seeing *through* the sensory world as opposed to looking *at* it; this sensory world therefore becomes transparent as a deeper (or higher) level is revealed. Thereafter even sensory reality is seen in a new light.

These considerations bring us back to the threads woven in the chapters on near-death experiences and unitive consciousness. As Capra points out above, the key terms are interconnectedness and interdependence within the unity of a dynamic system. If we apply this systems view to divine and metaphysical orders, the following picture emerges:

1. There is one Field of Consciousness in which we live and move and have our being.

2. Within this Field we are holons (relatively autonomous subtotalities), or thinking, feeling and willing beings.

3. Although we are inseparable from the Field, which constitutes our underlying identity as revealed in unitive consciousness, we are nevertheless distinct in form and may have the sensory illusion that we are in fact quite independent.

4. We act on and in the Field in such a way that the results of our thinking, feeling and willing return to us in a dynamic feedback loop.

5. The interconnectedness and interdependence within the Field are the ultimate context of our moral responsibility. The Field is not mocked.

6. The dynamics of the Field are such that they elicit Love, which is Its essential nature. The feedback of loving thoughts and actions in love and joy, while hatred and bitterness breed isolation and sorrow. Each feedback constitutes a lesson in learning the art of loving and realizing the inescapability of our interconnectedness as illustrated in the reciprocity of the Golden Rule.

These points will be expanded on in the rest of the chapter.

Towards a Living Ethic

Metaphysics and Ethics

Since the soul is clearly immortal, it can have no escape or security from evil except by becoming as good and wise as it possibly can.

SOCRATES

Socrates and Plato urge the closest possible links between the metaphysical and moral orders, as is traditional in the spiritual world-view.

We saw in Chapter 7 how these links have been severed for many people with the rise of the materialistic philosophy which denies the possibility of consciousness continuing beyond the grave. Such a view implies that there can be no metaphysical consequences or sanctions, so that all redress is the responsibility of the social order in this lifetime. It is all too apparent that many crimes go undetected and therefore unpunished; not to mention the hurts we inflict on each other in private which make up our unfinished emotional business. At all levels, then, it would be impossible to argue that the scores are even, that the seeds sown have been fully harvested.

It was the inconclusive nature of human affairs and justice that led many thinkers, including Kant, to formulate the moral argument for immortality: it is an outrage to the moral senses that there should be no ultimate redress or compensation for injustice, therefore such redress and compensation must be assumed to take place in the post-mortem metaphysical dimension. The other two postulates which complete the picture are God as the guarantor of justice, and freedom, without which no responsible moral choice can be made. The argument has failed to impress many philosophers, while in theology it occasionally appears in disguise as the proposition that God could not possibly extinguish such a fine creation as an individual human being who has only just begun to realize his or her inherent potential. Both arguments require a metaphysical order so as to complete a process begun in the physical order; similarly, they are *a priori* intuitions which are not empirically grounded in experience. Another line of attack would regard them as infantile wish-fulfilments, usually adding that one can hardly expect an indifferent universe to take notice of human moral sensibilities.

But is this the final word, the whole picture? Not if we take the data of the life-review seriously. The experiencing of events from another person's point of view provides a framework of moral order which is a sanction in the metaphysical order of the kind postulated by Kant; furthermore, it is not so much a moral intuition as an insight derived from human experience and therefore empirically grounded. The only question, unanswerable until we ourselves pass through death, is whether such an experience is universal. It would be strange if it were not so, given the need we all have to learn and arrive at a truer and wider perspective of our life-experience.

Traditional Christian eschatology, with its picture of death, sleep, resurrection, judgement and definitive consignment to heaven or hell, appeals to fewer and fewer contemporaries. The majority, if they give the matter any thought at all, probably assume that consciousness is extinguished at brain-death. As such, this scenario enables people to escape any ultimate responsibility for their actions; they are only accountable for as long as physical life lasts. The data examined in Chapters 1 and 2, however, imply that memories are retained, and puts us morally right on the spot: we are able, through empathetic resonance, to experience events from other points of view. The old metaphysical order may be out of date, but a new picture can be constructed through an understanding of the processes of human consciousness around and immediately after bodily death. The basic postulates of such a reconstructed metaphysical order are the overall unity of the Field in which we exist, our interconnection and interdependence within this Field, and empathetic resonance which mediates our conscious connections. In so doing, it illustrates the scope of our responsibility to each other.

Reverence for Life and Ethical Mysticism

The name Albert Schweitzer is synonymous for many with the dedication of a Western doctor in tropical Africa. Fewer people know his playing of Bach's organ works; fewer still about his contributions to theology, and scarcely anyone about his work in ethics, philosophy and comparative religion. Yet his whole life was of a piece, each aspect shedding light on the others. What concerns us specifically in this context is his ethical thought and its relation to mysticism.

The insight into his principle of reverence for life (*Ehrfurcht vor dem Leben*) arose in the unlikely context of a boat trip through a herd of hippopotami at sunset. It was the key he had long sought, the 'path through the thicket', an idea which implied world - and life - affirmation (not denial as in Indian thought) and ethics together. His fullest description of the principle uses an analogy: 'just as white light consists of coloured rays, so reverence for life contains all the components of ethics: love, kindliness, sympathy, empathy, peacefulness, power to forgive.'

Schweitzer's *cogito* is 'I am will-to-live, in the midst of life which wills to live.' In looking around the world, though, it is apparent that competition between the various life-forms cannot in itself form the basis of an ethic: 'The world is horror in splendour, meaninglessness in meaning, sorrow in joy', what Schweitzer calls 'the enigmatic contradiction in the will to live'. It is only human beings who are fully capable of rising above the fray, of 'achieving knowledge of shared experience and compassion, of transcending the ignorance in which the rest of creation pines'. Then, as thinking beings, humans can attempt to extend to every will-to-live the same reverence for life accorded to their own. Thus good consists in preserving and promoting life, raising it to its highest level of development; while evil is destruction, injury or repression of life which is capable of development. The consequence of such an attitude is an ever-widening sphere of responsibility, to include animals and plants as well as humans. All life is sacred, and decisions to favour one kind over another are made under pressure of necessity. As an example, Schweitzer cites his own experience of having to decide to kill fish for a young fish-eagle: the choice and responsibility are his, using the yardstick of empathetic concern.

In his study of Indian thought Schweitzer became aware of the non-equivalence of spirituality and ethics. He saw that mysticism tends to become supra-ethical in its cultivation of consciousness through meditation practices. In spite of this tension between mysticism and ethics, Schweitzer felt the need to reconcile the two at the deepest level: 'All profound philosophy, all deep religion, is ultimately a struggle for ethical mysticism and mystical ethics.' Mysticism is the calyx of the flower, while ethics itself is the flower. The mysticism of ethics takes place in devotion to other manifestations of the same Being. By entering into relationship as one manifestation of infinite Being with another such manifestation, one is entering into relationship with that Being which is God. Thus the ethic of self-devotion is at the same time an ethic of self-perfection: through loving service to others we are perfecting ourselves. In this way reverence for life leads to devotion to live which in turn implies a path to self-perfection and union with the divine Being behind all manifest life-forms. Responsibility knows no limits. In practical terms Schweitzer concludes that 'Whenever my life devotes itself in any way to life, my finite will-to-live experiences union with the infinite will in which all life is one, and I enjoy a feeling of refreshment which prevents me from pining away in the desert of life.' His own life was a powerful witness to this ethical mysticism of reverence for life, and proved an inspiration to UN Secretary-General Dag Hammarskjöld, among others, in combining a deep inwardness with active public service.

We can see that Schweitzer's scheme is at once an ecological and systems ethic which overcomes the polarities of contemplation and action by rooting action in an attitude of self-devotion and self-perfection. He considers the nature of the dynamic parts within the whole and perceives the harmony and synergy of the parts working for each other and thus for the good of the whole. The feedback loops will reinforce the qualities expressed in the actions, especially since our own fulfil-ment is aligned with our most creative contribution to the welfare of others. The division between self and not-self is gradually overcome through a deepening appreciation of self-fulfilment as self-devotion and self-perfection.

There is a reciprocity implied in the Golden Rule, whether expressed positively as doing to others as you would be done by or negatively as avoiding treating others in ways that you yourself would find hurtful. When the Golden Rule is understood within the context of an under-lying unity of Being, as in Schweitzer or the *Bhagavad Gita* (discussed earlier), its logic becomes inescapable: in benefiting others you benefit yourself and in harming others you harm yourself. This may not be im-mediately apparent, but seems to be fully revealed in the life-review, if not before. The great illusion of the explicate order is that we are sepa-rate consciousnesses who do not affect each other directly. Sometimes feedback is instant, while on other occasions we may not experience it for a long time. Schweitzer's scheme provides another framework of understanding for the reciprocal operation of the Golden Rule.

The reciprocity of reverence for life can be practised on many levels and either as avoidance of the negative or performance of the positive. If one takes as an example the injunction not to kill, this can be applied at different levels of the food chain – most West-erners do not extend it to animals apart from dogs and cats; then comes the question of capital punishment and distinctions between civilian murder and warfare – where does one draw the line? At an-other level it can refer to Gaia herself – the foolish shortsightedness of destroying the eco-system on which we and our descendants de-pend; and at the ultimate level it can be applied to the 'death of God' by severing our inner connection in an act of spiritual suicide. The truly ethical person would avoid inflicting unnecessary suffering on any sentient creature.

The positive expression of reverence for life is in love, compassion, empathy and forgiveness. The word love requires some elaboration in this context. Martin Luther King said that when he spoke of love 'I am not speaking of some sentimental and weak response. I am speaking of that force which all the great religions have seen as the supreme unify-ing principle of life. Love is somehow the key which unlocks the door which leads to ultimate reality.' Schweitzer himself stated that the eth-ic of reverence for life was the ethic of love widened into universality. It goes beyond the love of the neighbour to love and devotion to the whole of creation, which it recognizes as embodiments of the divine. The love of God is expressed not only in and of itself, but also towards the individual forms.

For Peter Deunov love can be analysed at four levels which represent the whole cycle of human evolution.

1. 'Aspiration in the heart', the love of ordinary family members for each other.
2. 'Feeling in the soul', the fraternal feeling between friends.
3. 'Force in the mind', present in those who are ready to live for and defend a divine cause, whatever the cost to themselves. There is a certain charisma in such people as King, Gandhi or Schweitzer, whose words carry precisely this force.
4. 'Principle in the spirit,' an all-embracing and ordering harmony which Deunov says is hardly perceptible as yet, but which is the closest link to divine perfection and fills life with meaning.

The first two stages, symbolically the root and the branch, are human, and the last two, flower and fruit, are divine. The devotion of reverence for life goes beyond sentiment and even fraternity, reaching into the energetic force which alone truly inspires transformation. The influence and example of saints and sages who have sacrificed themselves for a divine cause reverberates through time, creating a resonance of hope and inspiration to follow in their footsteps with our own small gift to the great work of the whole. The ethic of reverence for life, like the ethic of love, awaits the time when a sufficient number of human beings are ready to put it into practice. Some are ready now, while for others it is still a distant and therefore unrealistic prospect.

The Expansion of Consciousness and Ethics

A human being is part of the whole, called by us the 'Universe', a part limited in time and space. He experiences himself, his thoughts and feelings, as something separate from the rest – a kind of optical delusion of his consciousness. This delusion is a kind of prison for us, restricting us to our personal desires and to affection for a few persons nearest to us. Our task must be to free ourselves from this prison by widening our circle of compassion to embrace all living creatures and the whole of nature in its beauty.

ALBERT EINSTEIN

In English we have separate words for consciousness and conscience, and yet they derive from the same root meaning 'to know with'. If consciousness mediates knowledge, then so does conscience, but in a different way. There are many interpretations of the word, from the Freudian superego to the voice of God within, but all recognize the potential for an inner dialogue in the making of hard decisions. The link between consciousness and conscience is that between knowledge and ethics. It is through consciousness that we have a sense of meaning and identity, which may be more or less wide and comprehensive depending on our angle of vision. If we restrict ourselves to our material identity, we can only speak in terms of the physical and social orders. As soon as we postulate ourselves as souls, we have entered the metaphysical order and widened our sense of identity accordingly. We can then move on into the divine order of the imperishable spirit and recognize our essence as an individual spark or droplet in the ocean of divine Being. We can picture these identities as a series of concentric spheres: on one model the divine seed would be in the centre and the other levels around it; while, conversely, we could picture the divine spirit level as containing the other narrower identities. If we put the images together we have the Aristotelian definition of God as a sphere whose centre is everywhere and circumference nowhere.

Expanding Consciousness

Beyond a certain stage the evolution of consciousness can be equated with its expansion, but consciousness first has to individualize before it can begin to expand. We know from the work of Jean Piaget, Erich Neumann and Ken Wilber that there are discernible patterns in the development of self-consciousness and of the corresponding social attitudes. We can usefully use Peter Deunov's scheme to illustrate the general picture.

The first stage shows a lack of differentiation between the individual and the group, corresponding to infants not sharply distinguishing inner and outer, self and other; we can call it primitive collective consciousness. The next stage is individual self-consciousness which has distinguished itself as a separate identity; socially we see the rise of private property, demands for individual rights and freedom, the growth of individual conscience, and the growing prevalence of participatory democracy. At stage three – collective consciousness – there is once more an awareness of the group and of the relationship of the part to the whole. There is a danger of stopping the process at this point and becoming fixated on one's identity as a member of a group or movement. Neumann calls this recollectivization, while Reinhold Niebuhr demonstrates how individual altruism can be sublimated into an expression of collective national egotism. Arthur Koestler pursues this line even further when he examines the pernicious effects of the individual's integrative tendency in its pathological form. The three factors he cites are 'submission to the authority of a father-substitute; unqualified identification with a social group; uncritical acceptance of its belief-system'. In terms of our previous categories, the individual's sense of self-identity merges with the group as a subset of the social order: social or group identity becomes central and as such forms a substitute for the deeper metaphysical and divine levels. Moreover, such absolute allegiance encourages the individual towards fanaticism and inhuman treatment of those outside the group.

We have dwelt on the perversion of collective consciousness in order to show how development can be arrested at certain stages. The same could be said of those whose self-assertive tendencies fixate them at the individual consciousness level. These both point towards their synthesis and transcendence in the unfolding of what Deunov calls cosmic consciousness, which we have already encountered in descriptions of mystical experience. In this sense mystics are in the vanguard of the expansion of human consciousness: their present experience is the future for those at earlier stages of the process. The ultimate divine cosmic consciousness is likened to a magnet drawing all towards the convergence of what Teilhard de Chardin would call the Omega Point. The outward manifestation of cosmic consciousness – seeing the sacredness of creation in the organic unity of the whole – would be the kingdom of heaven, with love as 'a principle in the spirit' operating through mutual co-operation. Contact with immanent divine love through meditation, prayer, contemplation and centred awareness is the inner link. It is clear that only a handful of human beings have attained cosmic consciousness, but it nevertheless gives us a sense of orientation and a logical picture of the whole process of the expansion of consciousness, wherever we happen to be on the ladder. Only when love rules in the human heart as a principle will harmony reign in the outer world; there can be no kingdom of heaven on Earth without it first existing within us.

Psychology and Moral Development

From delusion lead me to Truth From darkness lead me to Light. From death lead me to Immortality.

BRIHADARANYAKA UPANISHAD

The spiritual path is often likened to a journey from darkness to light and from delusion (*maya*) to truth (*vidya*); also from bondage to freedom, and from indifference to compassion. These processes are parallel in such a way that advance in one area is reflected in corresponding progress in another towards the B-values described by Maslow as encountered in the NDE: love, wisdom, peace, beauty, joy. The well-known prayer of St Francis asks to be able to transform a negative into a positive such as sorrow into joy, hatred into love, despair into hope. When viewed through the lens of the expansion of consciousness it is possible to discern the web of connections: enhanced wisdom and insight implies increased freedom as we become aware of limiting patterns of behaviour; when we see these in ourselves and others, we learn compassion and forgiveness, enlarging our sympathies in the process. Paradoxically, though, wisdom brings with it the desire to be of service and to fulfil the will of God. From the outer point of view it may appear that freedom is being curtailed, but the person is actually becoming free inwardly as the realization dawns that the ordinary conception of free will amounts to little more than giving a free rein to desires and appetites. True freedom is inner independence from unconscious drives and outward circumstances.

Most philosophical debates about free will simply omit the psychological dimension unearthed by the inner pioneers of the early part of the century. Ethical discussions pay scant attention to the role of the unconscious and the necessary correlation between the processes of psychological integration and ethical maturity. The most significant work in this area has been the fruit of the Jungian tradition with its psychology of individuation and growth towards a wholeness in which the opposites are not ignored or repressed but reconciled. Alongside and independently has grown the study of moral development, which is able to arrive at certain broad cross-cultural patterns. In the following section I will use the insights of both approaches in the treatment of our theme of the expansion of consciousness and ethics.

I have already referred to the predominance of masculine values in modern Western culture; a similar statement can be made about the acknowledgement of the conscious side of our nature and the repression of the shadow aspect. Such repression, though, does not make the shadow go away. It is just displaced or projected outward on to something or someone else. The classic illustration of this split is the scapegoat or Lamb of God that carries the sins of the world: the evil within oneself or one's group is denied and perceived as outside. We find the development of the so-called 'enemy-image' so prominent in superpower relations until quite recently. For the USA, the USSR was the evil empire, while the USSR saw itself equally under threat from US 'imperialist expansionism'. Once they take hold, these attitudes are extremely hard to break, since every move is interpreted according to the enemy-image: thus an apparently constructive move can be dismissed as propaganda or deception, while the same initiative on one's own part is a gesture of genuine goodwill which the enemy will naturally misrepresent – after all, they cannot be trusted ... The central message of Erich Neumann's *Depth Psychology and a New Ethic* is the need for individuals to work through their own moral problems arising from the unconscious before they are in a position to play a responsible role in the collective. They will otherwise be subject to zealous fanaticism with its one-sided premise that their own group is absolutely right, and that their views must be imposed on others, if need be by force.

For Neumann the old ethic, which fails to take into consideration the tendencies and effect of the unconscious, is at best only partial; it 'accepts no responsibility for the unconscious actions of the group or the collective', such as outbreaks of fanatical nationalism. The aim of the new ethic is 'the achievement of wholeness', a state in which the 'purposive directedness of ego-consciousness is not undermined by the opposite tendencies of unconscious contents of which the ego and the conscious mind are entirely unaware'. For example the Christian religion of love cannot then be perverted into the cruel persecutions of the Inquisition. Neumann's formulation of values echoes in some respects that of Schweitzer: 'Whatever leads to wholeness is "good"; whatever leads to splitting is "evil". Integration is good, disintegration is evil. Life, constructive tendencies and integration are on the side of good; death, splitting and disintegration are on the side of evil.' Lest Neumann be accused of naïvety, he adds that modern people are aware of the indissoluble interdependence of the two principles, although processes of integration predominate: death may precede birth, disintegration may come before integration, and destruction before creation.

Some of the most important contributions to the philosophy of moral development have come from Lawrence Kohlberg, whose analysis I shall use here in order to discuss the various stages involved. Kohlberg distinguishes six stages of moral development and posits a seventh. His research has enabled him to establish a 'universal moral form successively emerging in development and centring on principles of justice'.

He therefore argues against relativism on the basis of the universal scope of his observations. Briefly, these are the stages.

> Stage 1: Punishment and obedience. Literal obedience to rules and authority, and the prudent attempt to avoid punishment.

> Stage 2: Individual instrumental purpose and exchange. Motivation is the desire for reward or benefit and may entail making deals in terms of fair exchange. Each pursues their own interest.

> Stage 3: Interpersonal conformity. The 'desire to meet the expectations of one's community and to do what is necessary to maintain relationships of affection and trust'. Following rules so as not to rock the boat.

> Stage 4: Social system and conscience maintenance. The social system is maintained by doing one's duty and upholding social standards, thus ensuring the coherence and continuity of the group.

> Stage 5: Prior rights and social contract. The recognition of the universal human rights of individuals and thus of respect for others and self-respect.

> Stage 6: Universal ethical principles. Such principles to be followed by all humanity, as for instance in Kant's moral imperative of treating people as ends in themselves and not as means.

Kohlberg characterizes the first two stages as preconventional, the next two as conventional and the final two as post-conventional or principled. There are trends from heteronomy towards autonomy, from egotism towards altruism, from the outer authority of communally approved law towards the inner authority of individual conscience based on ethical principles. The civil disobedience of Martin Luther King is quoted as an example of Stage 6 morality superseding as it did the social expectations of Stages 3 and 4, as well as the legalistic framework of Stage 5. King regarded it as his moral responsibility to obey just laws and disobey unjust laws 'openly, lovingly, and with a willingness to accept the consequences'. He defines an unjust law as one which degrades human personality and is not rooted in eternal law and natural law. As Kohlberg points out, King is straying into the metaphysical order by invoking eternal law and hinting at 'a parallelism between our consciousness of moral law and the nature of ultimate reality'.

This last remark leads us into a consideration of a possible seventh state rooted in a cosmic perspective which embraces all the preceding levels. The need for a seventh stage is indicated by the fact that 'universal ethical principles cannot be ... immediately justified by the realities of the human social order.' Kohlberg suggests that initiation into Stage 7 begins with a despair about the meaning of life which is resolved by adoption of and identification with the cosmic or infinite perspective: from the crisis of the dark night of the soul to the illumination of unitive consciousness. He goes on to maintain that the essence of a religious orientation lies in 'a sense of connectedness between the individual mind and heart and the larger cosmic whole or order which they call almost equally readily God, Nature, Life or ultimate reality'. Then, crucially, he adds: 'This sense of connectedness supports and inspires ... ethical action towards other human beings.' Put in quasi-Schweitzerian terms we could say that connectedness to life results in devotion to life.

As examples of Stage 7 moral thinking Kohlberg considers Spinoza and Teilhard de Chardin. Teilhard's presentation of seeing and vision goes right to the heart of the matter:

Seeing – we might say that the whole of life lies in that verb – if not ultimately at least essentially. Fuller being in closer union: such is the kernel and conclusion of this book. But let us emphasize the point: union increases only through an increase in consciousness; that is to say, in vision. And that, doubtless, is why the history of the living world can be summarized as the elaboration of ever more perfect eyes within a cosmos in which there is always something more to be seen.

The key words are seeing, vision, being, union and consciousness. The increase or expansion of consciousness is a widening of vision and a concomitant intensification of being and of the sense of unity. As Kohlberg rightly remarks, mystical experience assumes an underlying substance or ground of being in which all life and consciousness participates; and 'intuition of this ground of being transcends the duality of subject and object; it involves a sense of union between the knower and the known.' The boundaries of the holon within the Field are expanded to the dimensions of the Field itself; life and self are seen and experienced from the cosmic perspective; yet there is no loss of sense of self and reality, but rather an enhancement. Unitive vision increases proportionately with expanded consciousness; and, returning to our earlier points, freedom and compassion are likewise extended. The moral order finds its ultimate ground in actual experience of union with the divine order. The yearning for harmony is fulfilled in the experiential fusion of facts and values. For the mystic, the 'ought' is simply harmony with the 'is' of the divine order. Having tasted the plenitude of love, wisdom, beauty, peace and joy, how could they settle for less than attempting to carry these qualities in their consciousness and infuse them into their actions? This is the same spiritual impulse as that noted in the aftermath of the NDE.

The ethics of reverence for life, along with the application of love as a force in the mind, are also Stage 7 moral thinking, based as they are on the insight of interconnectedness within the whole or Field, and devotion to the forms of will-to-live which are equally manifestations of that same whole. An identical structure and process informs the life-review and the phenomenon of empathetic resonance: it is not ultimately possible to separate ourselves from other life-forms contained within the same Field, so that devotion to other forms is beneficial to oneself and the whole. The win-lose option is ruled out by the very nature of interconnectedness; only lose-lose and win-win remain, and the dynamics of the game eventually persuade us to harmonize with our own real best interests; these in turn can only be the best interests of the whole system.

Education

If the above account of the moral dynamics and metaphysical context of human life is even approximately correct, it has some far-reaching educational implications. The underlying assumptions of any educational system can only be those of the social order, which today is predominately secular. The keynotes are intellectual development and, to a lesser degree, a strengthening of the will in order to enable children to compete in the jungle conditions of the rat-race. Inner emotional, psychological and spiritual training are not priorities in a culture devoted to material acquisition at the expense of the cultivation of ethical sensitivity. The core (literally and ironically 'heart') curriculum stresses the necessary technical skills without giving children much insight into the nature and purpose of life, and the part that they might play in fulfilling themselves and the deepest aspirations of humanity towards a world of abundance, health and harmony. The following are some preliminary suggestions for a revised approach which does not neglect the strengths of the present set-up, but proposes some complementary themes:

1. The need to place human beings in a systems context of interconnectedness and responsibility at the biological, ecological, social, psychological and spiritual levels.

2. The need for children to see themselves primarily as citizens of the Earth and only secondarily as members of separate nationalities.

3. The need for a course in comparative world-views, both historical and contemporary, in order to foster mutual tolerance and understanding.

4. The need to understand a minimum of modern psychology, especially in the areas of masculine and feminine qualities within each person, and of the hazards of projecting enemy-images on to each other.

5. The need for each of us to learn ways of acquiring inner peace as a result of silence and meditation.

6. The need to cultivate a sense of beauty which stimulates the imagination and sympathies.

7. The need to understand the nature of physical, emotional, social, mental and spiritual health and the ways in which we can contribute responsibly to the maintenance of the requisite dynamic balance within our physical systems.

8. The need to learn of the power as well as the hazards of practical idealism in order to avoid on the one hand self-defeating fanaticism and on the other sinking into helpless apathy. The power of an ideal lies in its ability to co-ordinate our energies.

9. The need to study in depth the nature of love in its widest sense, and to work out how kindness, trust and co-operation can best be

fostered in the attempt to create a maximum of synergy within the world system.

10. The need to recognize the crucial importance of individual contributions through the study of the lives of remarkable men and women who continue to inspire us.

11. The need to develop a personal sense of moral responsibility within the context of our interconnectedness and interdependence, extending this on the principle of reverence for life.

The Power of Creative Thought

Complementary medicine is beginning to appreciate the power of creative visualization in activating the inner self-healing capacities of those with psychosomatic conditions. The mind has played its part in the genesis of the condition and may be equally capable of reversing the process. A commonly used technique is the imaginary bombardment of cancer cells by white T-cells. It seems that the mind is able to reorganize the energy of matter. We saw a similar phenomenon in healing as the transmission of an ordering and balancing force. Prayers use the power of thought positively, and curses negatively. Our imaginations are teeming with our own creations and thought-forms, some of which we may share with others by empathetic resonance. Perhaps the simplest image to use is that of a transceiver which both receives and emits signals and can tune in to various frequencies. We are responsible for the choice of station and for our emissions which can then be picked up by others. In meditation, for example, we can try to tune in to peace and light, even if part of our minds at first twists the knob back to the habitual station. Likewise, our emission of thoughts and feelings need not be automatic, but can gradually be controlled and channelled for the good of oneself and others in the course of our integration of the shadow side.

One of the most coherent and fascinating accounts of the power of thought can be found in the teachings of Daskalos, *The Magus of Strovolos*. A chapter on elementals defines the term as any thought or feeling projected by the individual. Most of these are produced unconsciously, and are called 'desires-thoughts', while consciously constructed ones are called 'thoughts-desires'. The quality of a person's being determines the corresponding quality of their elementals. Once projected, such elementals eventually return to the subconscious of their creator, and resurface into consciousness where they may be energized and projected once again. It is not hard to appreciate that the creation of benign elementals is a central task of the spiritual life and of healing. The spiritual aspirant is encouraged to make a nightly examination of the thoughts and desires which have arisen during the day; in this way it becomes easier to know and master them, and to re-energize harmful elementals through a technique of indifference.

Elsewhere in the book, Daskalos explains that elementals may grow so strong that a person can literally become a slave to their desires and a victim of the consequences of these desires. Purity of thought and feeling becomes paramount if aspirants are to detoxify their inner pollution. The punishment of creating evil elementals is inherent in the process, since they return to their originator with increased force. Construction of an elemental comes about through concentration and desire, and needs to be based on right thought and right feeling if we are to benefit ourselves and others. Nor can we in the end deceive our consciences. Daskalos remarks that we should not be afraid of others' opinions of us, but only of the judgement of our own inner selves, as we saw in the NDE life-review. And in listening to our inner selves we will be on the right path of creating only benevolent elementals under our full control.

Modern science has focused our attention on externals, neglecting the inner world of thought. Thought itself has been reduced by sophisticated neuroscience to chemical transfer across neuronal synapses; consciousness is entirely dependent on the material substructure and cannot possibly survive the dissolution of brain tissue. Human beings are determined by heredity, environment, unconscious drives or a combination of these factors. The logical corollary is a denial of moral responsibility and the removal of any coherent basis of moral order.

Yet the data of our study of near-death and other experiences point in the opposite direction. Thought and consciousness are mediated through but not dependent on physical matter. Our conscious self is capable of surviving bodily death and experiences an extension of consciousness rather than the oblivion of extinction. Moreover, we encounter and experience through empathetic resonance the results not merely of our actions but also of our thoughts and feelings in so far as they affect people in ways we did not even imagine or suspect. Our sense of responsibility is dramatically enhanced; and the greater the power, the more extensive the responsibility through indirect effects on many more people and even on animals and plants.

The rationale of this purging process of life-review – the why and the how – is what I have tried to sketch in this chapter by taking a systems view of life, consciousness and ethics: picturing human beings as dynamic and creative holons within the Field of life and consciousness; and stressing the nature of our interconnectedness which constitutes our inescapable responsibility to each other. The life-review is simply the display of this interconnectedness of which we are largely unaware during physical life, acting as we do on the assumption that our consciousnesses are separate. We have the illusory impression that we do not reap what we sow, an illusion compounded by the prevalent philosophy of extinction at bodily death. My analysis suggests that the moral order is not confined to the physical order but transcends it to participate in the metaphysical and divine orders, finding its ultimate context in those very values reported in the unity of mystical experience. As for the why of the dynamics of life, we can only guess. It seems to be a gradual learning process whereby we slowly come to realize within ourselves and then apply the law of love, the win-win option which gives us the feedback of self-perfection, inner peace and joy when we harmonize ourselves with it. If we take the reincarnation view, then our present circumstances and attributes are the feedback from previous existences and provide us with perfect learning opportunities through creative acceptance of our situation with its joys and sorrows, frustrations and breakthroughs.

Pascal argued that it was worth betting on immortality. What if we take our interconnectedness, dynamic interdependence and reciprocal moral responsibility as a working hypothesis illustrated in the phenomenon of the life-review? Our principal conclusion would be to apply the Golden Rule both positively and negatively: to do as we would be done by and not to harm others because we are in the end only harming ourselves. The distinction between our own best interests and those of others dissolves in the ocean of interconnectedness and empathetic resonance. At Stage 1 we would be acting out of fear of the consequences in the light of a post-mortem deterrent. There is nothing wrong with such an attitude except that it is not the last word in moral and spiritual development, as we have seen. Would the terrorist or criminal really go through with an act of violence if they knew for certain that they would eventually experience the event through the consciousness of the victim? Socrates maintained that no one did wrong knowingly. The key definition is that of 'knowingly'. If the central proposition of this book is true, that our consciousnesses are interconnected so that we eventually experience the consequences of our thoughts, feelings and actions, then most of us are acting ignorantly for most of the time; and the hardened criminal is wilfully ignorant, totally oblivious to what he is creating.

The drug trafficker is a case in point: addiction is secured in order to obtain a captive market; the drug-users stop at no crime for a fix, thus compounding the chain of suffering and woe. The drug barons behind the pushers make vast profits out of human weakness and curiosity. Imagine now the post-mortem life-review of such a drug baron: he would experience all the suffering for which he was directly or indirectly responsible, not to mention the consequences of his own destructive elementals. On the other hand, those who have spent their lives alleviating the suffering of others and bringing them new hope will experience joy and happiness; as will inventors and artists who have used their talents in a constructive way. It is up to us to choose our path.

At the top end of the scale of moral and spiritual development we found in Stage 7 a fusion of the moral order with the divine order, ethics grounded in mysticism and mysticism expressed in ethics: self-perfection through self-devotion. The One is displayed in the many, and the many united by participating in the One; the part is contained in the Whole, and the Whole immanent (literally dwelling) in the part. Christ in the neighbour and the neighbour in Christ. Our true meaning and vocation lie in answering the call to the wholeness and fulfilment of Love, the great integrating principle of the inner world, so that it becomes a harmonizing and radiant force in our feelings, thoughts and actions. Only then can we occasionally become one with the Whole and with each other. One thing is certain: we will not lack opportunities for practice; and only through such persistent practice can we hope to absorb the essential lessons of life and love.

BIBLIOGRAPHY

Aall, Anathon, *The Hellenistic Elements in Christianity,* University of London Press, 1931.

Adam, James, *The Religious Teachers of Greece,* Edinburgh, T. &. T. Clark, 1908.

Aivanhov, Omraam Mikhael, *Cosmic Moral Laws,* Frejus, Prosveta, 1984.

Aldwinckle, Russell, *Death in the Secular City,* London, Allen and Unwin, 1972.

Alger, W. R., *A Critical History of the Doctrine of a Future Life,* New York, Middleton, 1871.

Anderson, Bernhard W., *The Living World of the Old Testament,* London, Darton, Longman and Todd, 1988.

Anderson, Ray S., *Theology, Death and Dying,* Oxford, Blackwell, 1986.

Andrews, Valerie, Bosnak, Robert and Goodwin, Karen Walter, *Facing Apocalypse,* Dallas, Spring Publications, 1986.

Ariès, Philippe, *Western Attitudes Towards Death,* London, Marion Boyars, 1976.

Ariès, Philippe, *The Hour of Our Death,* London, Penguin, 1981.

Arkle, William, *A Geography of Consciousness,* London, Neville Spearman, 1974.

Assagioli, Roberto, *Psychosynthesis,* London, Turnstone, 1975.

Atwater, P. M. H., *Coming Back to Life*, New York, Dodd, Mead, 1988.

Badham, Paul, *Christian Beliefs about a Life after Death*, London, SPCK, 1978.

Badham, Paul, and Badham, Linda, *Immortality or Extinction*, London, Macmillan, 1982.

Badham, Paul, and Badham, Linda, *Death and Immortality in the Religions of the World*, New York, Paragon House, 1987.

Bailey, Alice, *Death: The Great Adventure*, London, Lucis, 1985.

Baillie, John, *And the Life Everlasting*, Oxford University Press, 1934.

Barrett, William, *Death of the Soul*, Oxford University Press, 1986.

Barrow, John D., and Tipler, Frank J., *The Anthropic Cosmological Principle*, Oxford, Clarendon Press, 1986.

Bateson, Gregory, *Mind and Nature*, London, Fontana, 1979.

Beard, Paul, *Survival of Death*, London, Psychic Press, 1966.

Beard, Paul, *Living On*, London, Allen and Unwin, 1980.

Beard, Paul, *Hidden Man*, Norwich, Pilgrim Books, 1986.

Bebek, Borna, *The Third City*, London, Routledge and Kegan Paul, 1982.

Berdyaev, Nicolas, *The Destiny of Man*, London, Bles, 1937.

Berger, Peter, *The Social Reality of Religion*, London, Penguin, 1967.

Bergson, Henri, *L'Energie spirituelle*, Paris, Presses Universitaires de France, 1919.

Bergson, Henri, *Matière et mémoire*, Paris, Presses Universitaires de France, 1932.

Bergson, Henri, *The Creative Mind*, New York, Citadel Press, 1946.

Bertalanffy, Ludwig von, *Problems of Life*, London, Watts, 1952.

Bertalanfiy, Ludwig von, *General Systems Theory*, London, Allen Lane, 1968.

Bland, Herbert, *Psychometry: Its Theory and Practice*, London, Rider, 1937.

Blavatsky, H. P., *The Secret Doctrine*, London, Theosophical Press, 1885.

Blavatsky, H. P., *The Key to Theosophy*, London, Theosophical Publishing House, 1968.

Bleier, Ruth (ed.), *Feminist Approaches to Science*, New York, Pergamon, 1986.

Bocock, Robert, and Thompson, Kenneth (eds.), *Religion and Ideology*, Manchester University Press, 1985.

Bohm, David, *Wholeness and the Implicate Order*, London, Routledge and Kegan Paul, 1980.

Bohm, David, *Unfolding Meaning*, London, Ark, 1987.

Bohm, David, and Krishnamurti, J., *The Ending of Time*, London, Gollancz, 1985.

Brandon, S. G. F., *Man and His Destiny in the Great World Religions*, Manchester University Press, 1962.

Brandon, S. G. F., *The Judgement of the Dead*, London, Weidenfeld and Nicolson, 1967.

Broad, C. D., 'Normal Cognition, Clairvoyance and Telepathy', *Proceedings of the Society for Psychical Research*, part 142, vol. XLIII, no. 3, October 1935, pp. 397—438.

Broad, C. D., *Lectures on Psychical Research*, London, Routledge and Kegan Paul, 1962.

Brown, Hanbury, *The Wisdom of Science*, Cambridge University Press, 1986.

Brunton, Paul, *The Wisdom of the Overself*, London, Rider, 1943.

Brunton, Paul, *The Spiritual Crisis of Man*, London, Rider, 1952.

Brunton, Paul, *Essays on the Quest*, London, Rider, 1984.

Brunton, Paul, *Perspectives*, New York, Larson, 1984.

Buchanan, James R., *Manual of Psychometry*, Boston, Holman, 1885.

Burnet, John, *Early Greek Philosophy*, Edinburgh, A. and C. Black, 1932.

Burr, Harold Saxton, *Blueprint for Immortality*, London, Neville Spearman, 1972.

Burtt, E. A., *The Metaphysical Foundations of Modern Science*, London, Routledge and Kegan Paul, 1924.

Bury, J. B., *History of the Freedom of Thought,* London, Williams and Norgate, 1928.

Butler, Samuel, *Erewhon,* London, Page, 1922.

Butterfield, Sir Herbert, *The Origins of Modern Science,* London, Bell, 1949.

Cameron, Sir Alexander, *The Power Within,* London, Rider, 1950.

Campbell, Joseph (ed.), *Man and Transformation,* London, Routledge and Kegan Paul, 1964.

Campbell, R. J., *The Life of the World to Come,* London, Longman, 1948.

Capra, Fritjof, *The Tao of Physics,* London, Fontana, 1976.

Capra, Fritjof, *The Turning Point,* London, Wildwood House, 1982.

Capra, Fritjof, *Uncommon Wisdom,* London, Century, 1987.

Carington, Whately, *Telepathy,* London, Methuen, 1945.

Catholic Dictionary of Theology, London, Nelson, 1963-71, 4 vols.

Cerminara, Gina, *The World Within,* New York, Sloane, 1957.

Cerminara, Gina, *Many Mansions,* London, Neville Spearman, 1967.

Charles, R. H., *The Doctrine of a Future Life,* London, A. and C. Black, 1899.

Charles, R. H., *Immortality,* Oxford, Clarendon Press, 1912.

Cherrie, Marie, *The Barbanell Report,* ed. Paul Beard, Norwich, Pilgrim Books, 1987.

Collin, Rodney, *The Theory of Eternal Life,* London, Shambahla, 1984.

Cooke, Ivan (ed.), *The Return of Arthur Conan Doyle,* London, White Eagle Press, 1968.

Copleston, Frederick, *Philosophies and Cultures,* Oxford University Press, 1980.

Copleston, Frederick, *Religion and the One,* London, Search Press, 1982.

Coxhead, Nona, *The Relevance of Bliss,* London, Wildwood House, 1985.

Cranston, Sylvia, and Williams, Carey, *Reincarnation: A New Horizon in Science, Religion and Society,* New York, Julian Press, 1984.

Crookall, Robert, *The Study and Practice of Astral Projection,* London, Aquarian, 1960.

Crookall, Robert, *The Supreme Adventure*, Cambridge, James Clarke, 1961.

Crookall, Robert, *What Happens When You Die*, London, Colin Smythe, 1978.

Cummins, Geraldine, *Beyond Human Personality*, London, Ivor, Richardson and Watson, 1935.

Daily, Starr, *Release*, London, Arthur James, 1950.

Dampier-Whetham, Sir W. C. D., *A History of Science*, Cambridge University Press, 1950.

Dean, Michael, and Neate, Tony, *The Guide Book*, Bath, Gateway, 1986.

Denton, William, *The Soul of Things*, London, Aquarian, 1988.

Deunov, Peter, *L'Enseignement de vie nouvelle*, Paris, Courrier du Livre, 1983.

Devall, Bill, and Sessions, George, *Deep Ecology*, Salt Lake City, Utah, Peregrine Smith, 1985.

Dewick, E. C., *Primitive Christian Eschatology*, Cambridge University Press, 1912.

Dossey, Larry, *Space, Time and Medicine*, London, Shambahla, 1982.

Dossey, Larry, *Beyond Illness*, London, Shambahla, 1984.

Dostoevsky, Fyodor, *The Brothers Karamazov* (2 vols.), London, Heinemann, 1975.

Douglas-Smith, Basil, *The Mystics Come to Harley Street*, London, Regency Press, 1983.

Draper, J. W., *History of the Conflict between Religion and Science*, New York, King, 1875.

Easwaran, Eknath (ed.), *The Bhagavad Gita*, London, Arkana, 1986.

Easwaran, Eknath (ed.), *The Dhammapada*, London, Arkana, 1987.

Eccles, Sir John, and Popper, Sir Karl, *The Self and its Brain*, London, Routledge and Kegan Paul, 1984.

Eccles, Sir John, and Robinson, Daniel N., *The Wonder of Being Human*, London, Shambahla, 1985.

Eddington, Sir Arthur, *The Nature of the Physical World*, Cambridge University Press, 1928.

Edwards, David L., *The Last Things Now*, London, SCM Press, 1969.

Eliade, Mircea, *Rites and Symbols of Initiation*, New York, Harper and Row, 1958.

Eliade, Mircea, *A History of Religious Ideas*, London, Collins, 1979 and 1982 (2 vols.).

Emerson, R. W., *Complete Works*, London, Routledge, 1897.

Emery, F. E. (ed.), *Systems Thinking*, London, Penguin, 1969.

Evans, R. F., *Pelagius: Inquiries and Reappraisals*, London, A. and C. Black, 1968.

Evans-Wentz, W. Y., *The Tibetan Book of the Dead*, Oxford University Press, 1960.

Ferguson, Marilyn, *The Aquarian Conspiracy*, London, Routledge and Kegan Paul, 1981.

Fiore, Edith, *You Have Been Here Before*, London, Sphere, 1980.

Fisher, Joe, *The Case for Reincarnation*, London, Granada, 1985.

Fortune, Dion, *Through the Gates of Death*, London, Aquarian, 1987.

Frankl, Viktor, *Man's Search for Meaning*, London, Hodder and Stoughton, 1964.

Frankl, Viktor, *Psychotherapy and Existentialism*, London, Penguin, 1973.

Frankl, Viktor, *The Doctor and the Soul*, New York, Vintage Books, 1973.

Frankl, Viktor, *The Unconscious God*, London, Hodder and Stoughton, 1975.

Frazer, Sir J. G., *The Belief in Immortality*, vol. 1, London, Macmillan, 1913.

Frazer, Sir J. G., *The Golden Bough*, London, Macmillan, 1937, 12 vols.

Freud, Sigmund, *The Future of an Illusion*, London, Hogarth, 1928.

Freud, Sigmund, *Totem and Taboo*, London, Routledge and Kegan Paul, 1950.

Freud, Sigmund, *Civilisation and Its Discontents*, New York, Norton, 1961.

Fromm, Erich, *The Fear of Freedom*, London, Routledge and Kegan Paul, 1942.

Fromm, Erich, *Man for Himself*, London, Routledge and Kegan Paul, 1949.

Fromm, Erich, *Psychoanalysis and Religion,* London, Yale, 1950.

Fromm, Erich, *The Sane Society,* London, Routledge and Kegan Paul, 1956.

Fromm, Erich, *To Have or To Be,* London, Cape, 1978.

Fromm, Erich, *Beyond the Chains of Illusion,* London, Abacus, 1980.

Fromm, Erich, *On Disobedience,* London, Routledge and Kegan Paul, 1984.

Gallup, George, Jr., *Adventures in Immortality,* London, Souvenir, 1983.

Gaskin, J. C. A., *The Quest for Eternity,* London, Penguin, 1984.

Geach, P. T., *God and the Soul,* London, Routledge and Kegan Paul, 1969.

Geach, P. T., *Providence and Evil,* Cambridge University Press, 1977.

Godman, David, *Be As You Are,* London, Arkana, 1986.

Goldbrunner, Josef, *Individuation,* London, Hollis and Carter, 1955.

Grant, Patrick, *A Dazzling Darkness,* London, Fount, 1985.

Grayeff, Felix, A *Short Treatise on Ethics,* London, Duckworth, 1980.

Greaves, Helen, *Testimony of Light,* London, Churches' Fellowship for Psychical and Spiritual Studies, 1969.

Greene, F. Gordon, 'A Glimpse Behind the Life Review', *Theta,* vol. 8, no. 2,1980.

Gregory, Richard (ed.), *The Oxford Companion to the Mind,* Oxford University Press, 1987.

Grey, Margot, *Return from Death,* London, Arkana, 1985.

Greyson, Bruce, and Flynn, Charles P., *The Near-Death Experience,* Springfield, Ill., Charles C. Thomas, 1984.

Griffiths, Bede, *The Marriage of East and West,* London, Collins, 1982.

Grof, Stanislav, and Halifax, Joan, *The Human Encounter with Death,* London, Souvenir, 1978.

Gromyko, Anatoly, and Hellman, Martin (eds.), *Breakthrough,* New York, Walker, 1987.

Grosso, Michael, *The Final Choice,* Walpole, NH, Stillpoint, 1986.

Guenon, Rene, *Crisis of the Modern World,* London, Lukacs, 1975.

Gurney, Edmund, Myers, F. W. H., and Podmore, Frank, *Phantasms of the Living*, London, Trübner, 1886.

Hampe, J. C., *To Die is Gain*, London, Darton, Longman and Todd, 1979.

Handbook of Marxism, ed. and pub. Victor Gollancz, 1936.

Happold, F. C., *Mysticism*, London, Penguin, 1963.

Hardy, Sir Alister, *The Spiritual Nature of Man*, Oxford, Clarendon Press, 1979.

Harman, P. M., *The Scientific Revolution*, London, Methuen, 1983.

Harman, Willis, *Global Mind Change*, New York, Knowledge Systems, 1988.

Hastings, James (ed.), *Encyclopaedia of Religion and Ethics*, Edinburgh, T. and T. Clark, 1913 (12 vols.).

Head, Joseph, and Cranston, S. L., *Reincarnation: The Phoenix Fire Mystery*, New York, Julian Press, 1977.

Hick, John, *Evil and the God of Love*, London, Macmillan, 1966.

Hick, John, *Death and Eternal Life*, London, Collins, 1976.

Hiley, Basil, and Peat, F. David, *Quantum Implications: Essays in Honour of David Bohm*, London, Routledge and Kegan Paul, 1987.

Hill, Brennan, *The Near-Death Experience: A Christian Approach*, Iowa, Brown, 1981.

Hoeller, Stephan A., *The Gnostic Jung*, London, Theosophical Publishing House, 1982.

Houlden, J. L., *Ethics and the New Testament*, London, Penguin, 1973.

Hulme, T. E., *Speculations*, London, Routledge and Kegan Paul, 1924.

Huxley, Aldous, *The Perennial Philosophy*, London, Chatto and Windus, 1946.

Huxley, Aldous, *The Human Situation*, London, Chatto and Windus, 1977.

Inge, W. R., *Christian Mysticism*, London, Methuen, 1899.

Inge, W. R., *The Philosophy of Plotinus*, London, Longman, 1929.

Jacobi, Jolande, *The Way of Individuation*, London, Hodder and Stoughton, 1967.

James, William, *Human Immortality*, London, Constable, 1899.

James, William, *The Varieties of Religious Experience*, London, Longman, 1903.

James, William, *Pragmatism*, London, Longman, 1921.

Jantsch, Erich, *The Self-Organising Universe*, London, Pergamon, 1980.

John, Da Free, *Easy Death*, London, Dawn Horse Press, 1983.

Johnson, Raynor, *The Imprisoned Splendour*, London, Hodder and Stoughton, 1953.

Johnson, Raynor, *Light of All Life*, Norwich, Pilgrim Books, 1984.

Journal of the Society for Psychical Research

Journal of the American Society for Psychical Research

Jung, C. G., *Psychological Types*, London, Kegan Paul, 1924.

Jung, C. G., *Modern Man in Search of a Soul*, London, Routledge and Kegan Paul, 1933.

Jung, C. G., *Memories, Dreams, Reflections*, ed. Aniela Jaffe, London, Routledge and Kegan Paul, 1963.

Jung, C. G., *Collected Works*, vol. 9, part 1, 'The Archetypes and the Collective Unconscious', London, Routledge and Kegan Paul, 1968.

Jung, C. G., *Collected Works*, vol. 8, 'The Structure and Dynamics of the Psyche', London, Routledge and Kegan Paul, 1969.

Jung, C. G., *Collected Works*, vol. 10, 'Civilisation in Transition', London, Routledge and Kegan Paul, 1970.

Jung, C. G., *Collected Works*, vol. 11, 'Psychology and Religion: East and West', London, Routledge and Kegan Paul, 1970.

Jung, C. G., *Letters*, vol. 1 (1906-50), London, Routledge and Kegan Paul, 1973.

Jung, C. G., *C. G. Jung Speaking*, London, Thames and Hudson, 1977.

Katz, Steven T. (ed.), *Mysticism and Philosophical Analysis*, London, Sheldon, 1978.

Kay, William, *Moral Development*, London, Allen and Unwin, 1970.

Keller, Evelyn Fox, *Reflections on Gender and Science*, Yale University Press, 1985.

Kelsey, Morton T., *Afterlife,* New York, Crossroads, 1988.

Khursheed, Anjam, *Science and Religion: Towards the Restoration of An Ancient Harmony,* London, Oneworld, 1987.

King, Martin Luther, *The Words of Martin Luther King Jr.,* New York, Newmarket Press, 1958.

Koestler, Arthur, *The Yogi and the Commissar,* London, Cape, 1945.

Koestler, Arthur, *The Sleepwalkers,* London, Hutchinson, 1959.

Koestler, Arthur, *Janus,* London, Hutchinson, 1978.

Kohlberg, Lawrence, *The Philosophy of Moral Development,* New York, Harper and Row, 1981.

Kolakowski, Leszek, *Religion,* London, Fontana, 1982.

The Koran, London, Dent, 1909.

Kropotkin, Prince, *Ethics,* Dorchester, Prism, 1924.

Kuhn, Thomas J., *The Structure of Scientific Revolutions,* Chicago University Press, 1970.

Küng, Hans, *Eternal Life?,* London, Collins, 1984.

Kunz, Dora, *Spiritual Aspects of the Healing Arts,* London, Theosophical Publishing House, 1985.

Langford, Michael J., *Providence,* London, SCM Press, 1981.

Lash, Nicholas, *A Matter of Hope,* London, Collins, 1981.

Leadbeater, C., *Clairvoyance,* London, Theosophical Publishing House, 1918.

Leggett, D. M. A., and Payne, Max, *A Forgotten Truth,* Norwich, Pilgrim Books, 1986.

Le Goff, Jacques, *The Birth of Purgatory,* London, Scolar Press, 1985.

Leith, John H. (ed.), *Creeds of the Churches,* Oxford, Blackwell, 1973.

LeShan, Lawrence, *Science and the Paranormal,* London, Aquarian, 1987.

Lethbridge, T. C., *ESP: Beyond Time and Distance,* London, Sidgwick and Jackson, 1974.

Lethbridge, T. C., *The Essential T. C. Lethbridge*, London, Routledge and Kegan Paul, 1980.

Lethbridge, T. C., *The Power of the Pendulum*, London, Arkana, 1989.

Lévy-Bruhl, Lucien, *The Soul of the Primitive*, London, Allen and Unwin, 1928.

Long, Max Freedom, *The Secret Science Behind Miracles*, Marina del Rey, Devorss, 1954.

Lorimer, David, *Survival? Body, Mind and Death in the Light of Psychic Experience*, London, Routledge and Kegan Paul, 1984.

Lovejoy, Arthur O., *The Great Chain of Being*, Harvard University Press, 1948.

Lovelock, James, *Gaia: A New Look at Life on Earth*, Oxford University Press, 1979.

Lovelock, James, *The Ages of Gaia*, Oxford University Press, 1988.

Lovin, Robin W., and Reynolds, Frank E., *Cosmogony and Ethical Order*, University of Chicago Press, 1985.

MacCulloch, J. A., *The Harrowing of Hell*, Edinburgh, T. and T. Clark, 1930.

MacGregor, Geddes, *Reincarnation in Christianity*, London, Theosophical Publishing House, 1978.

MacGregor, Geddes, *The Christening of Karma*, London, Theosophical Publishing House, 1984.

MacIntyre, Alasdair, A *Short History of Ethics*, London, Routledge and Kegan Paul, 1967.

MacIntyre, Alasdair, and Ricoeur, Paul, *The Religious Significance of Atheism*, London, Columbia University Press, 1969.

McKenzie, John, *Hindu Ethics*, Oxford University Press, 1922.

Macmurray, John (ed.), *Some Makers of the Modern Spirit*, London, Methuen, 1933.

Macquarrie, John (ed.), A *Dictionary of Christian Ethics*, London, SCM Press, 1967.

Margenau, Henry, *The Miracle of Existence*, London, Shambahla, 1987.

Markides, Kyriacos C., *The Magus of Strovolos*, London, Arkana, 1985.

Markides, Kyriacos C., *Homage to the Sun*, London, Arkana, 1987.

Mascaró, Juan (ed.), *The Bhagavad Gita*, London, Penguin, 1962.

Mascaró, Juan (ed.), *The Upanishads*, London, Penguin, 1965.

Mascaró, Juan (ed.), *The Dhammapada*, London, Penguin, 1973.

Maslow, Abraham, *Motivation and Personality*, New York, Harper and Row, 1954.

Maslow, Abraham, *Religion, Values and Peak Experiences*, New York, Viking, 1964.

Maslow, Abraham, *The Farther Reaches of Human Nature*, New York, Viking, 1971.

Masterson, Patrick, *Atheism and Alienation*, London, Penguin, 1973.

Matthews, W. R. (ed.), *King's College Lectures on Immortality*, University of London Press, 1920.

Maxwell, Nicholas, *From Knowledge to Wisdom*, Oxford, Blackwell, 1987.

May, Robert M., *Physicians of the Soul*, New York, Amity House, 1988.

Medawar, Sir Peter, *The Limits of Science*, Oxford University Press, 1986.

Meeks, Wayne, *The Moral World of the First Christians*, London, SPCK, 1987.

Mellone, S. H., *Eternal Life Here and Hereafter*, London, Lindsay Press, 1916.

Milgram, Stanley, *Obedience to Authority*, London, Tavistock, 1973.

Miller, J. G., *Living Systems*, New York, McGraw Hill, 1970.

Minogue, Kenneth, *Alien Powers: The Pure Theory of Ideology*, London, Weidenfeld and Nicolson, 1985.

Mitchell, Basil, *Morality: Religious and Secular*, Oxford, Clarendon Press, 1980.

Monod, Jacques, *Chance and Necessity*, London, Collins, 1974.

Moody, Raymond, *Life after Life*, New York, Mockingbird Books, 1975.

Moody, Raymond, *Reflections on Life after Life*, New York, Mockingbird Books, 1977.

Moody, Raymond, *The Light Beyond*, London, Macmillan, 1988.

Muller, F. Max, *The Vedanta Philosophy*, London, Longman, 1894.

Muller, Robert, *New Genesis*, New York, Doubleday, 1984.

Mullin, Glenn, *Death and Dying: The Tibetan Tradition*, London, Arkana, 1986.

Murdoch, Iris, *Acastos*, London, Chatto and Windus, 1986.

Neumann, Erich, *The Origins and History of Consciousness*, London, Routledge and Kegan Paul/New York, Bollingen, 1954.

Neumann, Erich, *Depth Psychology and a New Ethic*, London, Hodder and Stoughton, 1969.

Niebuhr, Reinhold, *Moral Man and Immoral Society*, New York, Scribner, 1936.

Niebuhr, Reinhold, *An Interpretation of Christian Ethics*, London, SCM Press, 1936.

O'Brien, Elmer (ed.), *The Essential Plotinus*, Indiana, Hackett, 1964.

O'Grady, Joan, *Heresy*, Shaftesbury, Element, 1985.

Oldroyd, David, *The Arch of Knowledge*, London, Methuen, 1986.

Ornstein, Robert E., *The Psychology of Consciousness*, London, Penguin, 1975.

Ornstein, Robert E., *Multimind*, London, Macmillan, 1988.

Ornstein, Robert E., and Sobel, David, *The Healing Brain*, London, Macmillan, 1988.

Osborne, Arthur, *Ramana Maharshi and the Path of Self-Knowledge*, London, Rider, 1954.

Osty, Eugene, *Supernormal Faculties in Man*, London, Methuen, 1923.

Palmer, Martin, *Genesis or Nemesis*, London, Dryad Press, 1988.

Pauchard, Albert, *The Other World*, Norwich, Pelegrin, 1987.

Paulsen, Friedrich, *A System of Ethics*, New York, Scribner, 1899.

Peacocke, Arthur, and Gillett, Grant, *Persons and Personality*, Oxford, Blackwell, 1987.

Peck, M. Scott, *The Road Less Travelled*, London, Century, 1983.

Penfield, Wilder, *The Mysteries of Mind*, Princeton University Press, 1975.

Perry, Michael, *Psychic Studies: A Christian's View*, London, Aquarian, 1984.

Pittenger, Norman, *After Death, Life in God*, London, SCM Press, 1980.

Plato, *Phaedrus*, ed. R. Hackforth, Cambridge University Press, 1952.

Plato, *The Last Days of Socrates*, ed. Hugh Tredinnick, London, Penguin, 1954.

Plato, *The Republic*, ed. Sir Desmond Lee, London, Penguin, 1955.

Plato, *Protagoras and Meno*, ed. W. K. C. Guthrie, London, Penguin, 1956.

Plato, *The Laws*, ed. Trevor J. Saunders, London, Penguin, 1970.

Plotinus, *The Enneads*, ed. Stephen Mackenna, London, Faber and Faber, 1962.

Polanyi, Sir Michael, *Personal Knowledge*, London, Routledge and Kegan Paul, 1923.

Popper, Sir Karl, and Eccles, Sir John, *The Self and its Brain*, Heidelberg, Springer International, 1977/London, Routledge and Kegan Paul, 1984.

Potter, Karl H., *Presuppositions of India's Philosophies*, Delhi, Prentice-Hall, 1965.

Pringle-Pattison, A. S., *The Idea of Immortality*, Oxford, Clarendon Press, 1922.

Proust, Marcel, *A la Recherche du temps perdu*, Paris, Gallimard, 1919, 14 vols.

Radhakrishnan, Sir S., *An Idealist View of Life*, London, Allen and Unwin, 1932.

Radhakrishnan, Sir S., *Eastern Religions and Western Thought*, Oxford University Press, 1939.

Radhakrishnan, Sir S., *Religion and Society*, London, Allen and Unwin, 1947.

Radhakrishnan, Sir S., *The Present Crisis of Faith*, Delhi, Orient, 1970.

Radhakrishnan, Sir S. (ed.), *The Bhagavad Gita*, London, Allen and Unwin, 1948.

Radhakrishnan, Sir S. (ed.), *The Dhammapada*, Oxford University Press, 1950.

Radhakrishnan, Sir S. (ed.), *History of Philosophy, Eastern and Western*, London, Allen and Unwin, 1952, 2 vols.

Radhakrishnan, Sir S. (ed.), *The Principal Upanishads*, London, Allen and Unwin, 1953.

Radhakrishnan, Sir S. (ed.), *The Brahma Sutra*, London, Allen and Unwin, 1960.

Rashdall, Hastings, *The Theory of Good and Evil*, Oxford University Press, 1924.

Ratsch, Del, *Philosophy of Science*, Illinois, Inter-Varsity Press, 1986.

Rawlings, Maurice, *Beyond Death's Door*, London, Sheldon, 1978.

Rawls, John, A *Theory of Justice*, Oxford University Press, 1971.

Richards, H. J., *Death and After*, London, Fount, 1980.

Richards, Stewart, *Philosophy and Sociology of Science: An Introduction*, Oxford, Blackwell, 1987.

Ring, Kenneth, *Life at Death*, New York, Coward, McCann and Geoghagan, 1980.

Ring, Kenneth, *Heading toward Omega*, New York, Morrow, 1984.

Ritchie, George, *Return from Tomorrow*, London, Kingsway, 1978.

Roberts, Jane, *Seth Speaks*, London, Bantam, 1974.

Robertson, Roland (ed.), *Sociology of Religion*, London, Penguin, 1969.

Rogo, D. Scott, *Life after Death*, London, Aquarian, 1986.

Rohde, Erwin, *Psyche*, London, Kegan Paul, Trench and Trübner, 1925.

Roubiczek, Paul, *Existentialism: For and Against*, Cambridge University Press, 1964.

Rowell, Geoffrey, *Hell and the Victorians*, Oxford, Clarendon Press, 1974.

Russell, Bertrand, *The Scientific Outlook*, London, Allen and Unwin, 1931.

Russell, Bertrand, *History of Western Philosophy*, London, Allen and Unwin, 1946.

Russell, Bertrand, *Human Society in Ethics and Politics*, London, Allen and Unwin, 1954.

Russell, Bertrand, *Why I am not a Christian*, London, Allen and Unwin, 1957.

Sabom, Michael, *Recollections of Death*, London, Harper and Row, 1982.

Salmond, S. D. F., *The Christian Doctrine of Immortality*, Edinburgh, A. and C. Black, 1899.

Scheler, Max, *The Nature of Sympathy*, London, Routledge and Kegan Paul, 1954.

Schiller, F. C. S., *Riddles of the Sphinx*, London, Swan Sonnenschein, 1891.

Schiller, F. C. S., *Humanism*, London, Macmillan, 1903.

Schopenhauer, Arthur, *Essays and Aphorisms*, London, Penguin, 1970.

Schroedinger, Erwin, *What is Life? Matter and Mind*, Cambridge University Press, 1967.

Schumacher, E. F., *A Guide for the Perplexed*, London, Cape, 1977.

Schweitzer, Albert, *Christianity and the Religions of the World*, London, Allen and Unwin, 1923.

Schweitzer, Albert, *Memoirs of Childhood and Youth*, London, Allen and Unwin, 1924.

Schweitzer, Albert, *The Mysticism of Paul the Apostle*, London, A. and C. Black, 1931.

Schweitzer, Albert, *My Life and Thought*, London, Allen and Unwin, 1933.

Schweitzer, Albert, *Indian Thought and its Development*, London, Hodder and Stoughton, 1936.

Schweitzer, Albert, *The Decay and Restoration of Civilisation*, London, A. and C. Black, 1947.

Schweitzer, Albert, *Civilisation and Ethics*, London, A. and C. Black, 1949.

Schweitzer, Albert, *The Teaching of Reverence for Life*, London, Owen, 1966.

Schweitzer, Albert, *Reverence for Life,* London, SPCK, 1970.

Serrano, Miguel, C. G. *Jung and Hermann Hesse: A Record of Two Friendships,* London, Routledge and Kegan Paul, 1966.

Sharma, I. C., *Ethical Philosophies of India,* London, Allen and Unwin, 1965.

Sharma, I. C., *Cayce, Karma and Reincarnation,* London, Theosophical Publishing House, 1975.

Sheldrake, Rupert, *A New Science of Life,* London, Blond and Briggs, 1981.

Sheldrake, Rupert, *The Presence of the Past,* London, Collins, 1988.

Sherrard, Philip, *The Rape of Man and Nature,* Cambridge, Golgoonooza, 1987.

Sherrington, Sir Charles, *Man on His Nature,* Cambridge University Press, 1942.

Sherwood, Jane, *Post-Mortem Journal of T. E. Lawrence,* London, Neville Spearman, 1964.

Sherwood, Jane, *The Country Beyond,* London, Neville Spearman, 1969.

Sidgwick, Henry, *History of Ethics,* London, Macmillan, 1886.

Siegel, Bernie, *Love, Medicine and Miracles,* London, Rider, 1986.

Siemons, Jean-Louis, *Mourir pour Renâitre,* Paris, Albin Michel, 1987.

Simon, Ulrich, *Heaven in the Christian Tradition,* London, Rockliff, 1958.

Skolimowski, Henryk, *Eco-Philosophy,* London, Boyars, 1981.

Smart, Ninian, *The Religious Experience of Mankind,* London, Fontana, 1971.

Smart, Ninian, *Beyond Ideology,* London, Collins, 1981.

Smart, Ninian, *Religion and the Western Mind,* London, Macmillan, 1987.

Smith, Huston, *Forgotten Truth,* New York, Harper and Row, 1976.

Spengler, Oswald, *The Decline of the West,* London, Allen and Unwin, 1934.

Sperry, Roger, *Science and Moral Priority,* Oxford, Blackwell, 1983.

Stace, W. T., *Religion and the Modern Mind,* London, Macmillan, 1953.

Stace, W. T., *Mysticism and Philosophy*, London, Macmillan, 1961.

Steiner, Rudolf, *Theosophy*, London, Rudolf Steiner Press, 1922.

Steiner, Rudolf, *Karmic Relationships*, London, Anthroposophical Publishing Company, 1955, 5 vols.

Steiner, Rudolf, *Cosmic Memory*, New Jersey, Rudolf Steiner Publications, 1959.

Steiner, Rudolf, *Reincarnation and Karma: Their Significance in Modern Culture*, London, Anthroposophic Press, 1960.

Steiner, Rudolf, *Reincarnation and Karma: How Karma Works*, New York, Anthroposophic Press, 1962.

Steiner, Rudolf, *Knowledge of the Higher Worlds*, London, Rudolf Steiner Press, 1963.

Steiner, Rudolf, *Occult Science*, London, Rudolf Steiner Press, 1963.

Steiner, Rudolf, *Theosophy of the Rosicrucians*, London, Rudolf Steiner Press, 1966.

Steiner, Rudolf, *Life between Death and Rebirth*, New York, Anthroposophic Press, 1968.

Stevenson, Ian, *Twenty Cases Suggestive of Reincarnation*, New York, American Society for Psychical Research, 1966.

Stevenson, Ian, *Children Who Remember Previous Lives*, Charlottesville, University of Virginia Press, 1987.

Streeter, B. H. (ed.), *Immortality*, London, Macmillan, 1917.

Swedenborg, Emanuel, *Arcana Celestia*, London, Swedenborg Society, 1909,12 vols.

Swedenborg, Emanuel, *The True Christian Religion*, London, Swedenborg Society, 1950.

Swedenborg, Emanuel, *Heaven and Hell*, London, Swedenborg Society, 1958.

Swedenborg, Emanuel, *The Last Judgement*, London, Swedenborg Society, 1961.

Tagore, Sir Rabindranath, *Sadhana*, London, Macmillan, 1914.

Tawney, R. H., *Religion and the Rise of Capitalism*, London, John Murray, 1926.

Taylor, A. E., *Elements of Metaphysics*, London, Methuen, 1924.

Taylor, A. E., *Plato*, London, Methuen, 1926.

Taylor, A. E., *The Faith of a Moralist*, London, Macmillan, 1937.

Teilhard de Chardin, Pierre, *The Phenomenon of Man*, London, Fontana, 1965.

Teilhard de Chardin, Pierre, *Let Me Explain*, London, Fontana, 1974.

Tenhaeff, W. H. C., *Telepathy and Clairvoyance*, Springfield, Ill., Charles C. Thomas, 1972.

Thomas, Sir Keith, *Religion and the Decline of Magic*, London, Penguin, 1973.

Thomson, Alexander, *Tradition and Authority in Science and Theology*, Edinburgh, Scottish Academic Press, 1987.

Tischner, R., *Telepathy and Clairvoyance*, London, Kegan Paul, 1925.

Toffler, Alvin, *Previews and Premises*, London, Pan, 1984.

Toon, P. (ed.), *Puritans, The Millennium and the Future of Israel*, London, James Clarke, 1970.

Toynbee, Arnold, *An Historian's Approach to Religion*, Oxford University Press, 1956.

Toynbee, Arnold, *A Study of History*, vol. 12, Oxford University Press, 1961.

Toynbee, Arnold, *Surviving the Future*, Oxford University Press, 1971.

Toynbee, Arnold, and Ikeda, Daisaku, *Choose Life*, Oxford University Press, 1976.

Toynbee, Arnold (ed.), *Man's Concern with Death*, London, Hodder and Stoughton, 1968.

Toynbee, Arnold (ed.), *Life after Death*, London, Weidenfeld and Nicolson, 1976.

Turner, Victor, *Dramas, Fields and Metaphors*, New York, Cornell, 1974.

Tylor, Sir Edward, *Primitive Culture*, London, John Murray, 1903, 2 vols.

Tyrrell, G. N. M., *Grades of Significance,* London, Rider, 1947.

Tyrrell, G. N. M., *Apparitions,* London, Duckworth, 1953.

Underhill, Evelyn, *Mysticism,* London, Methuen, 1911.

van Gennep, Arnold, *Rites of Passage,* London, Routledge and Kegan Paul, 1960.

Von Franz, Marie-Louise, *On Dreams and Death,* London, Shambahla, 1984.

von Rad, Gerhard, *Wisdom in Israel,* London, SCM Press, 1972.

Walle, Anton van der, *From Darkness to Light,* London, SCM Press, 1984.

Wallis Budge, Sir E. A., *The Egyptian Book of the Dead,* London, Routledge and Kegan Paul, 1969.

Wambach, Helen, *Life before Life,* London, Bantam, 1979.

Wambach, Helen, *Reliving Past Lives,* London, Hutchinson, 1979.

Ward, Keith, *Images of Eternity,* London, Darton, Longman and Todd, 1987.

Warnock, Mary, *Existentialist Ethics,* London, Macmillan, 1967.

Weber, Renée, *Dialogues with Scientists and Sages: The Search for Unity,* London, Routledge and Kegan Paul, 1986.

Weil, Simone, *Intimations of Christianity among Ancient Greeks,* London, Ark, 1987.

Werbach, Melvyn R., *Third Line Medicine,* London, Arkana, 1986.

Werner, Karel, *Yoga and Indian Philosophy,* Delhi, Banasidass, 1977.

Westerman, Claus, *Creation,* London, SPCK, 1974.

White, Ruth, and Swainson, Mary, *Gildas Communicates,* London, Neville Spearman, 1971.

Whitehead, A. N., *Science and the Modern World,* Cambridge University Press, 1928.

Whitehead, A. N., *Process and Reality,* London, Macmillan, 1929.

Whitehead, A. N., *Adventures of Ideas,* New York, Collier Macmillan, 1967.

Whiteman, J. H. H., *The Meaning of Life,* London, Colin Smythe, 1986.

Whitmont, Edward C., *Return of the Goddess,* London, Routledge and Kegan Paul, 1983.

Whitton, Joel L., and Fisher, Joe, *Life between Life,* London, Collins, 1986.

Wilber, Ken, No *Boundary,* London, Shambahla, 1979.

Wilber, Ken, *The Atman Project,* New York, Theosophical Publishing House, 1980.

Wilber, Ken (ed.), *The Holographic Paradigm,* London, Shambahla, 1982.

Wilber, Ken (ed.), *Quantum Questions,* London, Shambahla, 1984.

Wilber, Ken, Engler, Jack, and Brown, Daniel P. (eds.), *Transformations of Consciousness,* New York, Shambahla, 1986.

Wilder, Amos N., *Ethics and Eschatology in the Teaching of Jesus,* New York, Harper Bros, 1950.

Willey, Basil, *The Seventeenth Century Background,* London, Ark, 1986.

Wilson, Colin, *Mysteries,* London, Granada, 1979.

Wilson, Colin, *The Psychic Detectives,* London, Pan, 1984.

Wilson, Ian, *The After-Death Experience,* London, Sidgwick and Jackson, 1987.

Wynne-Tyson, Jon (ed.), *The Extended Circle,* Fontwell, Centaur Press, 1985.

Yates, Frances, *The Rosicrucian Enlightenment,* London, Paladin, 1975.

Young, J. Z., *Philosophy and the Brain,* Oxford University Press, 1987.

Zaehner, R. C., *Mysticism Sacred and Profane,* Oxford University Press, 1961.

Zaleski, Carol, *Otherworld Journeys,* New York, Oxford University Press, 1986.

Paperbacks also available from
White Crow Books

Elsa Barker—*Letters from
a Living Dead Man*
ISBN 978-1-907355-83-7

Elsa Barker—*War Letters from
the Living Dead Man*
ISBN 978-1-907355-85-1

Elsa Barker—*Last Letters from
the Living Dead Man*
ISBN 978-1-907355-87-5

Richard Maurice Bucke—
Cosmic Consciousness
ISBN 978-1-907355-10-3

Arthur Conan Doyle—
The Edge of the Unknown
ISBN 978-1-907355-14-1

Arthur Conan Doyle—
The New Revelation
ISBN 978-1-907355-12-7

Arthur Conan Doyle—
The Vital Message
ISBN 978-1-907355-13-4

Arthur Conan Doyle with
Simon Parke—*Conversations
with Arthur Conan Doyle*
ISBN 978-1-907355-80-6

Meister Eckhart with Simon Parke—
Conversations with Meister Eckhart
ISBN 978-1-907355-18-9

D. D. Home—*Incidents in my Life Part 1*
ISBN 978-1-907355-15-8

Mme. Dunglas Home; edited,
with an Introduction, by Sir
Arthur Conan Doyle—*D. D.
Home: His Life and Mission*
ISBN 978-1-907355-16-5

Edward C. Randall—
Frontiers of the Afterlife
ISBN 978-1-907355-30-1

Rebecca Ruter Springer—
Intra Muros: My Dream of Heaven
ISBN 978-1-907355-11-0

Leo Tolstoy, edited by Simon
Parke—*Forbidden Words*
ISBN 978-1-907355-00-4

Leo Tolstoy—*A Confession*
ISBN 978-1-907355-24-0

Leo Tolstoy—*The Gospel in Brief*
ISBN 978-1-907355-22-6

Leo Tolstoy—*The Kingdom
of God is Within You*
ISBN 978-1-907355-27-1

Leo Tolstoy—*My Religion:
What I Believe*
ISBN 978-1-907355-23-3

Leo Tolstoy—*On Life*
ISBN 978-1-907355-91-2

Leo Tolstoy—*Twenty-three Tales*
ISBN 978-1-907355-29-5

Leo Tolstoy—*What is Religion
and other writings*
ISBN 978-1-907355-28-8

Leo Tolstoy—*Work While
Ye Have the Light*
ISBN 978-1-907355-26-4

Leo Tolstoy—*The Death of Ivan Ilyich*
ISBN 978-1-907661-10-5

Leo Tolstoy—*Resurrection*
ISBN 978-1-907661-09-9

Leo Tolstoy with Simon Parke—
Conversations with Tolstoy
ISBN 978-1-907355-25-7

Howard Williams with an Introduction
by Leo Tolstoy—*The Ethics of Diet:
An Anthology of Vegetarian Thought*
ISBN 978-1-907355-21-9

Vincent Van Gogh with Simon Parke—
Conversations with Van Gogh
ISBN 978-1-907355-95-0

Wolfgang Amadeus Mozart with Simon
Parke—*Conversations with Mozart*
ISBN 978-1-907661-38-9

Jesus of Nazareth with Simon Parke—
Conversations with Jesus of Nazareth
ISBN 978-1-907661-41-9

Thomas à Kempis with Simon
Parke—*The Imitation of Christ*
ISBN 978-1-907661-58-7

Julian of Norwich with Simon
Parke—*Revelations of Divine Love*
ISBN 978-1-907661-88-4

Allan Kardec—*The Spirits Book*
ISBN 978-1-907355-98-1

Allan Kardec—*The Book on Mediums*
ISBN 978-1-907661-75-4

Emanuel Swedenborg—*Heaven and Hell*
ISBN 978-1-907661-55-6

P.D. Ouspensky—*Tertium Organum:
The Third Canon of Thought*
ISBN 978-1-907661-47-1

Dwight Goddard—*A Buddhist Bible*
ISBN 978-1-907661-44-0

Michael Tymn—*The Afterlife Revealed*
ISBN 978-1-970661-90-7

Michael Tymn—*Transcending the
Titanic: Beyond Death's Door*
ISBN 978-1-908733-02-3

Guy L. Playfair—*If This Be Magic*
ISBN 978-1-907661-84-6

Guy L. Playfair—*The Flying Cow*
ISBN 978-1-907661-94-5

Guy L. Playfair —*This House is Haunted*
ISBN 978-1-907661-78-5

Carl Wickland, M.D.—
Thirty Years Among the Dead
ISBN 978-1-907661-72-3

John E. Mack—*Passport to the Cosmos*
ISBN 978-1-907661-81-5

Peter & Elizabeth Fenwick—
The Truth in the Light
ISBN 978-1-908733-08-5

Erlendur Haraldsson—
Modern Miracles
ISBN 978-1-908733-25-2

Erlendur Haraldsson—
At the Hour of Death
ISBN 978-1-908733-27-6

Erlendur Haraldsson—
The Departed Among the Living
ISBN 978-1-908733-29-0

Brian Inglis—*Science and Parascience*
ISBN 978-1-908733-18-4

Brian Inglis—*Natural and Supernatural:
A History of the Paranormal*
ISBN 978-1-908733-20-7

Ernest Holmes—*The Science of Mind*
ISBN 978-1-908733-10-8

Victor & Wendy Zammit —*A Lawyer
Presents the Evidence For the Afterlife*
ISBN 978-1-908733-22-1

Casper S. Yost—*Patience
Worth: A Psychic Mystery*
ISBN 978-1-908733-06-1

William Usborne Moore—
Glimpses of the Next State
ISBN 978-1-907661-01-3

William Usborne Moore—
The Voices
ISBN 978-1-908733-04-7

John W. White—
The Highest State of Consciousness
ISBN 978-1-908733-31-3

Stafford Betty—
The Imprisoned Splendor
ISBN 978-1-907661-98-3

Paul Pearsall, Ph.D. —
Super Joy
ISBN 978-1-908733-16-0

All titles available as eBooks, and selected titles available in Hardback and Audiobook formats from www.whitecrowbooks.com

www.ingramcontent.com/pod-product-compliance
Lightning Source LLC
Chambersburg PA
CBHW032150080426
42735CB00008B/647